Straw Bale Building

How to plan, design & build with straw

"*Straw Bale Building* is an excellent addition to the growing body of literature and knowledge on straw bale construction. The authors' experiences are combined with those of many others in a practical and thoughtful guide to this burgeoning building system. Chris Magwood and Peter Mack continue the tradition of providing useful technical and general information about straw bale building in a humane and environmentally aware context."
— David Eisenberg, co-author of *The Straw Bale House* book, Director of the Development Center for Appropriate Technology

"*Straw Bale Building* is the first major book published in the 'second wave' of the straw-bale resurgence, joining such valuable classics as *The Straw Bale House, Build It With Bales,* and *Buildings of Earth and Straw.* If you're thinking about building a straw-bale house, this book will be a valuable tool in your investigation and education."
— Mark Piepkorn, *The Last Straw,* the Journal of Strawbale and Natural Building

"What a technological leap was the straw baler, in the later 1800s! And how boldly and quickly did the Nebraskan pioneers apply straw bales and plaster to create good walls for their houses. It took us most of a century to seize their idea of building with dry-packed 'waste' fiber. Only now, entering the 2000s, are we inspired to advance further, with 'blockmakers' using sugar cane, wood fiber, straw, elephant grass, *agave* ... for walls and roofs. Magwood and Mack bring a wealth of experience, and a rare mix of soul and common sense, into the creation of *Straw Bale Building.* Their uniquely useful book does full honor to the great deal of work and thought that it takes to build a good house, and to the Nebraskan pioneers."
— R. E. Platts, P. Eng., housing engineer

Straw Bale Building

How to plan, design & build with straw

Chris Magwood & Peter Mack

Illustrated by Elisabeth Ohi

NEW SOCIETY PUBLISHERS

Cataloging in Publication Data:
A catalog record for this publication is available from the National Library of Canada.

Third printing July, 2002.

Cover design by Miriam MacPhail from original photographs by Peter Mack, Chris Magwood, and Greg Magwood.

Printed in Canada on acid-free, partially recycled (20 percent post-consumer) paper using soy-based inks by Transcontinental/Best Book Manufacturers.

New Society Publishers acknowledges the support of the Government of Canada through the Book Publishing Industry Development Program (BPIDP) for our publishing activities, and the assistance of the Province of British Columbia through the British Columbia Arts Council.

BRITISH
COLUMBIA
ARTS COUNCIL
Supported by the Province of British Columbia

Paperback ISBN: 0-86571-403-7

Inquiries regarding requests to reprint all or part of *Straw Bale Building: How to Plan, Design and Build with Straw* should be addressed to New Society Publishers at the address below.

To order directly from the publishers, please add $4.00 shipping to the price of the first copy, and $1.00 for each additional copy (plus GST in Canada). Send check or money order to:

New Society Publishers
P.O. Box 189, Gabriola Island, BC V0R 1X0, Canada

New Society Publishers aims to publish books for fundamental social change through nonviolent action. We focus especially on sustainable living, progressive leadership, and educational and parenting resources. Our full list of books can be browsed on the worldwide web at:

NEW SOCIETY PUBLISHERS   www.newsociety.com

First comes knowledge, then the doing of the job.
And much later, perhaps after you're dead,
something grows from what you've done.
— Rumi, *Mathnawi,* V, 1053

CONTENTS

A Note from the Authors

Neither of us set out to become straw bale builders. That we are now writing a book about straw bale construction is a surprise to both of us. We arrived at our respective decisions to build with bales out of a common human desire to make ourselves homes that suited our needs, our esthetics, and our values. For both of us, straw bales seemed to fit perfectly into this scheme.

As it turned out, we loved the work itself, not just the finished product. We first met as owner/builder and volunteer helper, and our relationship is founded on the joy of making buildings, challenging ourselves, and seeking the best, most efficient ways of doing things.

In our headlong dive into the excitement of building with straw bales, we made a fair number of mistakes and many observations that led us toward better methods and more efficient uses of time and materials. We began to share those lessons in a series of workshops and with other bale builders. It became obvious that every project in this very young style of building was adding important knowledge to the common pool of bale building wisdom. This book is our attempt to make that accumulated knowledge available to others who are inspired to build with straw.

We hope you find the information in this book useful and its tone inviting and friendly. We've made a lot of friendships based on our work with straw bales and hope that some of the spirit of fun, adventurousness, and accomplishment make the translation to paper. Without the humor and inventiveness we've been able to apply to straw bale construction, neither of us would still be stacking bales and loving it so much. We owe a lot of thanks to a lot of people who helped, coaxed, cajoled and encouraged us along, and 'baled' us out when we really needed it.

Writing this book has been an exciting process for us. We hope that you enter its pages with the same kind of excitement, and that it does not fade after you are cozily tucked into your new straw bale home.

Chris and Pete

Acknowledgements

The authors would like to thank the following people a whole bunch:
Julie Bowen
Emma Jane Bowen
Tina Therien
Tina Terrion
Elisabeth Ohi
Russell Scott and everybody at the Ecology Retreat Centre
Bob Platts
Eric Hart
Kim Thompson
Laura Ponti-Sgargi
Dahl Atin
Catherine Wanek
Mark Piepkorn
Don Fugler
Ross and Patti Kembar
Martin Liefhebber
David and Anne-Marie Warburton
Torch, Mills, Mary, Gab and Co.
Marlene Burnett and Judy Lever
Linda and Robert Smith
Elisabeth and Bear
Michael Greenbough and Co.
All of Pete's parents
Michael Liebson
Uncle Reggie
Gary Magwood
Sandy Z
Gary Heuvel
Leslie, Peter and Duff
Callum McKee and the Paradise Lake Environmental Learning Centre
Spatch Noseworthy
Teresa Morrow

John Marrow

Kim 'Slammer' Place

Gavin Dandy

Heide Bateman

Rodney Me Me Me Litigio

Sidewalk Jay

Smokin' Joe

John Dixon

Andrea MacNeil

All our workshop 'graduates'

Lego blocks

and for their inspiring, pioneering work in straw bale construction,
David Eisenberg, Athena and Bill Steen, David Bainbridge, Matts Myhrman,
Steve MacDonald, and Bruce King.

Photo Credits: all photographs are by Peter Mack or Chris Magwood, unless otherwise indicated. Special thanks to Kristin Donaldson, Eric Hart, Ross Kembar, John Marrow, Kim Thompson, and Rich Schreiber of the East Coast Alternative Building Center (21, Quail Run Road, York PA17402 USA, E-mail: ecabc@juno.com).

Disclaimer

While we have made every effort to ensure that the information presented in *Straw Bale Building* is as reliable as possible, straw bale builders are subject to the same rules of common sense and safety that apply to all those in the construction industry. Accordingly, neither the authors, the illustrator, the other contributors, nor New Society Publishers accept any liability or responsibility for damages, injury, or loss incurred as a result of following the practices described or illustrated in this book. The information in *Straw Bale Building* does not over-ride any applicable building codes or regulations. We encourage straw bale builders to undertake the construction of building code-approved structures and to build responsibly and conscientiously to further the credibility and acceptance of straw bale building.

Introduction

WHAT TO EXPECT FROM THIS BOOK

In less than twenty years, straw bale building has come from complete obscurity to widespread attention. Spreading from its revival roots in the American Southwest, there are now thousands of bale homes and structures across North America — and in many other parts of the world — with the number of new starts rising exponentially every year. From remote rural locations and small towns to suburbs and inner-city housing, straw bale construction keeps making more and more sense to more and more people.

Why this remarkable growth in popularity? Well, the novelty of the idea has certainly attracted a great deal of mainstream media attention — every journalist loves a Three Little Pigs headline! — but once the novelty wears off, many people remain intrigued and fascinated with straw bale construction. Impressed by the high energy-efficiency, lowered environmental impact, and beautiful simplicity of building with straw bales, many people have been willing to commit their time, effort, and money to building with bales. But whether the straw bale project is a small, owner-built bungalow or a contractor-built luxury home, the need exists for clear, straightforward, and accurate information. That's what we are attempting to present in this book.

This is a Book of Options and Thinking Tools

There is no such thing as 'the straw bale standard.' Modern straw bale building is relatively young; each new project and personality adds to a collective knowledge — a warehouse of ideas and possible answers. Instead of accepting or rejecting any viable option, we have set out to define the questions you will face as you go through the exciting process of building. At each moment of debate, we attempt to outline a number of possible solutions and give an honest appraisal of the cost, complexity, efficiency, and environmental implications of each choice. We don't want you to build our dream home; we want you to have the thinking tools with which to build — or commission — your own.

Cost, complexity, efficiency, environmental impact, and building code compliance are all important factors in every home builder's decision-making process; they are all addressed at each stage in this book. Only you can balance these factors in the way best suited to your needs. You may, however, notice a tendency toward environmentally-friendly options, and for this bias we offer no apology. Many modern building practices waste precious resources, and we believe wholeheartedly in doing everything possible to

Straw bale construction can create 'windows' into new ways of thinking about the buildings in which we live.

John Marrow

lighten the load our buildings place on the planet. Choosing to use straw bales as a building material is an important step toward more sustainable building practices, but the ideal can — and should — be pursued more vigorously.

Helpful Resources

In this book, we give specific, step-by-step instructions for designing, building, and finishing straw bale walls. While we attempt to address all the crucial elements of designing and creating foundations, roofing, plumbing, wiring, and all the other myriad tasks of building a structure, we do not attempt to instruct you in the particulars of building each stage of your home. A book of straw bale building options must address concerns beyond the actual bale walls themselves. Your straw walls must be integrated into a complete package.

One of the advantages of straw bale building is its easy integration with the familiar building practices which are well-known and understood by talented people in your local area and well-documented in books, manuals, and videos. We've included a resource list at the end of each chapter to suggest directions for your further research. These are references that we have found useful, but by no means do they represent the full depth of information available. Use these sources as a jumping-off place, and search for the resources that speak most clearly to your intentions.

In many chapters, you will find sidebars, written by people with a particular straw bale building experience to share. These are individual takes on specific areas of concern, both technical and personal. As a growing movement, straw bale building is developed and passed on by so many knowledgeable, creative people that we thought a sampling of voices from the field would prove useful to those who are currently being introduced to the idea.

A Note to Experienced Builders and Straw Bale 'Junkies'

The world currently contains a disproportionate number of first-time bale builders compared to those who have experience! We've written this book principally as a guide for people who are undertaking a bale structure for the first time. For builders who have a depth of experience in straw bale building or other styles of construction, there will inevitably be some redundant information. Hopefully, there will also be much that is either new or approached from a new angle. We hope you take the time to find what's useful to you. If you are a building professional, we encourage you to try some bale work, and then offer it to your future clients as an option. You might be surprised at the level of interest that's out there.

Bales Aren't Just for Houses

Throughout this book, we often use the word 'house' to describe bale buildings, but by no means is the use of straw bales limited to single-family dwellings. From tiny garden sheds to large factories or warehouses, bales can be used in many ways to create many structures, using the principles outlined here. If you find working with bales as addictive as we do, you'll start creating needs just to have an excuse to make another bale building!

Taking the First Step and Engaging Your Brain

Building your own home is a sprawling process of input, suggestion, passion, necessity, compromise, error, change, and refinement. We hope that this book inspires and assists those who wish to leap into that sprawl, immerse themselves, and emerge on the other side with a home to be proud of.

So, in the name of inspiration, it's onward we go.

CHAPTER 1

Why Build With Straw?

Straw bale builders must repeatedly answer the question, "Why?" "Why bother using straw bales?" There are many answers, and we'll start by addressing the most common reasons for building with bales.

STRAW AS A BUILDING MATERIAL

Not a Building Newcomer

Despite its relatively new status as a building material in North America, straw has been used in construction for thousands of years. Durable, flexible, and grown close to the building site, un-baled straw is still widely used around the world in a variety of flooring, wall, and roof systems.

Straw in 'Block' Form

The horse-driven baling machine, invented and introduced into the grain-growing regions of the North American West in the 1870s, had the unintentional side effect of turning loose straw into large, effective building blocks. The settlers of the Nebraskan sandhills, who faced a lack of lumber and suitable sod with which to build their new homes, were the first to put these building blocks to use. Some of these early bale structures are still standing - a testament to the durability of straw bale walls. The enduring and effective homes the settlers created are responsible for the bale building we do today.

Straw Bales: The Waste that Rocked the World

Enough straw is currently produced every year in North America to meet all our residential building needs. There would be plenty of good reasons to move toward using this abundant renewable resource for construction purposes even if it held no particular advantage over other building materials. Straw bale buildings can out-perform buildings made from other materials, and straw bale construction can lighten our load on the planet and at the same time, lighten the load on our pocketbooks.

The authors shoulder the basic building block: straw in baled form.

EFFICIENCY BENEFITS

Whether it's a concern for the environment or for the bottom line of our monthly heating and cooling bills, the high level of energy-efficiency achieved by straw bale

What's in an 'R'?

"Let me offer a slightly different take on what is likely happening with the R-value of a straw bale wall. I question whether the best, most controlled scientific testing would show anything like the R-50 that we have all heard about for [three-string, 24" wide] straw bales. The test used gives a fair first approximation, but is widely recognized as being less accurate than ASTM236 Hot Box testing. That said, the difference between R-50 and R-30 is really not that great. It is certainly less than the difference between R-10 and R-30, an apparently equally distant pair of values. This is because R-value (a derived number from U-value) is the ability of a substance to resist heat flow. To understand how that plays out in actual performance, we need to convert R-values BACK to U-values, the measure of how heat flows through a substance under a predefined set of conditions.

An R-10 wall will allow 1/10 of one Btu (0.10 Btus) through one square foot of wall in an hour if there is a one degree (Fahrenheit) temperature difference between the two sides of the wall. An R-30 wall will allow 1/30 of a Btu (0.033 Btus) through under the same conditions. An R-50 wall will allow 1/50 of a Btu (0.02 Btus) through. Obviously, if your wall is R-10, you are going to make a much bigger dent by increasing the R-value to R-20, than if your wall is R-30 and you move to R-50. It's the law of diminishing returns. At some point, common sense and the pocket book say it's good enough. (cont. on pg 9) ▶

homes is often the foremost reason for choosing straw bales over other building materials. The enviable energy-efficiency is due to the highly insulating properties of straw bales. The role of insulation is to prevent the migration of heat from the inside of a structure, where you live and burn fuel to maintain the temperature, to the outside of a structure, where heat and cold are at the whim of nature. The better the insulation, the more slowly heat is lost to the outside, and the less energy will be required to maintain a desired temperature. Through a combination of thickness, the amount of air they entrap, and the fairly low conductivity of straw itself, straw bales offer insulation values that can exceed even those of modern, well-insulated, frame-walled homes.

R-What?

Insulation values are most commonly expressed as 'R- values', a measurement that denotes the ability of a material to resist the flow of heat. R-values for residential wall systems typically range between R-12 and R-20, depending on climatic conditions, building code regulations, and type of insulation. Bales have R-values ranging from R-35 to R-50, depending on their width.

No Gaps, No Leaks

Not only do bale walls offer excellent insulation value, but a well-built bale wall creates an unbroken surface of high insulation. In a traditional frame wall, the space between the studs might be insulated to R-20, but the studs themselves only offer approximately R-1 per inch, or R-5.5 for a common 2x6-inch stud. The thermal efficiency of the building is broken by these regular 'cold bridges', and problems can arise with settling and improper installation of various insulation materials.

Reduce Your Heating and Cooling Bills

By significantly reducing the energy required to heat and cool your home, straw bale walls will save you a great deal of money over the lifetime of your home. These savings are ongoing and can allow for sizable changes in the amount of money you currently require to heat and cool your living space.

LOWER CONSTRUCTION COSTS

We have devoted an entire chapter to 'The Hotly-Debated, Often-Distorted Question of Cost,' so here we will only point out that bale walls are less expensive than other common wall systems. By doubling as both wall structure and insulation, they play a dual role at a very reasonable cost. Whether you can translate this lower cost into a less expensive building project is a matter that will be determined by your particular plans and the way you go about realizing them.

A significant cost advantage can be realized if you raise your own walls without the assistance of professional builders. It takes much less time and specific knowledge to build a bale wall than a wooden frame wall, and you can save money by doing it yourself.

Cost will always be an important factor as we consider different building possibilities in this book. Our aim is to allow you to build to your needs while meeting your particular budget requirements.

DESIGN BENEFITS

Many alternative building systems require builders to adapt to new and often complicated construction techniques in order to achieve the benefits of the system. These same buildings can also require the occupants to adapt to new living conditions and configurations. These adaptations are not necessarily undesirable, but they are a significant factor in the decision-making process.

John Marrow

Rich Schreiber

From the square lines and conventional finishes of a professionally-built modern bungalow in Smithville, Ontario, *(above)* to the hexagonal load-bearing walls of this cottage in Davidsonville, Maryland, *(left)* or the rounded walls of an owner-built retreat in Ship Harbour, Nova Scotia, *(below)* straw bale design offers remarkable adaptability.

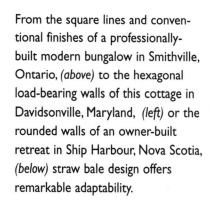

Straw bale construction is easily adaptable to a wide variety of design configurations - from the norms of traditional suburban homes to round, curved, or other unusual designs. Regardless of the design, the insulating and cost benefits of straw bale walls are always evident. Where building codes require new homes to blend with current fashions, or where homebuilders prefer established designs, straw bales can be used to upgrade the performance of those homes. At the same time, bales leave the field wide open to spatial innovations of all stripes.

Kim Thompson

John Marrow

Interior finishes in straw bale homes can vary from rough and round to straight and square.

Beautiful, Adaptable Walls

Straw bale walls can be built to suit a variety of esthetics. From rounded and lumpy to straight and elegant, straw walls can take on many shapes and textures depending on how they are detailed. Finishing choices are almost unlimited, and different effects can be applied to different walls in the same home. Especially attractive to many builders are the deep window openings, which can be finished in a number of ways to provide seats, plant shelves, or decorative sills.

Bales Suit Human Dimensions

Bales are unusually — though unintentionally — well suited to human dimensions. On work sites, builders will find that a single bale makes a comfortable seat, two bales a comfortable stool, and three bales an excellent leaning post. These friendly dimensions can be incorporated into your design in unique and comfort-making ways.

Quiet and Comfortable

Straw bale walls are excellent sound barriers, making them an attractive choice in urban settings where ambient noise can be distracting and unhealthy. Inside a straw home, the nature of the walls provide a pleasant sound, feel, and ambiance unavailable from flat, drywalled rooms.

ENVIRONMENTAL BENEFITS

Straw bale construction affects the environment in positive ways. The significant reduction of energy needed to heat and cool bale buildings combines with the annual renewability of straw to make a persuasive environmental argument for the use of

John Marrow

straw bale wall systems. Reduced energy consumption for heating and cooling means less fuel is required and fewer emissions are produced from burning finite natural resources. Straw harvesting is much less energy-intensive than the lumber harvesting and manufacturing of insulation and other products used to build frame walls. At the same time, energy expended in straw production produces grain crops, resulting in a two-for-one energy saving. Straw is available locally in a wide variety of climatic regions; using locally-produced bales saves energy that would otherwise be consumed in transportation.

Lowering the 'Embodied Energy'

Environmentalists refer to the energy used in producing materials as 'embodied energy.' It can be quite an eye-opener to see the amount of energy industry expends on creating and supplying building materials. Unlike most other building supplies, straw can be grown and harvested annually. This means the same fields can continue to produce building material year after year — unlike forests that take upward of fifty years to regenerate and rarely return to their former levels of production.

Environmental Benefits that Don't Cost More...

It is unusual to find an environmentally-friendly alternative that does not require sacrifices in terms of costs, appearance, or availability. Straw bale building provides that magical, and increasingly necessary, alternative to wasteful, unsustainable modern practices.

...And Just Might Be Better For You

Straw bale walls offer a potential solution for those who find that the paints, chemicals, glues, and toxins embedded in manufactured building materials negatively affect their health. Organically grown straw coated with earth-based and cement/lime plasters have received positive feedback from environmentally-sensitive people, though further study is required to substantiate the anecdotal evidence.

BALES AREN'T MAGIC

Any conventional building method, if used to build walls of the same thickness as a bale wall, would provide similar levels of performance, albeit at greater cost. When the mystique of building with bales has been stripped away, the truth is that straw bales simply allow for the creation of very thick walls without consuming the quantity of resources frequently used to make equally thick walls of wood, fiberglass, or other materials. Bales work — cheaply and sustainably!

While the benefits of building with bales are clear, straw bale building is still in its infancy. Techniques and concepts that will further enhance the practical and sustainable use of straw bales as a construction material are constantly being sought, tried, and studied, bringing us closer to the best possible uses of labor, time, and materials.

IF BALES ARE SO GOOD, WHY DOESN'T EVERYBODY USE THEM?

The obvious advantages of building with bales gives rise to this common question. Passive resistance to bale construction comes from two sources: homeowners and the building industry.

Who Wouldn't Want a Bale Home?

Big financial commitments like the building of a house usually inspire conservatism in even the most adventurous spirits. Conventional frame houses are widely accepted as the safest financial choice. Even those who are willing to invest in new ideas

(cont. from pg. 6) However, the tested R-value has little to do with how the wall performs in the real world. This is much truer for straw bale walls than for stud walls. Thermal bridges occur with regularity in stud walls — in fact, at every stud. Straw bale walls have fewer thermal breaks, by far. Moreover, the R-value is measured under what can be called static conditions: you can only take your readings once the wall surface temperatures have stopped changing. This takes about twenty minutes for the average window, an hour or two for a wall, and three to seven days for a straw bale wall. In other words, the conditions at the two wall surfaces must not change for days on end, or the R-value is invalid. Well, how often in the real world does that happen with one's house? The time it takes heat to travel through a straw bale wall is about 12-15 hours. By the time the heat has made that journey, diurnal (daily) temperature swings are driving the heat the other way in the wall."

- Nehemiah Stone is currently building his own straw bale house in Penryn, California. He has adapted this explanation of R-values and straw bale walls from his posting to the straw bale building news group on the Internet. The news group is a lively and interesting place to hear from builders and to engage in debate on all aspects of straw bale construction. To subscribe, e-mail majordomo@crest.org, no subject, and include "subscribe strawbale" in the body of the message. ❖

Before you tackle an entire house, a small, simple building project is a good way to learn straw bale construction techniques.

US Department of Energy Straw Bale Assessment

Research summarized in the forty-page final report by Lawrence Berkeley Laboratory (LBL) on the Navajo Test Project shows that the program currently undertaken by the Navajo Nation has the potential to improve the energy efficiency and thermal comfort of new residences when compared to those currently being built on the reservation.

LBL analyses show that:
"(1) there are alternative construction technologies that provide equal or better energy performance than current practice;
(2) the demonstration building, with a few modifications, could be substantially more energy efficient and comfortable than current practice, while meeting other program goals ❯

can face significant resistance from spouses, family, friends, lenders, architects, building inspectors, building supply yard employees, and a host of other cautious types. It takes a fair bit of spirit and resolve to overcome such personal obstacles, and many people do not pursue their ideals in the face of such resistance.

There's No Money in Them There Straw Houses

The building industry has not yet embraced straw bale construction because it offers limited opportunities for profit. Bales cannot be patented, nor would it be immediately feasible for a building supply company to go into straw bale production. Most advances in building technology come from companies who develop products, test them, then use their testing results to obtain building code approval — or better yet, code requirement — for the product. Straw bales have little or no immediate chance of receiving the high-budget testing afforded by big companies or the promotional dollars that would convince contractors to use them. Until widespread bale building begins, prefabricated products — top plates, curbs, lintels, and stucco meshes — that would speed the building process are unlikely to become available. Until consumers begin demanding highly efficient, environmentally-responsible homes in sufficient quantity, straw bale construction will remain a marginal percentage of new home starts.

Be a Pioneer

If you decide that a straw bale home is what you want, then plunge in and do it. While you may feel like an isolated nut case at first, you will be opening doors to a whole new and lively community that will spring up around your efforts. Friends you didn't know you had will emerge to help out, and connections will be fostered with other like-minded people, both in your immediate area and around the world. Once you're settled into your house, these people will continue to make your life richer. It's an opportunity you won't want to miss.

REFERENCES

Books on Straw Bale Building

Bainbridge, David A., Athena Swentzell Steen and Bill Steen. *The Straw Bale House.* Chelsea Green Publishing Company, 1994. ISBN 0-930031-71-7.

King, Bruce P.E. *Buildings of Earth and Straw: Structural Design for Rammed Earth and Straw Bale Architecture.* Ecological Design Press, 1996. ISBN 0-9644718-1-7.

Myhrman, Matts and S.O. MacDonald. *Build It with Bales, Version 2.* Out on Bale, 1997. ISBN 0-9642821-1-9.

Thompson, Kim. *Straw Bale Construction: A Manual for Maritime Regions.* Straw House Herbals. ISBN 0-96805526-0-6.

The Last Straw Journal. P.O. Box 42000, Tucson AZ 85733-2000 USA.

Books on Other Alternative Building Methods

Bee, Becky. *The Cob Builder's Handbook.* Groundworks, 1997. ISBN 0-9659082-0-8.

Easton, David. *The Rammed Earth House.* Chelsea Green Publishers, 1997. ISBN 0-9652335-0-2.

Roy, Robert L. *Cordwood Masonry Housebuilding.* Sterling Publishing Co., 1995. ISBN 0-8069-8590-9.

Wells, Malcolm. *The Earth-Sheltered House: An Architect's Sketchbook.* Chelsea Green Publishers, 1999. ISBN 1-890132-19-5.

Journals

The Last Straw (The Quarterly Journal of Strawbale and Natural Building), HC66 Box 119, Hillsboro NM 88042 USA. Tel: 505-895-5400; Fax: 505-895-3326. E-mail: thelaststraw@strawhomes.com

Videos

Building With Straw Series, Vol. 1–3. Black Range Films, Star Rt. 2, Box 119, Kingston New Mexico 88042 USA.

How to Build Your Elegant Home with Straw Bales. Videotape. Produced by Sustainable Systems Support. P.O. Box 318, Bisbee AZ 85603 USA.

Straw Bale Construction. Produced by Straw House Herbals. RR 1, Ship Harbour NS B0J 1Y0 Canada.

Web Sites

Camel's Back Construction: www.mwsolutions.com/straw

Black Range Films: www.StrawBaleCentral.com

Surfin' Strawbale: www.moxvox.com/surfsolo

The Last Straw: www.strawhomes.com

▶ *of architectural interest and long term environmental sustainability; and*

(3) straw-bale construction, along with appropriate building conservation technologies and simple passive solar design, could provide up to a 60 percent reduction in building heating loads over current practice.

Straw-bale building technology offers the best energy performance of any of the new construction typologies currently being considered, with 15 percent improvements in overall building energy-efficiency in heating for the climates on the Navajo reservation.

Energy-related testing of straw-bale buildings in the field is warranted. Infiltration characteristics and the effects of moisture on energy performance need further evaluation."

The above information is from *House of Straw: Straw Bale Construction Comes of Age,* a publication produced by the U.S. Department of Energy (DOE/G010094-01, April 1995); it is available on-line at http://www.eren.doe.gov/EE/strawhouse/ The project, created in 1990, was funded through the Department of Energy/Department of Housing and Urban Development initiative on Energy Efficiency for Housing. For more information, contact the Energy Efficiency and Renewable Energy Clearinghouse (EREC) at 1-800-DOE-EREC or doe.erec@nci-inc.com, or visit www.eren.doe.gov and search for "straw bale" or "consumer info." ❖

CHAPTER 2

What Are Straw Bales?

As bales are the essential building blocks for your home, it is important to know your bales. Understanding how they are made and what qualities to look for are important if you are going to make the right choices.

SPEAKING OF STRAW

Rectangular bales dotting the fields in midsummer is a familiar sight to a lot of people. An essential rural icon, a field of bales is often a symbol for wholesome rural ideals. But are those bales straw or hay?

Straw Is Not Hay!

It is common for people to confuse straw with hay. While bales of the two are the same size and shape, they are quite different substances. Hay refers to any combination of field grasses that are grown to maturity, cut while still relatively green, and baled to use as livestock feed when fresh grasses are not available. High in moisture content, food energy — a full-course meal for critters big and small! — and having the potential to sustain microbial activity that can cause rotting and mold, hay is not what you want in your walls. Build your house with straw. Feed the hay to your livestock!

"I'll Grind Your Seeds to Make My Bread..."

Straw refers to the dried stems of grain-bearing grasses. Straw is harvested as a by-product of cereal grain farming. The nutritious seed head is cut — threshed — from the top of the plant once the plant is fully mature. With the seed head gone, the stalks are dried and baled.

Farmers may use their straw as bedding for livestock, and gardeners use straw to mulch crops. But grain production by far outstrips our current minimal usage of straw; it is largely considered a waste by-product of grain production.

Tiny Trees in Fast Growing Forests

Each stalk of straw resembles a long, thin, hollow tree trunk. The resemblance is more than skin deep, for trees and straw share a similar chemical structure — cellulose and lignin — and a similar strength and durability.

Any grain crop can produce straw suitable for construction. Wheat, oats, barley, and rye are among the common varieties of straw in northern climates. Where it's grown, rice straw can also be excellent for construction. As commercial hemp crops are re-introduced, baled hemp may also become available.

Get to Know Some Straw

Each little tree trunk is remarkably strong. Straw is capable of quickly dulling metal cutting-blades and is hard to tear apart by hand. It also resists decomposing quite well, which anyone who has mulched with it will confirm. Pick up a piece of straw — even long, dry grass at the edge of your lawn will do — and you'll be amazed at its strength and resilience. Imagine thousands of these rugged tiny trees packed tightly together to create your building bales.

ABOUT BALES

The Harvesting Process

Commercial grain fields are harvested by a combine. This machine cuts the grain stalks close to the ground, then threshes the seed heads from the plant stalks. The bare stalks — straw — are deposited on the field in straight lines to await baling.

A baling machine is pulled over the field, sweeping the lines of straw up into a chamber where a mechanical plunger compacts the loose straw into thin square 'flakes.' (You'll hear a lot about flakes later on.) A number of these flakes are pressed together and tied into a bale. The bale is either re-deposited onto the field or kicked into a trailing wagon. Different baling machines produce bales of differing quality. Even bale quality from the same machine can vary dramatically, depending on the sharpness of the cutting blades and the adjustments made for the tightness of the strings.

Wheat straw is being baled and kicked into a wagon while the post and beam frame in the background is being prepared for the wall-raising.

How to Find Bales

Unlike most other building supplies, you can't order bales from the local construction supply yard — not yet, anyway! So, when it comes to finding your bales, you're on your own. However, anywhere grain is harvested, so is straw. Chances are good that there is straw within a reasonable distance of your chosen building site, even if the site is urban. Many cities are built near or on prime farmland, and the farmers who have maintained their land near these areas are often producing some grain crops. But how to find the right farmer with the right bales?

Go Where the Farmers Are

You can look for bales in several ways. One way to find bales is to approach a local feed mill, farmer's co-op, or grain elevator. They will know who is growing grain and might be able to put you in contact with an appropriate source. They may be willing to broker the sale for you, although they will add a percentage to the cost for providing the service. Farmer's markets, agricultural fairs, farm equipment sales centers, or any other places that farmers frequent can be good places to start. An advertisement in a few small town newspapers or want-ad flyers can also put you in direct contact with farmers who have bales.

Old Bales, New Bales, No Bales

You can use bales that have been in storage from previous harvests, or you can pre-order your bales from the current grain harvest. Remember that bales are an agricultural product and therefore are susceptible to fluctuations in weather, crop prices, and demand. There are always lean and abundant bale years. Where grain production is modest in scale, farmers will sometimes reserve their entire harvest for their own use. For this reason, it is best to source your bales as early as possible.

Round Bales Don't Work

In recent years, baling machines that create large, round bales have come into favor with many farmers. However, you can't build with round bales. You'll have to specify that you need square bales. If contacted prior to harvest, some farmers who currently bale round might use their old square baler in order to make the sale to you. It can sometimes be frustrating to see literally tons of straw at hand but in a form you can't use. Be persistent — somebody out there has square bales for you.

Two-String versus Three-String Bales

Much of the pioneering work in reviving straw bale construction was done in the southwestern United States. There, large three-string bales are common. In areas of small-scale grain farming, two-string bales are the norm. Both are suitable for building purposes; the kind you use will be determined by the baling standard in your local area.

THE THREE BALE BASICS

When faced with a towering mound of hundreds or thousands of bales, it's good to know what to look for. You have three basic concerns: tightness, dryness, and size. Before making your purchase, be sure you are satisfied on all three counts.

Tightness

You want your bales tight. Bales can be tied with polypropylene string, sisal twine, or metal wire. Polypropylene string or metal wire are the better choices, since sisal twine is prone to rot. It is the solidity of a straw bale that allows it to be used as a building material, and that solidity — or lack thereof — is a direct result of how tightly the bale has been tied. A farmer can adjust the baling machine to vary tightness. Really tight bales use less twine or wire to bale an entire field but are heavier and harder to handle. If you are pre-ordering your bales, be sure to specify that you want them on the tight side. But what exactly is tight?

Methods for assessing tightness vary from the low tech to the scientific. For the low tech method, pick up the bale by its strings and check that they don't separate from the bale by more than 4–5 inches. The bale should also maintain its integrity when you lift it by just one string. Be sure you sample a number of bales from different places in the stack.

Some attempts have been made to more scientifically quantify tightness. The Arizona and California Straw Bale Codes specify that "bales shall have a minimum calculated dry density of 7.0 pounds per cubic foot" [see Appendix: Arizona Straw Bale Building Code, Section 7 2041.6]. Densities over 8.5 pounds per cubic foot are felt to lower the insulation value of the bale by eliminating spaces between the stalks that entrap air. In order to calculate the dry density of a bale, we need to address the second important quality of a building bale.

Dryness

Start with dry bales. You want to avoid building 'compost' walls and, like any organic material, straw will decompose if the right conditions of moisture and temperature exist.

Like methods for determining tightness, methods for determining moisture content vary in complexity. For the low tech option, open the strings on several different bales and look inside. Is the straw moist to the touch? Does it smell damp? Are there any hints of black mold on the straw? Study the storage facility. Is the roof good? How about the floor and walls? Ask the farmer about the weather conditions when the straw was baled. Was it a damp summer with lots of rain?

If you want to be more scientific, use a moisture meter to get an accurate reading of moisture content. The farmer may own a meter or may be able to borrow one from a neighbor or from a co-op. Moisture meters are most often used on hay bales but can give accurate readings for straw as well. Moisture content of 20 percent is considered the safe maximum for a building bale. To calculate the dry density of a bale, subtract the weight of the moisture from the overall weight of the bale.

Keep in mind that farmers don't want wet bales either. Moist bales will mold in the barn and make for lousy bedding for the livestock. While it's possible to worry about whether your newly purchased bales are dry or not, it is common practice to bale straw under good, dry conditions, and to keep it dry once it has been baled.

Size

Size is the least important concern for building bales. As long as the bales are of consistent height and width, their exact dimensions are not so important. Two-string bales, as shown in Illustration 2.1, are generally 14 inches high, 30–40 inches long and 18–20 inches wide. Three-string bales are 14–17 inches high, 32–48 inches long and 23–24 inches wide. It doesn't matter if your bales vary from these numbers, as long as they are consistent with each other so that your bale wall doesn't vary greatly in height or width.

Illustration 2.1
Common bales come in either two- or three-string sizes, with roughly standard dimensions.

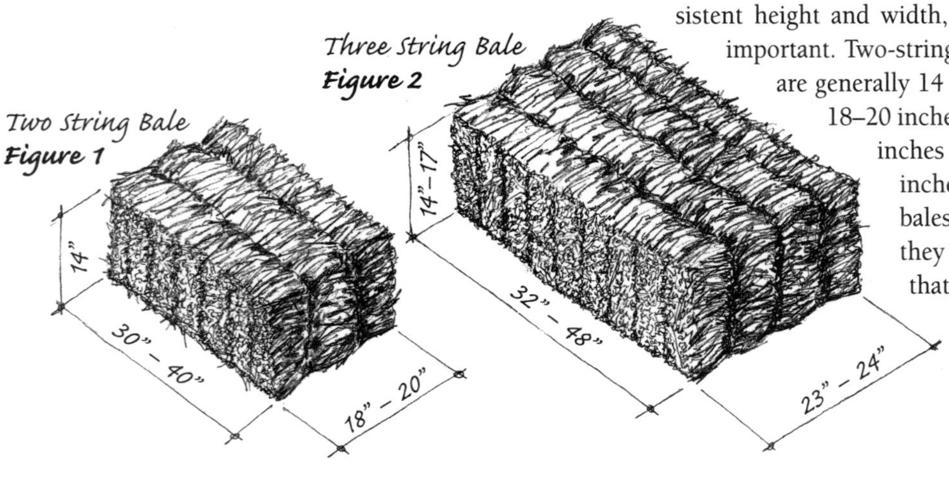

Three String Bale
Figure 2

14"–17"

32" – 48"

23" – 24"

Two String Bale
Figure 1

14"

30" – 40"

18" – 20"

OTHER FACTORS TO CONSIDER

Before You Buy

Some general concerns about bales should be addressed. Many modern combines chop the straw as it is harvested. This chopped straw can be baled, but the bales are not as strong and are much more difficult to cut, shape, and trim. Less air is entrapped in chopped straw, lowering the insulation value; the best bales contain long, unbroken straw.

Balers affect bale quality, too. An improperly adjusted baler will tighten one string more than the other, producing lopsided, curved bales. If there are many such bales, avoid purchasing. Each bale has a 'cut' side and a 'folded' side. The folded side will always be shaggier than the cut side. Examine both sides to see if they are relatively smooth and even. 'Smooth' bales will require less trimming later on, and are more desirable.

Check bales to be sure that there is not too much grain left mixed in with the straw. While some seed heads inevitably make their way into bales, large pockets of seed or a high percentage of straw with seed heads intact are grounds for declining the purchase. These seed heads attract pests and can activate microbial activity in your finished wall.

Grain crops are often treated with chemical fertilizers and sprays. While studies exist to prove the safety of such products, you may wish to find out which products have been used on any straw you purchase. It is possible to find organically-grown straw or straw that has been grown with a minimum of chemical interference.

What Price, Fair Bale?

As an agricultural product, straw bales vary in price from season to season and from region to region. Common prices vary from Can$1–4 per bale. If you live close to the source, the farmer may be willing to deliver the bales at quite a reasonable cost, or you might be able to make a few trips with a truck and trailer. If not, the farmer might be able to suggest appropriate transportation.

If a commercial carrier is your only option, negotiate carefully. Bales require a lot of effort to move, stack, and load, and they make a big mess. If you have a crew on hand to load and unload a truck, it will save time and may be necessary before some transport operators will consider moving straw.

Storing Your Mound of Straw

Once you've bought your bales, you must decide where you're going to put them. It is best if bales can arrive at your construction site very close to the time of the wall-raising. If you or the farmer is transporting the bales, time the move for the day of use. If the bales arrive early, they must be stored.

You'll want to ensure that stored bales stay as dry as possible. This can take a fair bit of planning and preparation — unless you have a suitable barn or shed on-site. Post and beam builders can erect their framework and stack the bales under the roof.

Some simple rules apply to the making of a good stack of bales, as shown in the illustration and the photo below.

Purchase More than You Need

Plan to have extra bales on hand to compensate for broken, poorly tied, or damp bales in the stack. Extra bales can come in handy around the building site as step-stools, makeshift work benches, boot scrapers, and comfortable seats during breaks.

Handling Bales

It doesn't hurt to take some simple precautions when you are working with bales. Bales are lifted by their strings, and gloves are recommended to avoid pinched or sliced fingers. Long sleeved shirts cut down on straw scratch to your arms. Remember to use proper lifting techniques to avoid hurting your back. Depending on how they were stored and harvested, your bales may be quite dusty; if so, use adequate breathing masks. Other than that, don't worry. The color, size, shape, and smell of bales make them unlike any other building material. They're fun to play with, so go ahead and play.

REFERENCES

See Appendix A for the Arizona Straw Bale Building Code.

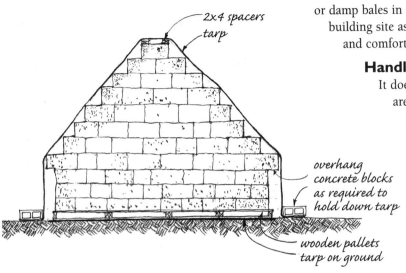

2x4 spacers
tarp

overhang
concrete blocks
as required to
hold down tarp

wooden pallets
tarp on ground

The illustration shows an ideal stack of bales, while the photo shows a good real-world example. Note the use of a swimming pool cover and Typar house-wrap.

CHAPTER 3

The 'Red Flag' Questions

What about fire? What about moisture? What about insects and pests? What about mortgages and insurance? What about longevity? These are the most frequently asked questions about straw bale construction. They all have answers that should alleviate your concern.

WHAT WE REALLY MEAN WHEN WE SAY 'STRAW BALE WALLS'

Before addressing common concerns about straw bale walls, we need to clarify what we mean by 'straw bale wall.' The term should really be 'plastered straw bale wall.' Without the coats of plaster — or stucco — applied to the inside and outside face of the bales, we wouldn't have straw bale walls. The plaster — and there are many different kinds — is what seals the bales against fire, rain, wind, bugs, and big bad wolves. The plaster also gives the wall its rigidity and strength, creating what engineers call a 'stressed skin panel' with impressive structural capabilities. As you read on, remember that all references to the performance of straw bale walls include the inherent characteristics of the plaster coating as well.

This building is structurally sound with plain bale walls, but it's not until plaster is applied that the impressive performance of plastered straw bale walls is achieved.

FIRE

Straw bale walls have been tested for fire resistance. In these tests, straw bale walls have proved themselves far superior to standard wood-framed walls.

Why Don't They Burn?

Straw bale walls are naturally fire resistant. While the dry straw that makes up a bale is easily combustible, the compact nature of a bale does not entrap enough air to readily support combustion. A good analogy can be drawn by comparing the combustibility of a single sheet of newsprint to that of an entire telephone directory. The single sheet will ignite and burn quickly, but if you drop a phone book on your fire, you'll probably put out the fire. The plaster coating effectively seals the already fire-resistant bales inside a non-combustible casement. A fire would have to burn through the plaster in order to reach the straw. When plaster is combined with the thickness of a bale wall, fire resistance is enhanced. Bale walls are not a drawback!

The Straw Bale/Plaster Stressed Skin Panel

"The proven Nebraska [load-bearing] structure is not, despite appearances, a stacked block structure. At most, the straw bales take little more than the dead loads only, while the rigid skins — stucco or plaster, chicken wire reinforced — must accept all of any live loads. Any imposed in-plane loads will be taken by the relatively high modulus skins with very little further deflection; such small further

▸

Don't Ignore the Real Fire Hazard

All of the above is true of baled, plastered straw. Unbaled straw, however, is extremely combustible, and the large amounts of loose straw that accumulate during construction are a serious fire hazard. Smoking, welding, grinding, or any other spark- or flame-producing activities should not be undertaken in the vicinity of loose straw. During construction, always be sure to have fire extinguishers and enough water available to deal with potential fires in your loose straw. Also, keep loose straw raked away from the walls to minimize the risk of any accidental fire spreading into the unplastered walls. Loose straw makes excellent garden mulch. Rake it up, keep it under control, and don't let it catch on fire.

Spontaneous Combustion

Concerns about spontaneous combustion do not apply to straw bale walls. The significant microbial activity within hay bales can result in spontaneous combustion under extreme conditions of humidity, temperature, and storage. Straw bales stacked in walls, however, will not support spontaneous combustion.

MOISTURE

Moisture is the enemy of all builders, regardless of which materials they are using. Wood, brick, and even concrete will deteriorate when exposed consistently to moisture. Bales, like any other building material, must be kept as dry as possible throughout the life of the building. Wet straw molds and eventually decomposes, creating an unpleasant odor, potentially harmful spores, and possible structural failures. Dry is important.

Many excellent building practices have been established over the years to help solve key moisture problems, and it is important to apply these practices to bale buildings. Moisture can enter the walls of a building in two ways: through vapor penetration and through direct air leaks. Straw builders must be aware of both in order to take adequate protective precautions.

Vapor Migration Through Walls

Think about blowing up a balloon. You force warm, moist air from your lungs into an air-tight container, creating a higher pressure than exists outside the balloon. Nature's incessant balancing act insists that the warm, moist air will do its best to leave the balloon and join the surrounding atmosphere. Your house is essentially the same as the balloon. When you heat your living space, you fill your house, which is relatively air-tight, with warm, moisture-laden air. Warm air naturally carries more moisture than cold, and you also add extra moisture by breathing, cooking, bathing, et cetera. That air will do its darnedest to get out of the house and give its heat and moisture to the cold air outside.

Why not just wave the moisture good-bye?

The warm, moist air that wants to travel through your walls does not stay warm and moist. At some point in its journey to the outside, it will begin to cool. If it cools enough, the water vapor it is carrying can condense back to liquid. (The point at which this condensation occurs is known as the 'dew point.') If liquid is deposited in your walls and allowed to remain without drying out, it will reduce the efficiency of your insulation and eventually lead to molding and rotting. In hot southern climates, the whole process can happen in reverse, especially if you use air-conditioning indoors.

Why aren't more old houses molding and rotting?

In earlier times, leaky windows, doors, walls, roofs, and floors kept relative humidity indoors below problem levels. Those same homes also required more energy to heat, because the heated air escaped the building, dissipating into the atmosphere. As better windows, doors, insulation, and building practices — especially the use of continuous plastic vapor barriers — began to make houses more air-tight, the need grew to prevent moisture from migrating directly through the walls.

Direct Air Leaks

Moisture can also enter your walls through direct air leaks. The Canadian Home Builders' Association estimates that, over a single winter of heating, air leakage through a hole with an area of less than one square inch could allow up to eight gallons of water to pass through a wall. Moisture concerns are hotly discussed among bale builders. Most of the testing done to date confirms what conventional builders already know: cracks, openings, and penetrations into the wall pose much greater risks for moisture damage than does vapor migration.

So What About Bale Walls?

Bale walls stack up well as moisture deterrents. The minimal amount of moisture that will migrate directly through the wall itself has not been shown to be a concern for moisture damage to bales. The plaster coating on bale walls is an effective barrier against damaging air leakage. If properly detailed to tie in with conventional polyethylene vapor barriers installed in the ceiling and under the floors, a bale house can be made air-tight.

Throughout this book, we will address proper detailing for creating a leak-free bale home without using a plastic vapor barrier over the straw wall.

Barriers

Why build without a vapor barrier?

Building without a vapor barrier simplifies the building process. Attaching a vapor barrier to a straw wall offers some complications. The barrier can only be attached to the top and bottom of the wall, making it hard to maintain a taut surface unless wooden attachment points are added to the wall. A vapor barrier prevents the plaster coating from attaching itself directly to the straw. This not only makes plastering much more difficult — and will likely require more metal reinforcement for the plaster — but eliminates the substantial structural benefits of bonding the plaster to the straw. Remember, bonded together, the two materials create a stressed skin panel far

---

Moisture Due to Vapor Penetration

Tests for moisture content in straw walls have been conducted in two locations in Canada. The testing of four houses without vapor barriers in Nova Scotia indicates that well-detailed straw bale buildings can be air-tight, and that moisture migration through plastered straw bale walls does not lead to a significant build-up of moisture within the wall:

"The results of the moisture monitoring... indicate that there is a higher moisture content at the mid-point of the bales in stuccoed walls during the summer in Nova Scotia. This rise in MC (moisture content) begins in March (avg. reading: 7.5% MC) and peaks in July (avg. reading: 12.2% MC), then falls through the heating season until December/January (avg. reading: 6.8% MC). The summertime peak does not come close to the 20% MC level, which is regarded as the "crisis" point for bale walls, and which, when coupled with consistent temperature levels of 20C (70F), could offer a prime colonizing environment for organisms which could destroy the integrity of the bale walls. This would indicate that straw bale construction is viable in Nova Scotia." — as reported in *Moisture in Straw Bale Housing, Nova Scotia* by SHE Consultants, in 1998. ❖

stronger than the sum of their independent elements. A straw wall without a vapor barrier is less time-consuming to build and eliminates the use of a manufactured product with a high embodied energy. Finally, straw, metal stucco mesh, and plastering tools all increase the risk of introducing punctures to the vapor barrier.

To barrier

There is no doubt that a properly installed vapor barrier is an effective tool in preventing moisture penetration through your walls. Though moisture migration has not been shown to be a problem in straw bale walls, a builder might choose — or be forced by local building officials — to spend the extra money and time and forego the structural strength and environmental bonuses of building a straw wall without a vapor barrier.

A middle ground

If you choose not to use a vapor barrier, you might want to use vapor-retardant paint. Apply it to the interior plaster of your walls to achieve a high degree of protection against moisture migration while avoiding the difficulties of working with a vapor barrier. You might also decide to apply different vapor-retarding strategies in different areas of your home. Bathrooms and kitchens are especially prone to high humidity and can be sealed with more vigor than other areas.

Build to your level of comfort

Bale homes have been built both with and without vapor barriers. To date, only direct water leakage into the wall or rising damp from foundations have resulted in damaging deterioration of the straw. But with no complete set of data from which to work, you must decide how to build to your own level of comfort and protection. Real-life experience has indicated that both types of homes operate within reasonable levels of moisture content due to vapor penetration.

Building Practices that Minimize Rainwater Penetration

Many simple, effective building techniques are used to protect bales from exposure to moisture. Generous roof overhangs and proper eaves-troughs eliminate most direct rainfall and splash-back from reaching your walls, as shown in Illustration 3.1.

Illustration 3.1
Simple techniques like increasing roof overhangs on walls exposed to frequent rains can adequately protect the bales from moisture.

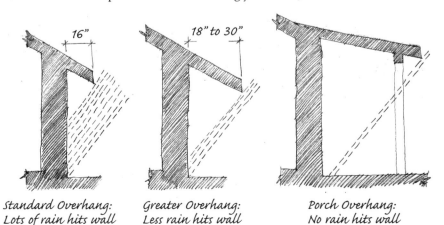

Standard Overhang: Lots of rain hits wall   *Greater Overhang: Less rain hits wall*   *Porch Overhang: No rain hits wall*

A bale wall that is raised on a wooden curb on the foundation or floor allows any spills or floods inside the house to drain away before they soak into the walls. Plastic or tar paper placed along the top of the walls helps shed any water that may some-day come through your roof. Windows and doors can be detailed to incorporate proper flashing and drip edges that shed water away from the walls.

INSECTS AND PESTS

Let's face it: we share this planet with billions of other creatures, both large and small. To say that a particular house or style of construction is 'pest-proof' is to ignore the intelligence and persistence of our little neighbors.

What are Pests Looking For?

To be suitable for sheltering pests, our homes must offer doors, nests, and food to prospective house guests. Plastered bale walls are short on all three, since their plas-ter coating seals the bales from foundation to roof with a difficult-to-chew barrier. Should a gap be left open in the plaster, the bales themselves are too densely packed to make comfortable housing for mice and other rodents. All those comfy spaces in your neighbor's frame walls, lightly packed with batt insulation, make a much more inviting home.

There is little food for any living creature in a straw wall; even termites tend to eschew straw. An inordinate amount of seed head in the straw does provide a good source of food, which is why you should check your bales for excess seed content before purchasing them. Care should be taken — as with any style of construction — to keep pests out during the building process. Your bales and — more susceptible to pests — your roof and/or floor framing will be open and accessible during this time.

MORTGAGES, INSURANCE, AND RESALE

The construction standards required by local building codes and those required by lending agencies are not necessarily the same. Sometimes, commercial lenders are even more conservative than building officials. Just because your building inspector approves your plans doesn't mean your lending institution will back them with dollars.

It's Not Impossible to Get $$

Don't panic! Many bale builders have obtained financing from regular sources. In general, it takes thoughtful preparation and patience to explain straw bale construc-tion to a lender. The U.S. Department of Energy has published positive findings about straw bale construction, and other government agencies have also done pre-liminary studies on straw bale. The CMHC (Canada Mortgage and Housing Corporation) that helps set many of the standards used by lending institutions in Canada is quite supportive of straw bale construction, and their data can be used when negotiating for a loan. Government facts, figures, and opinions can be power-ful tools when you're dealing with lenders.

How to Avoid Borrowing

"If you plan a modestly-sized home and do the building yourself, you can potentially eliminate the need to borrow, or at least reduce your borrowed amounts significantly. The freedom allowed by living without a mortgage is considerable, and it may be worth the effort to build yourself and trim size and 'flash' from your project.

When planning the budget for a building, consider these thoughts :

Even if you get a good rate for your mortgage — for example, $71,250 for 25 years at 5.9 percent, for which you'll repay $136,336.90 — the bank will make over $0.91 in interest for every dollar of principle. Considering the income tax and other payroll deductions many of us pay, it is not uncommon to have to earn at least $2.50 in order to spend $1.00 on a 5.9 percent mortgage. Start looking at 10 percent and 12 percent mortgages and one gets into having to earn $3.50 plus per dollar of principle!

If a family member or friend can loan you money, they can give you a more reasonable rate than a mortgage and still earn more on the investment than they would get almost anywhere else. Looking at it this way makes me think that pulling in the reins a bit would make sense. Possibly, you could wait to install flooring and trim, a dishwasher, or the second bathroom. Alternatively, you could design your house to be expanded once the mortgage is under control. Fortunately, you can take solace in ▶

Research Lending Options

There are many excellent references available that describe methods and means for obtaining financing. Read widely before you plunge in — and remember, numerous options are still available to you should you receive an initial negative response. Talk to other straw bale homeowners about their financing, especially if they are in your region.

Insurance

Insurance companies are concerned with facts and figures. The existing research for straw bale homes scores positively with most insurers, especially the excellent fire ratings. Many insurance companies already have these test results on file; others are willing to consider them if you submit them with your application.

Building code approval is usually the only structural requirement of insurers, so with a permit and fire test ratings, insurance is attainable. Some bale homes have even been insured at rates lower than similarly sized conventional homes.

Some builders want to have their project insured during construction. In this case, the fire hazards of loose and unplastered straw may cause rates to be higher than with more conventional projects.

Resale Values

In current real estate markets, chances are good that a straw bale home will receive a lower resale value estimate than its frame wall equivalent. However, low appraisals do not necessarily mean lower resale prices. Home buyers looking for a strong, unique, and super-insulated house may decide that the attractions of a straw bale house are worth more to them than its appraisal indicates. As a side benefit, lower official appraisals often mean lower property taxes!

LONGEVITY

The current resurgence of interest in bale construction is due in part to the recent attention that has been drawn to bale homes in Nebraska dating from the early 1900s, in which the walls have remained strong and relatively unchanged from the day they were built.

The conditions that make for a long and healthy life cycle are the same for any style of construction. Do not expect a bale home to have a shorter life cycle than a wood-framed home. Kept dry, warm, and well-maintained, a bale home can last for a hundred years or more. After all, the molecular structure of straw is remarkably similar to that of wood — remember, each bale is thousands of tiny trees bundled together!

ETERNALLY ANSWERING QUESTIONS

Straw bale construction excites a lot of curiosity, and with curiosity comes questions. Be prepared to answer 'red-flag' questions frequently, since everybody from your mother to the grocery clerk is going to ask them. Consider your patient answers — and your tolerant smile for the inevitable Three Little Pigs joke — an important educational service on behalf of straw bale enthusiasts everywhere!

REFERENCES

Reports

Aprovecho Research Centre. *Testing Strawbale Construction in the Soggy Northwest* Send sase to 80574 Hazelton Rd., Cottage Grove, Oregon 97424 *apro@efn.org* *www.efn.org/~apro/strawbale.html*

Bolles, Bob and Boert Gay. *Strawbale Exterior Pinning Report* (1998). The system described has been approved by the Pima County (Arizona) officials. Report includes illustrations and photos. A. Evans, PO Box 826, Sonoita, Az 85637

Chapman, Linda and Bob Platts. *Developing and Proof Testing a 'Prestressed Nebraska' Method for Improved Production of Baled Fibre Housing* (1996). Test report documents development and testing of a prestressed SB wall system. CMHC, 682 Montreal Rd. Ottawa, Ontario K1A 0P7 ph 613-748-2367 *www.cmhc-shcl.gc.ca/*

Gibson, Scott. "Air Vapor Barriers." *Fine Homebuilding* 8 (May 1994): p. 48. The Taunton Press, 63 S. Main St., P.O. Box 5506, Newton CT 06470–5506 USA.

Jolly, Rob. *Straw Bale Moisture Monitoring Report*. Montreal: Canada Mortgage and Housing Corporation, 1998. 700 Montreal Rd., Ottawa ON K1A 0P7 Canada.

SHB AGRA, Inc. *Report of Transverse Load Test and Small Scale E-119 Fire Test on Un-Coated Straw Bale Wall Panels and Stucco Coated Straw Bale Wall Panels*. Document, 1993 available from Black Range Films, Star Rt. 2, Box 119 Kingston NM 88042 USA.

SHE Consultants. *Moisture in Straw Bale Housing,* Nova Scotia, 1998. RR3, Comp. 308, Wolfville NS B0P 1X0 Canada.

Straw Crafters Bale Wall Compression Testing Program lab tested 2-string and 3-string walls in 1998. Some surprising findings that present some new questions about just how straw bale walls work structurally. Straw Crafters, PO Box 1797, Boulder Colorado 80306 ph 303-546-6822 *jruppert@envision.net*

Thompson, Kim, K.C. Watts, K.I. Wilkie, J. Corson. *Thermal and Mechanical Properties as they Relate to a Straw House,* (1995). Reports on structural testing of bales and thermal and moisture monitoring of a strawbale house in Nova Scotia. Straw House Herbals, RR#1 Ship Harbour, Nova Scotia, Canada B0J 1Y0 ph 902-845-2750 *kimt@chebucto.ns.ca* *www.chebucto.ns.ca/~aa983strawhouse.html*

These reports, and many others, are listed in the annual "Resources" issue of *The Last Straw*. Back issues provide many otherwise unpublished results of all manner of lab-certified and back-yard tests of straw bales and straw-bale systems. Contact: *The Last Straw*, HC66 Box 119, Hillsboro NM 88042 USA. Tel: 505-895-5400; Fax: 505-895-3326 www.strawhomes.com

Videos

Building With Straw Vol. 3: Straw Bale Code Testing. Black Range Films Star Rt. 2, Box 119, Kingston New Mexico 88042 USA.

◗ *the fact that a straw bale home will save a significant amount of money on heating and cooling over the lifetime of the building, and that's money that can be put into paying down a mortgage!"*

— Peter Mack dreams of one day starting his own bank and loaning people friendly money for cool projects. ❖

CHAPTER 4

Building Permits

Many potential bale builders are concerned about getting a building permit for a straw bale structure. The willingness of code officials to accept the use of straw bales in construction is the single largest hurdle facing the growth of bale building at this time.

ABOUT CODES

If you are committed to building with bales, you will be able to get a permit for a soundly designed structure. It may be issued with a minimum of concern and hassle, or it may take several months — or more, in rare cases — to meet the demands of code officials. With each new project that gains approval, however, a greater precedent is set for the acceptance of straw bale construction.

What Is the Building Code?

Building codes are fascinating, and no two are exactly alike. Most civil authorities require a permit before builders are allowed to construct or renovate a building. This permit is issued when a project is deemed to meet all the necessary provisions of the building code.

Both the United States and Canada have a national building code, determined by the federal government. States and provinces fine tune these codes to suit their own purposes. Local governments — charged with the authority to implement, regulate, and enforce the codes — can fine tune them even further. Regional variations to the codes usually address specific climatic concerns such as seismic activity, snow loads, depth of frost penetration as well as zoning or property use issues. Considerations such as minimum and maximum building size, appearance restrictions, and water and waste management are also decided regionally. A building permit, once issued, also provides information to the municipality for the assessment of property taxes.

Straw bale building is not currently prescribed by any national building codes, although some state and regional prescriptions do now exist in the United States — including all or parts of Arizona, California, Colorado, and New Mexico. As the demand for straw bale structures grows, more national, state, provincial, and regional building codes will begin to adopt provisions for straw bale construction, and the process of obtaining permits will be greatly simplified. Until such time, most straw bale builders will have to apply for permits on a case-by-case basis.

Same Code, Different Interpretations

The building code is enforced by individual code officials, all of whom have varying levels of knowledge, experience, and comfort with new ideas. The exact same building code can receive different treatment, depending on the personality of the official

---

From a Skeptic to a Believer

"During a class at the 1994 Annual Business Meeting of the International Conference of Building Officials (ICBO) in Indianapolis, I experienced a major change in my views of code interpretation. The instructor, Mr. Brent Snyder of ICBO, brought to our attention the preface page of Volume I of the newly formatted 1994 Edition of the Uniform Building Code (UBC).

He asked us to read the first paragraph of this preface page. He pointed out that this was the 'mission statement' of the UBC. The second sentence of this statement really caught my attention. It reads as follows: "The code is founded on broad-based principles that make possible the use of new materials and new construction systems." This simple statement brought me up short. I realized that I had an obligation to look at all systems with an open mind.

In December, I was given the task of hosting the Colorado ICBO Chapter meeting slated for August, 1995. I was even given the theme of 'alternative building systems.' So I asked several members, "What kind of ▶

alternative systems are you interested in?" The answers were usually, "Oh, you know, those tire houses and straw houses." I had heard of tire houses, but straw houses? "You've got to be kidding," I thought. Fate and chance were going to play a role in my search for these systems in the months ahead. A trip to Cortez, Colorado to visit my son brought me into direct contact with my first straw-bale structure. My son was helping to build it!

What I saw impressed me. "Where did you find out about this?" I asked. "From Out On Bale in Tucson, Arizona," was the reply. Bingo, I had a contact, a starting point.

Back in Pueblo I used the phone to locate Out On Bale and was advised by a friendly person there to contact Matts Myhrman and David Eisenberg. I left a message for either of them to call me. A call from Matts quickly indicated to me that I was dealing with a very knowledgeable and professional person. Matts was very interested in being part of the program in Pueblo. He even suggested I meet him at a seminar he was doing in Carbondale, Colorado in mid-June, just weeks away. In spite of the favorable impression I had of Matts, my skepticism about straw as a viable building material was still high. I told him I'd see him there and we'd iron out the details for the program in Pueblo.

The program was outstanding. Over 52 building officials from across ◗

or officials involved; larger municipalities will have an entire building department, with numerous inspectors.

We have all received both good and bad service from public officials in our lives, and working with a building inspector is open to the same wide range of service. Depending on where you live and your local inspector's level of interest in alternative building practices, you may be dealing with somebody who has never heard of bale construction before or with somebody with a high degree of awareness and interest. Chances are, though, your path to getting a straw bale building permit will likely involve some educating of your building inspector.

Get to Know Your Code

Most states and provinces publish their codes in builder-friendly editions or make the relevant sections available through the municipality. The time you take to familiarize yourself with the code can be worth its weight in gold. You might find that there are special provisions for alternative or experimental building systems in your code, or perhaps there is an 'owner/builder' clause that removes liability from the municipality and places it back on you. These options are easy to research — call your local building department. You may not need to fit your straw bale design into the parameters of conventional construction as much as you think. Knowing your local code will help you appear knowledgeable and responsible when you enter into discussions with your inspector and can go a long way to helping you receive favorable treatment.

DEALING WITH OFFICIALS

Approaching Inspectors

Inspectors aren't prone to give out answers on speculation. Often, the liability-driven nature of the building inspection profession will prevent you from getting many direct answers from your inspector until you have working plans to present. If you are reluctant to proceed through the planning process without some positive indications from your inspector, you must be sure to ask answerable questions. Otherwise, it is usually best to proceed with your plans and work things out with your inspector over the plans themselves.

If you approach your inspector early, inquire about his or her familiarity with bale construction. Ask if he or she is aware of other bale structures in the region — you should already know the answer! Ask which code provisions you should be aware of that affect straw bale design — again, it helps to know already. Ask if he or she would like any information about straw bale design and research. Expect noncommittal answers. There is very little chance a code official will say, "Yes, by all means build with straw bales. I'd have no problem with that." Still, you may observe enough about his or her personality and openness to make it easier for you to go ahead.

Being Open and Friendly

It is best to maintain an open, friendly attitude toward your building inspector.

Remember, it's his or her job to allow building, not to prevent it. Ideally, inspectors are there to assist as you build the home you want. Begin with this attitude, rather than with a confrontational one. Try to avoid criticizing conventional construction, since inspectors are closely connected to conventional practices. Express a general familiarity with the building code. Stress the many positive reasons for choosing straw bale, and let your inspector know that you are willing to be a reasonable working partner in achieving code compliance for your straw bale plans. While there is plenty of opportunity to go over the head of your inspector, this should be used as a last resort only.

The Straw Bale Precedent

As more bale buildings are erected, precedent makes it more likely that permits will be issued. Being prepared with facts, figures, and contact names and numbers — especially of other inspectors who have approved straw buildings — is important. While the existing straw bale building codes have no legal status outside their jurisdictions, a building inspector provided with such information may be more willing to proceed, using the terms of those codes as a starting place for his or her understanding of bale construction. If you should happen to find a building inspector who is enthusiastic about straw bale, you have a valuable resource on your hands. Ask if he or she is willing to be used as a reference for other bale builders in the same state or province.

The Architect's Stamp

One easy way to sidestep many of the concerns that building officials raise is to present plans that have been stamped by an architect and/or an engineer. A registered professional's approval removes the weight of liability from the building official's shoulders and places it on the professional. Your building inspector may require professional plans before approving a bale design, in which case you don't have much choice but to commission them. While this can add time and expense to your project, you may be able to benefit from the contributions of an architect, as well.

Good Plans Are the Key to a Building Official's Heart

Comprehensive, clear, and accurate plans are the key to impressing a building inspector; the merit of your plans will determine his or her final decision. Be sure to provide references for all aspects of your design that can be related to the building code. Especially on home-drawn plans, these references prove that you have done your homework and don't intend to circumvent the code. Plans should be large, legible, and contain explanatory notes or supplementary drawings where details vary from standard practice. Many aspects of your plans are likely to be straightforward adaptations of the conventional building practices familiar to building officials. As the unusual element in your plans, bale wall details should be presented clearly and precisely and contain references to existing standards and tests where applicable.

▶ *Colorado listened intently as Matts and David put on their program, which was very well received. The next day we had a hands-on program and built a straw-bale wall. In the minds of those who participated, straw-bale construction took quantum leaps. Its validity as a building material passed the test. I had learned that the word 'alternative' was a misnomer. Here was a material that was environmentally acceptable and would offer an R-factor of as much as 50. I was hooked.*

I saw it as a material we could use in our often frustrating search for affordable housing. Here was a material that didn't require a lot of expertise to install and isn't labor intensive either.

One of my children, after hearing me expound on the virtues of straw as a building material, said, "My old rednecked, conservative dad is turning into an environmentalist!" I would rather they call me a practical man. But it's a fact that our infatuation with timber is reaching crisis stage. An average single family home uses 55 mature trees in its framing and trim lumber. I feel, as Building Official and Code Enforcement staff, we have, as our mission says, a real responsibility to look at these emerging alternative systems."

— Clint Tawse, Regional Building Official for both the City and County of Pueblo, Co. ❖

The Building Code Can Be Your Friend

"The building code can be an excellent ally for the owner/builder during construction. Although certain people will object to certain prescribed practices, the code contains lessons learned by professional and amateur builders over generations of home construction. Open to improvement — and debate — the building code can clarify various construction techniques and help you to ensure that your home is a safe, sturdy place. Similarly, your building inspector can be called upon for advice, direction, and guidance as you work on your house. Since he or she is not commercially affiliated with any supply store or contracting company, his or her advice may be among the most practical and impartial you will find."
— Chris Magwood ❖

An Interview with Bob Fowler by David Eisenberg

Bob Fowler, FAIA, RE, C.B.O., is The Chief Building Officer for Pasadena, California, and a past chairman of the board of the International Conference of Building Officials (ICBO), a member of the board of The World Organization of Building Officials (WOBO), and one of the founders of the International Code Council. He was interviewed by David Eisenberg for an article in *The Last Straw*.

D.E.: *Why have you been willing to support the efforts of the straw-bale* ▸

Safety is a key issue for building inspectors, so include references to safety-oriented clauses — sizing and placement of indoor and outdoor stairways and handrails, entrances and exits from the building, smoke and carbon dioxide detectors, et cetera. Make note of the span charts used for major framing components — floor joists and roof. If you are using manufactured trusses, be sure to note this on your plans. Approved drawings from the truss company can be supplied at a later time, as long as you inform the inspector.

The role of the building inspector is not to prevent you from building but to ensure that your building is structurally safe. It is very rare for a building inspector to completely reject a viable set of plans. In most jurisdictions, building is encouraged because you will be adding to the permanent tax base of the municipality. More than enough evidence now exists to prove the safety and viability of straw bale construction. Getting approval is a matter of providing enough of this evidence to satisfy your particular inspector.

The Hassle Factor

Don't be discouraged by a negative response to your plans to build with straw. Be prepared to persist; many permits have been issued after an initial rejection of the idea. There are answers to all of your building inspector's questions and concerns, but you will have to make the effort to supply them. Keep in mind that getting approval from your building department is not a one-shot, win-or-lose affair. It can be a process of change and exchange, in which modifications are made until both you and the building official are satisfied with the results.

Rejections and Appeals

In the rare case when approval from a local building official is not forthcoming, an appeals process is usually available. The manner of appealing will vary between jurisdictions. Often you will find someone at a higher level of authority who is willing to recognize the validity and importance of building with bales. The process might be short and informal, requiring only a call to a state or provincial politician, or it may be long and legal, involving internal appeals processes. Either way, if your plans are valid, the chances that you will be allowed to build are weighted in your favor and grow more favorable with each new approval that's issued for a straw bale design.

Approval Can Take Time

Whatever you do, don't rush your building inspector by imposing your own deadlines and time-frames. Approval can take one day or, in extreme cases, a year or more. Even if the inspector has no problem with straw bale construction, other adjustments to your plans may be required. Be patient and courteous during this process. Building inspectors wield a fair bit of authority and can seriously delay your project if they should so choose. Maintaining a positive attitude is your best defense. Gaining permit approval can be a bit nerve-wracking, but it shouldn't deter you from putting your plans into action.

A NOTE ON STRAW BALE AND CODIFICATION

Many efforts have been made to have straw bale construction included in building codes. As time goes on, these efforts are likely to meet with greater and greater success. Success creates both benefits and disadvantages to bale builders. Inclusion in the building code allows owner/builders to use the code to create their own plans with some confidence that they will receive approval. The elimination of architects and engineers from the planning process removes a significant cost from straw bale projects. On the down side, straw bale building is still at a very young stage in its development. While codification could make approvals simpler to obtain, it also poses the risk of freezing the technique before adequate experimentation leads us to sound, standard practices.

Were building codes flexible in nature, immediate codification of straw bale would be an undeniable asset. However, the tendency with codes is to simplify, over-protect, and narrow options. It remains quite likely that as techniques, approaches,

---

An Interesting Comparison of Materials

This excerpt from the website of The Development Centre for Appropriate Technology (DCAT) offers a startling perspective on the codification of bales.

"When we think about materials and their acceptance, we should consider the reality in which we already operate. Joe Lstiburek, of Building Sciences, Inc., a building consultant of the highest regard, has put the situation into perspective by describing the realities of the use of wood as a building material. He points out that wood, were it being introduced today as a new building material, could never get into the building codes. It has nearly every problem a material could conceivably have. There are hundreds of species. The strength and durability is dependent on the species, as well as some of the environmental conditions that occurred while it was growing. The strength is dependent on things like the orientation of the grain, the age of the wood, how it was dried, moisture content, and the size, location and frequency of knots. It burns, it rots, insects like to eat it. It is *dimensionally unstable, it splits. And yet, in spite of all these problems, it is the material of choice in this country for residential construction, even though there are huge environmental problems associated with its profligate use. Of course it is a wonderful material. And there are reasons it is so widely used. But if a new material [like straw bale] is introduced with any one of the problems that wood has, it is nearly impossible to get it accepted into the codes."*

— David Eisenberg's *Straw Bale Construction and the Building Codes: A Working Paper* is an excellent document concerning the ongoing process of making straw bale building viable. The printed version can be ordered from the Development Center for Appropriate Technology, PO Box 41144, Tucson AZ 85717, or you can view DCAT's excellent website at: www.cyberbytes.com/dcat/

---

construction community to re-introduce this building method?

B.F.: There are probably a dozen reasons. First, I have an adventurous spirit, and see the need for finding more sustainable ways to build. I also have a farming background and know the properties of straw and the disposal problems straw in the field presents to farmers. So I appreciate that these problems can be turned into assets. As an architect and an engineer, as well as a builder, I find straw-bale something I can really get excited about. Not just for the fact that you can build very good looking buildings with it, but for the environmental reasons, the energy efficiency, and the affordability of it.

D.E.: The straw-bale construction revival has been unique in that it is a very popular older building material that lacks the large quantified base of data we have for most other building systems. As a building official who has been supportive of this way of building, how do you respond to this?

B.F.: When someone comes in with a material that has a documented history, but no certified testing data, my suggestion is that we let them build an experimental structure, within our code jurisdiction. This is an opportunity to raise the level of comfort of the building officials. I'd also encourage doing a house, rather than a non-residential structure. A residence will be a better demonstration of the technology and there are so many good things about straw-bale construction that I'd prefer a house ▶

were built to be lived in. People are more likely to be influenced by a beautiful straw-bale home, because they will be able to relate to a home better than other buildings.

D.E.: What suggestions would you have for people when introducing the idea of straw-bale construction to building officials who have never heard of it?

B.F.: I think a wide variety of approaches is necessary. It's an education process. Let the building official know that this isn't a crackpot idea but a tried-and-true building method that's been used for years. Give the officials adequate material and don't push too hard. They see a lot of snake-oil artists and you don't want them to think you're pushing them into something. Give them time to review the information, put on a program to show them photos or books or videos. Use as many approaches as you can to educate them about it. You have to elevate their level of comfort.

D.E.: What suggestions would you have for those building officials?

B.F.: Keep an open mind. We all need to understand that we have to embrace different methods of construction. We must find low cost sustainable methods to build housing. Here is an opportunity to use a waste product. Express your concerns, ask your questions. Take the time to really look at it and learn about its history. I'm convinced that if you do, you'll get excited about it, too." ❖

and our understanding of how bales work as a building material change for the better, they will outstrip the provisions of any existing codes and require a willingness on behalf of code officials to change and update their regulations.

We look forward to the day when straw bale construction is an accepted and widespread practice. We're also glad to still have some of the freedom made possible by the case-by-case nature of project approvals. Let the learning continue.

REFERENCES

Books

Eisenberg, David. *Straw Bale Construction and the Building Codes: A Working Paper.* Development Center for Appropriate Technology, 1996. Available from: PO Box 27513, Tucson AZ 85726-7513 USA. Tel: 520-624-6628; Fax: 520-798-3701; E-Mail: dcat@azstarnet.com website: www.azstarnet.com/~dcat/

Interview

Eisenberg, David. "An Interview with Bob Fowler," *The Last Straw* 13 (spring 1996): p.4. HC 66 Box 119, Hlilsboro NM 88042 USA. Tel: 505-895-5400; Fax: 505-895-3326; E-Mail: (thelaststraw@strawhomes.com) www.strawhomes.com

Your local library, building department, and/or book store should have copies of the relevant building codes for your jurisdiction. Be certain you are obtaining the correct code and the correct version of the code.

See Appendix A for the full text of the Arizona Straw Bale Code.

CHAPTER 5

The Hotly-Debated, Often-Distorted Question of Cost

"So what does one of those straw bale houses cost?" Such a common question, such a difficult answer. The issue of cost is complex, and while bale building can be done less expensively than conventional framing, so much is up to you.

Much that is written and even more that is rumored about straw bale building hails it as the perfect option for people wanting to build on the cheap. Before we get into the specifics of designing and building your straw bale house, we'd like to address the hotly-debated, often-distorted question of cost.

ALL ABOUT MONEY

There is No Such Thing as 'Cheap'

Building a house is an expensive proposition. This is true whether you are using straw bales or other materials. From the cost of the property on which you build andpermit and start-up costs, right through to the hinges, knobs, and handrails of the finished house, the list of expenses is long and weighty. There is no way to avoid expense, especially when you are building for longevity, efficiency, and to meet codes.

The 'Less Expensive' House

Since truly cheap housing — lean-tos, shacks, or tents — is not what we deem suitable in North America, we prefer to use the term 'less expensive' housing when talking about straw bale building. Many people have heard of the $10 per square foot straw bale house. Be assured, a $10 per square foot house is very simple, roughly finished, not necessarily efficient, and definitely not erected where a building code is enforced. Building a home to modern standards can never be considered 'cheap.'

Money — or lack thereof! — is always a central concern when you design and build your house. Building your house is going to absorb whatever budget you allocate for it, even if the total dollar figure is not sky-high. Rather than focusing on how 'cheap' straw bale building can be, it makes more sense to focus on creating a building that can be completed within your means. At every juncture in this book, we will be assessing costs and trying to point out ways to save money.

How Can Bales Save Money?

Straw bale buildings can certainly hold a cost advantage over conventional styles. By replacing both wall-framing lumber and insulation — plus vapor barriers, nails, glues, et cetera — with a single, inexpensive material, the cost of building super-insulated walls can be lowered. The interior and exterior plaster cladding can, depending on the choice of ingredients and method of its application, be comparable with other cladding systems such as drywall, vinyl or wood siding, brick, etc.

You might also save money on framing. Because bales are more user-friendly than other wall systems, like stud-framing, many people are encouraged to put up their own walls, which can cut down on costs. If you are hiring people to build straw walls for you, you won't necessarily save money on labor. However, an experienced framing crew can knock together a frame wall quite quickly. Since most bale projects seem to include owner built walls — and why not? putting up straw walls is fun! — a cost saving in this area is often assumed.

The U.S. Department of Energy's Navajo Test Project

The Navajo Project has demonstrated that straw-bale construction can be inexpensive compared to other materials. The cost of the finished 988 square-foot home equates to $58 per square foot, not including the cost of utility hookups (water, power, and sewage). A similar sized wood-frame house constructed in the same area would probably have cost about the same as the demonstration prototype. However, future straw-bale homes should cost considerably less than the prototype because of required changes and modifications during building of the prototype. In addition, the labor-intensive double adobe walls of the hearth area added more than $3,000 to the project. Had the exterior walls been entirely straw-bale, the over-all costs would have been lower. Straw bales were supplied at a cost of $2.50 a bale, including transportation.

Normally, the cost of a bale wall is about one-fourth the cost of a comparable, superinsulated wall built with conventional materials.

Life cycle cost estimate for conventional vs. straw-bale houses

CONSTRUCTION	FINANCE	ENERGY	TOTAL	SAVINGS
Conventional				
$82,500	396,000	120,000	532,500	———
Straw Bale				
$78,375	376,000	60,000	451,675	83,875
Straw Bale*				
$40,000	192,000	60,000	260,000	272,500
*owner-built walls, finishing, roofing				

Notes:

Life cycle = 100 years.

Finance cost = construction cost minus down payment of twenty percent at an annual interest rate of six percent over the one hundred year life cycle (does not include closing costs when the house is sold).

Energy = the average cost for heating and cooling a conventional home for this analysis to be $100 per month.

Total = Amount of down payment plus energy and finance.

Source: Working Group Reports, Plastered Straw Bale Conference, "Roots and Revival," Arthur Nebraska, September, 1993.

The Buck Stops at the Top of Your Wall — Underneath It, Too!

With the exception of the exterior walls, all the rest of the construction costs for a straw bale house are identical to any other building style. Most contractors estimate the cost of the wall system at about 15 percent of the total budget. As a building material, your straw bales are going to directly reduce only that percentage of the total cost. To truly save money, a straw bale builder must turn his or her attention to all the other aspects of the building at hand, and lower costs at each stage. Fortunately, straw bale construction lends itself to the use of plenty of alternatives that can bring down the overall cost of a project.

Kim Thompson

How to Really Save Money

The choices you make concerning labor, materials, and finishing will determine whether or not you are able to build within a certain budget. Labor costs will have a big impact on your construction budget. Doing it yourself will eliminate labor costs. Doing some work yourself and hiring for some will raise costs. Having your home entirely built for you will increase costs even further. Remember that if you build the house yourself, you will have to make a serious commitment of time. While you may not be paying for labor, you are losing your own earning potential. It is quite possible to mix-and-match your talents and interests with those of local professionals and find a good balance between your budget, time, and level of expertise. Finding the right blend of personal 'sweat equity' and hired help is crucial as you establish an accurate budget.

Friends and family are almost always willing to be part of a bale-raising, but other tasks, like raising a post and beam frame, can also be done without professional help.

Kim Thompson

Your choice of materials will similarly cause wide variations in cost. Salvaged, used, and homemade materials can cost less but often involve more labor.

Interior finishing also makes up a significant portion of a typical house budget. Take into account what kinds of flooring, doors, windows, kitchen cabinets, appliances, curtains, rugs, bathroom fixtures, etc., you want. The same basic shell can be finished in wildly different ways, resulting in astronomically different budgets.

If you're looking for the lowest possible costs, take care to weigh the advantages of bottom-dollar prices with other factors. Used, single pane windows may be dirt cheap, but you will pay for that choice with higher heating costs for the rest of the building's life, and many building codes do not allow single pane windows. Similarly, salvaged materials can require large amounts of time to clean, prepare, and fit, which can offset any cost advantage. Conversely, a bit of extra legwork may produce excellent and inexpensive options for many building materials.

Over-Budget Is the Norm
The building that is completed without going over-budget is rare. Never plan to spend everything up to your last available penny at the budgeting stage. There are always problems, delays, or unforeseen costs, and they can add up significantly. Be sure to leave yourself plenty of breathing room. It is better to plan more modestly and finish your project than to plan grand and fall short of completion.

The Real Savings Are Long Term
Your straw bale house will inevitably save you significant amounts of money when it comes to heating and cooling costs. Long after you've finished the house, those savings will keep multiplying for you. So even if you don't build the cheapest house in the world, you will be building the cheapest house in which to continue living in the long term.

The Final Word
Well, there really isn't a final word on cost. Each house is unique — even when created from the exact same set of plans — and only you can make all the ongoing, complicated decisions about cost. The price tag is up to you, but we hope you'll find some good advice in this book to help you keep it as low as possible.

REFERENCES
Roy, Rob. *Mortgage-Free! Radical Strategies for Home Ownership*. Chelsea Green Publishers, 1998. ISBN 0-930031-98-9.

Landscaping and exterior detailing are important cost factors that many builders forget to consider when preparing a budget.

CHAPTER 6

Getting Focused

Most owner built homes start with a dream and a basic desire to shelter oneself affordably, creatively, and adequately. But as soon as you decide to realize those dreams, actually getting started can be daunting. You've entered the thinking stage, and now it's time to get focused.

Whether you intend to build every part of your house by yourself or hire a contractor to build it all for you, it is important to get focused and answer some basic questions very early in the process.

WORK SMART

Putting Thinking Ahead of Building

When most people envision building their home, they picture themselves with a hammer in hand, hoisting a bale, or in some other way being actively engaged in the physical building process. For those who have never built before, acquiring manual skills and technical building knowledge appears to be the most daunting part of such a project. In this book, we work with the assumption that the major difficulty faced by potential builders is articulating what they want from a building and learning what will be required to achieve their goals. The thinking tools are the most important tools you will acquire. In comparison, actual construction — whether done by you or by hired labor — is a matter of basic, achievable mechanics.

Wrong Turns, Bad Decisions, and Mistaken Assumptions

Every builder inevitably has a list of 'I shouldas' at the end of a project. It identifies points where knowledge and understanding came after the physical process of building was finished or at least well underway. It's impossible to predict and understand every variable a house building project will throw your way, and the only way to keep the 'I shouldas' from overwhelming your project is to allow yourself plenty of thinking time. Even builders with decades of experience will take away something new from each project; it is this acquired knowledge that often allows them to do things faster, better, and more economically than novices.

THE THREE BIG QUESTIONS

Why Build at All?

The potential answers to this question are as many and varied as the people asking. Write down your answers on a list, and keep coming back to it as you progress through the thinking stage. If your reasons for building are not being adequately addressed by the designing and planning you are doing, it's time to reassess. Don't allow the project to fuel itself — keep track of why you are doing what you are doing.

For example, if one of your primary reasons for building is to lower your current shelter costs, then be sure you are thinking toward a detailed budget. If, during the thinking process, you realize you won't be able to build within budget, you may need to reconsider. You may want to scale back your ambitions, rethink your financing, alter your time frame, or perhaps abandon your project for the time being until your pre-conditions for building have been met.

What Do I Really Want?

Closely tied to the first question, answers to "What do I really want from the house I build?" will provide a foundation for the thinking and planning you do. Make sure your answers to questions one and two are compatible. If not, your wishes and desires will outstrip your intentions. Plan to spend quite a while answering this question.

If you have the ability, sketch the kind of space you dream of inhabiting.

Don't assume that any point is too small or too obvious to include on your list. In fact, you can divide the list into large and small concerns. On the large side, take note of locations where you'd like to build, the kind of surroundings you'd like, and what exterior appearance you want your home to have. On the small side, keep a list of specific design details that are important to you. It will be a long time before some of the smaller details become a real concern, but get to know them early.

Ask yourself what rooms you envision for your house. Write down the names of those rooms and list of attributes you associate with each one. Do not limit yourself to what you already know and have experienced. This is a time to consider your ideals. Does your kitchen serve a central role, functioning as a place for food preparation, art work, and long, intimate tea-times? Is your bedroom only a place where you sleep, or do you enjoy certain activities — reading, writing, or watching television — in that room? Do you want a dining room? Is your bathroom merely functional, or is it your personal getaway? All these considerations are important. Include contradictions if they arise; they will be solved later.

If you find that a traditional room does not appear on your list, don't force it to be there. Perhaps the typical living room function will be served by your kitchen, or by a den or library. Invent new room names if necessary.

Room uses, furniture items, ambiance, noise levels, views, storage capacity, and counter space — whatever presents itself as important to you should be included. Be exhaustive, and allow yourself time to add to, change, and modify the lists.

Mapping your movements

Take the time to study and think about traffic circulation in your home — if you have kids, it may be more along the lines of air traffic control! What works in your current home? What needs improvement? You can begin this process by studying different kinds of movement. Movement in and out of the house is important; movement within key public rooms — especially kitchens — is also important. Examine traffic patterns between rooms, noting which patterns are most common. Make lists and notes about circulation. Do you often entertain crowds? If so, what happens to human movement under these conditions? Does movement change with the seasons?

Be sure to note all your current gripes! If you know what's wrong, keep track of the negatives. Solutions will be forthcoming.

Keep your eyes wide open

Don't limit your examination to your current home, but think about other residences you've lived in or places you've visited. Every time you are in a building, be conscious of its layout, the features of its rooms, and its traffic patterns. Take notes wherever you go, either mental or written. Building a home gives you the opportunity to blend the best and avoid the worst of everything you've ever known or experienced, so keep your eyes wide open.

This is not a chore!

Don't look at this stage of your design process as a chore. We call it the Design Game because it can be a lot of fun. You have access to a rich architectural and cultural history. Enjoy it! Revel in it! When you finally stop seeing new things and being excited by possibilities, you're probably at the end of the process.

Don't forget your family

Your family will be sharing the house with you, so involve them in the process. You'll be amazed at how attentive to detail kids can be if they are told what to look for! Think back to when you were young. Whose house did you like to visit? Why? What did you like and dislike about your own childhood homes? Think about your future needs. Will children be arriving? Will parents, siblings, or friends be moving in? Will your home be accessible to people with physical challenges? If you have children, you'll have to do some thinking about their future needs, too. Inevitably, conflicts between various needs will arise. Let them come to the fore, and soon enough you'll be able to start making compromises. Planning for everybody who will share the house is vital if it's going to work well for all concerned.

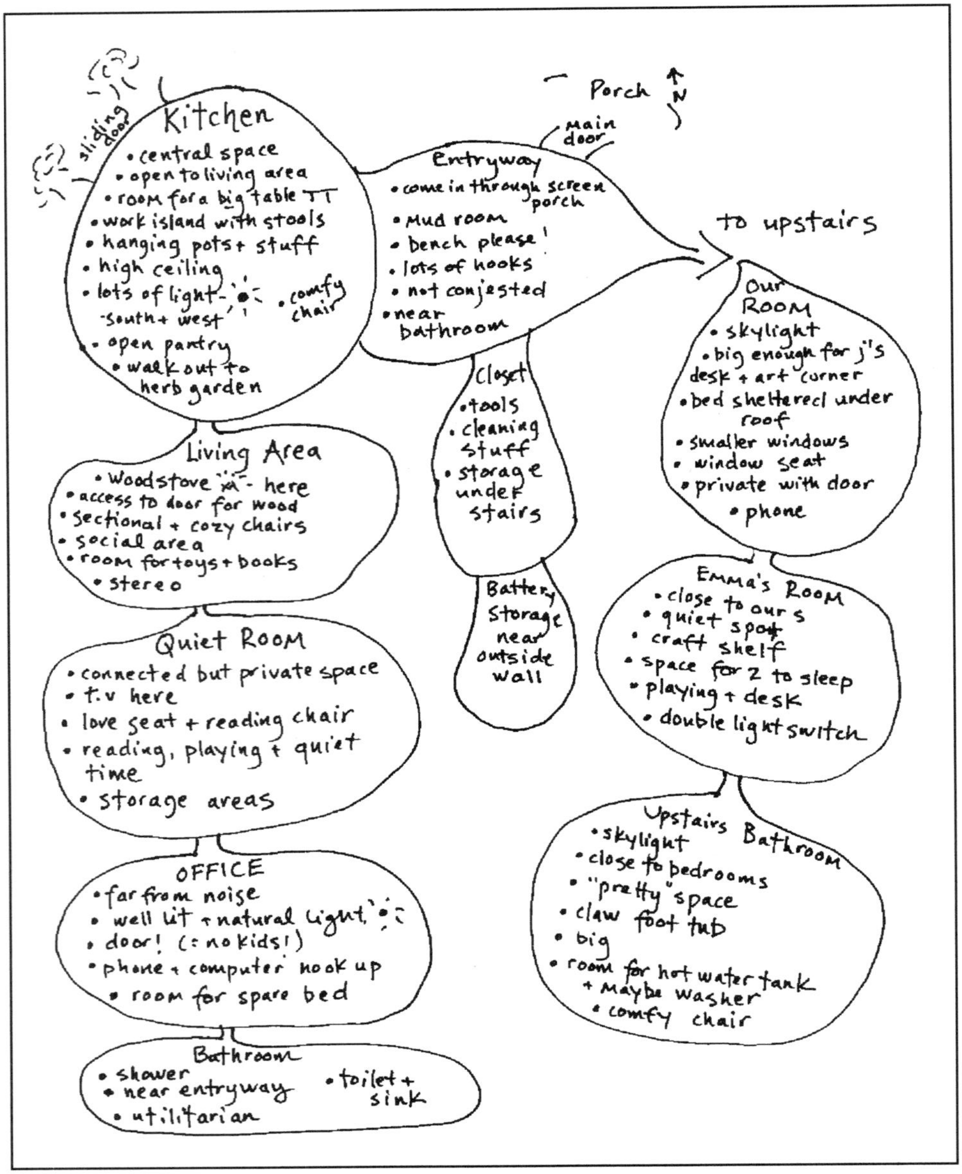
Porch
N
main door
sliding door
Kitchen
• central space
• open to living area
• room for a big table
• work island with stools
• hanging pots + stuff
• high ceiling
• lots of light - south + west
• comfy chair
• open pantry
• walk out to herb garden
Entryway
• come in through screen porch
• Mud room
• bench please!
• lots of hooks
• not conjested
• near bathroom
to upstairs
Our Room
• skylight
• big enough for j's desk + art corner
• bed sheltered under roof
• smaller windows
• window seat
• private with door
• phone
Closet
• tools
• cleaning stuff
• storage under stairs
Battery Storage near outside wall
Living Area
• Woodstove here
• access to door for wood
• Sectional + cozy chairs
• social area
• room for toys + books
• stereo
Emma's Room
• close to ours
• quiet spot
• craft shelf
• space for 2 to sleep
• playing + desk
• double light switch
Quiet Room
• connected but private space
• t.v here
• love seat + reading chair
• reading, playing + quiet time
• storage areas
Upstairs Bathroom
• skylight
• close to bedrooms
• "pretty" space
• claw foot tub
• big
• room for hot water tank + maybe washer
• comfy chair
OFFICE
• far from noise
• well lit + natural light
• door! (= no kids!)
• phone + computer hook up
• room for spare bed
Bathroom
• shower
• near entryway
• utilitarian
• toilet + sink

You can use a hand-drawn 'bubble' list for initial room arrangements. You might want to assign each room a bit of proportion, according to its function.

Once you know what rooms you want and how they will be used, start arranging them in ways that accommodate your movement patterns. One way to achieve this is to write the names of your rooms on individual pieces of paper, including key features and arrows that indicate the kind of traffic flow you expect that room to handle, as shown in the illustration at left.

Start arranging these pieces of paper in different ways until they start to make sense to you. When you find an arrangement that seems suitable, make a drawing of it. Then start over again. There are many possible arrangements that might work, so don't stop at one. As with each stage in the Design Game, give yourself lots of time. You can even make your puzzle the center of an evening with friends and family. Invite everybody to create their own house out of your individual elements — their designs will bring fresh perspectives to your own puzzling.

It's not a matter of life and death!

It is easy to become so wrapped up in the Design Game that you feel you must have everything perfect. Don't sweat it. Every house is full of compromises — even warm-spirited, inviting, and comfortable homes have their share of little problem areas and 'shouldas.' Some people — those who don't have building code concerns! — just start laying things out on the ground, and design as they build. That, too, can work. By the time you work your way through the Design Game, you'll have learned an awful lot about what you want your house to be like. This awareness — even when it's an awareness of flaws — is invaluable. It is your first important thinking tool.

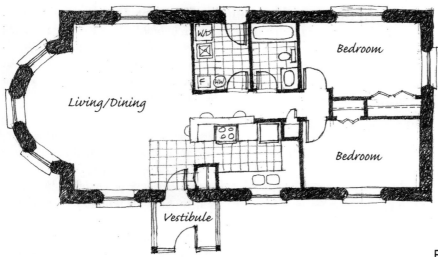

Planning For Phase Building

Early floor plans can be hand-drawn and are not etched in stone.
Floor plan drawings can reflect current budgetary restraints while allowing for future planning.
It is a good idea to start thinking about the thickness of bale walls.

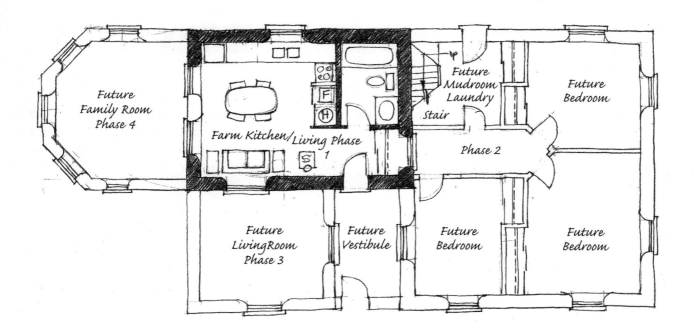

Where to Build — City, Suburbs, Town, or Country?

If you do not currently own property on which to build, you are facing a task about which entire books have been written. Chances are, you'll already have made a decision to live within a certain region due to family ties, employment, love of the landscape, or some other personal reason. When buying property, it is helpful to define a boundary for yourself and concentrate your search within it.

City sites

City builders must consider issues of lot size and availability, local zoning and building restrictions, neighborhood quality, availability of services, proximity to employment and schools, and transportation networks. Don't forget to research the city's development plan to see whether or not your prospective neighborhood is slated for major zoning changes. Talk to people who live in the area and find out what they have to say.

If the lot you are considering has been empty for a long time, find out how it has been used in the past. Be suspicious of former industrial sites or sites that have been used for gas stations or other polluting businesses. Paying for a soil analysis is not a bad idea if you harbor any suspicions or concerns. Don't forget to consider light pollution. Excessive shading of your site by other buildings, proximity to high-wattage street lights, signage or factory lighting, and car headlights can become constant irritants for urban dwellers.

To date, straw bale homes have been idealized. Straw bale construction, however, works well as urban housing. The remarkable sound-proofing nature of thick bale walls can significantly lower the amount of ambient noise in your home, making it a more relaxing environment. Used in duplexes or other multiple unit dwellings, straw bales can form dividing walls between units. By virtually eliminating noise transfer, straw bale housing removes a major disadvantage of shared-living structures. Furthermore, flexible bale construction allows for design adaptations to surrounding home styles without requiring higher expenditures for conventional materials.

While the associations of clean, environmental living that are identified with straw bale homes might seem incongruous in urban settings, urban living offers us many opportunities to lower our personal environmental impact. Using public transportation and bicycles make as valuable an environmental contribution as does building with bales.

Suburban sites

If an urban site does not appeal to you, you may want to build in the suburbs. Suburban sites offer builders more opportunity to take advantage of passive solar gain than do many urban sites. Exterior appearance is often highly regulated in suburban neighborhoods. Fortunately, straw bale designs can easily be made to blend in with dominant architectural styles, allowing builders to retain maximum efficiency without resorting to conventional building practices.

In general, suburban sites represent the most environmentally-unfriendly option for building. Due to the separation between residential and commercial areas, suburban residents are forced to use automobiles whenever they go out.

Town sites

Small towns can offer a balanced compromise between urban and rural choices. Prices for town lots can be very reasonable and edge-of-town lots can be quiet and very rural in feeling. There are likely to be fewer appearance restrictions and building code limitations in smaller towns. Environmentally, town living can cut down on automobile use.

Country sites

Rural isolation and straw bale homes seem well suited to one another. Rural sites have many advantages. Under proper conditions a builder can harvest both straw and lumber from his or her own property. Code restrictions are usually least imposing — or possibly nonexistent — in rural areas. Be careful not to jump into rural life without adequate forethought, especially if you are a long-time urban dweller. While rural life can be quiet, beautiful, and inspiring, it also requires adaptations in lifestyle. From an environmental perspective, rural homes are often the most energy-intensive dwellings. Automobiles must be used frequently, fuel sources need to be transported long distances, and road construction and maintenance consume vast amounts of energy. If you are committed to lowering your environmental impact, think carefully about how you plan on living after you've built your straw bale home in the country.

ABOUT PROPERTY

Find Property that Agrees With You

Allow yourself some room for intuition when choosing property. If a particular site feels good and meets your price and location needs, go with that choice. Similarly, if a site meets all your requirements but simply doesn't turn your crank, then let it go and keep looking elsewhere. If possible, visit your potential site several times and over a few seasons: seasonal changes can transform the land of your dreams into a dismal mess. Anticipate the view when the trees are with and without leaves. Examine the ground for signs of spring flooding and water movement.

You Can 'Grow' Your Site

Remember that sites are not unchangeable nor unchanging. Sites that do not currently appear naturally beautiful can be grown into lush, attractive sites over time. That lot with the two gorgeous, mature oak trees may be nice now, but how will it look when those trees inevitably come down as they die? Try to look ahead. You can always transform your site to meet your needs, and if the lot you're interested in is clear, beginning with a clean slate is not always a bad thing.

Wherever You Build, Think About More Than Your House

Regardless of your choice of location, don't forget to plan for more than just your house. Assess the property for its natural characteristics, including trees, bushes, hills, and other features. Harmonize friendly outdoor spaces with your plans. Think about storage buildings and workshops, and leave room for such outbuildings even if you don't need them now. Situate the house to make gardening possible.

Property Hunting Schemes

Searching for property can be a long frustrating process. Real estate agencies are a good place to start your hunt, but be sure to let agents know all your requirements early on. Listings for vacant lands are considered the doldrums at most real estate offices. Be sure to ask for complete listings in your preferred area; otherwise, you may only be shown newer listings or those an agent is keen to push. Expect to see a lot of what you don't want. You can also place ads in local newspapers, specifying your needs and price range. Quite often, the prospect of a keen buyer can motivate property owners into selling lots that are not currently on the market. Tax foreclosures, property dealers, and re-zoned lands are all worth researching, too.

Don't Design Too Early

Without a piece of property on which to build, don't spend too much time creating a finished design for your home. The land should — and will — be responsible for shaping your design.

REFERENCES

Books

Allen, Edward. *How Buildings Work: The Natural Order of Architecture.* Oxford University Press, 1995. ISBN 0-19-509100-0.

Brooks, Hugh. *Illustrated Encyclopedic Dictionary of Building and Construction Terms.* Prentice-Hall, 1976. ISBN 0-13-451013-5.

Brown, Azby. *Small Spaces: Stylish Ideas for Making More of Less.* Kodansha International, 1993. ISBN 4-7700-1495-3.

Crowther, Richard L. *Ecological Architecture.* Butterworth Architecture, 1992. ISBN 0-7506-9171-9.

Holloway, Dennis and Maureen McIntyre. *The Owner-Builder Experience: How to Design and Build Your Own Home.* Rodale Press, 1986. ISBN 0-87857-643-6.

Preston, Edward. *How to Buy Land Cheap (4th Edition).* Loompanics Unlimited, 1991. ISBN 1-55950-064-6.

Rybczynski, Witold. *The Most Beautiful House in the World.* Penguin Books, 1989. ISBN 0-14-010566-2.

Taylor, John S. *A Shelter Sketchbook: Timeless Building Solutions.* Chelsea Green Publishers, 1997. ISBN 1-890132-02-0.

Woods, Charles G. *A Natural System of House Design: An Architect's Way.* McGraw-Hill, 1996. ISBN 0-07-071736-2.

CHAPTER 7

Design Considerations

After playing the Design Game, you'll have come to certain conclusions about the house you want. Before you move on to a scaled drawing or design, there are some technical considerations to be addressed. It's time for you to become aware of some key design considerations.

The results from your Design Game are an important beginning. You will have gained some clear understanding about your future home and learned about the kinds of compromises that must be made along the way. Depending on your level of experience and the range of your personal concerns, you may or may not have addressed certain technical issues in your version of the Design Game. These elements must be addressed before the Game is over and the working design is created.

SOME NEW PIECES FOR THE DESIGN GAME

Passive Solar Design

Early cave dwellers knew about it, wild and domestic animals know about it, and some cultures still practice it, but passive solar design has long been forgotten in modern home design. Incorporating passive solar elements into your house is easy to do and the rewards are significant.

Ever watched a cat or dog stretch out on the floor in a beam of warm sunlight? Passive solar design maximizes your home's exposure to those warm rays and gives them a chance to heat your home, as shown in Illustration 7.1 on the next page. At the same time, good passive solar design ensures those same rays are kept out when you are trying to keep your home cool. By simply taking advantage of the sun's position in the sky, winter heating costs and summer cooling costs can be lowered dramatically.

Passive solar design is a three-step process. The first step is to align your house so its longest side faces south — reverse for Southern Hemisphere. This southern alignment can be scientifically calculated or approximate. Many passive solar designs favor a slight eastward leaning, which brings in early morning warmth and cuts out late afternoon overheating. The second step is to arrange the majority of your larger windows on this elongated south face, so sunlight can enter. The third step is to ensure that your south facing windows are shaded against summer sun, while allowing winter sun

This is a good example of effective passive solar design. South facing windows on both floors are shaded, and the roof is slanted at a good angle for mounting solar panels.

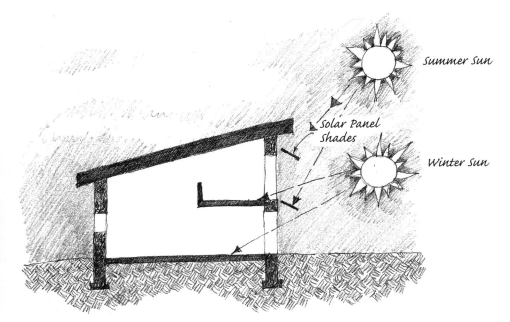

Summer Sun

Solar Panel Shades

Winter Sun

Illustration 7.1
The basics of passive solar design are easy to comprehend. You want to maximize exposure to your southern windows during winter, when the sun is lower in the sky, and minimize or eliminate the exposure those windows get at the height of summer.

to enter freely. Awnings, nose roofs, vine trellises, blind systems, deciduous trees, and bushes — any of these can be used, individually or in conjunction with one another, to block the summer sun when it is high in the sky. The winter sun, crossing the sky at a much lower angle, can enter below the awnings.

How you accomplish your own version of passive solar gain will depend on your location, building style, and climate. For now, add this new aspect to your current efforts in the Design Game. Align your rooms along an east-west axis, and figure out which rooms will benefit from larger, south facing windows and which will function well without. It is also a good time to think about sunrise and sunset and which rooms you'll want to receive morning and evening light. If you're an early riser, a bedroom with an eastern exposure will fill your room with morning sunshine. If you dread the sun's arrival, go west. Consider when certain rooms will most be used, and make an effort to match natural lighting to room use.

Bungalow or Multi-Story?

You may already have decided whether you are building your home on one or two levels. (Three stories plus a basement is the maximum allowable by many residential building codes.) If you haven't decided, now is a good time to consider your options. Size alone may dictate whether your building is one or two stories. Tiny houses don't need an extra level, while very large buildings usually do. However, with a moderately sized building — 1200–2400 square feet — you have the option of going either way.

It may seem that the added complexity of an extra level would be more costly to construct, but a reduction in footprint size can often cancel out such cost factors. For example, a 2000-square-foot building constructed on one level will require a large foundation, a large floor area — more concrete if it's a slab, more framing if it's wooden — and a large roof. However, if you build two 1000-square-foot stories, you not only halve the size of the foundation and roof but halve the building's footprint size as well. You will end up adding expenses for stairs, second-floor joists, and flooring materials, but your overall costs may balance in favor of the two-story option. It can also be easier to move heat, water, and power around a two-story building. Square footage, construction complexity, footprint size, and cost must all be considered as you decide how you're going to build.

Rounded and Curved Elements

Square buildings are the norm in our culture, but you might want to stray from the norm and incorporate round or curved walls in your design. Modern construction avoids curves because wooden framing, plywood, and drywall do not lend themselves easily to curved details. Bale walls are quite adaptable to curves, allowing for design possibilities foreign to most modern home plans. Keep in mind that your round or curved bale wall will still have to blend with your foundation and roof, both of which are likely to use straight materials.

The potential for using rounded or curved walls is a benefit when designing bale walls. Remember that although bales are easily curved, other building materials aren't necessarily so adaptable. The results of taking the time to design and build curved walls is evident in this guest lodge at the Spoutwood Farm CSA in Glen Rock, PA.

LEARNING TO JUGGLE

As you will discover as you begin this part of the design process, there is nothing simple or easy about it. It can be, in turns, fun, challenging, and frustrating. The number of ideas, considerations, and technical requirements you have to juggle will only keep growing as you delve deeper into the design of your home. Don't worry if you drop an item or two as you juggle. Work at a pace that is comfortable to you, and progress at a rate that matches your understanding. Expect to ride an emotional roller coaster, with high highs and low lows. In the end, remember that you are building a house, not attempting to reach a state of perfection. There is plenty of room for learning — and for mistakes — as you move forward. The more you think about the design of your house now, the easier the building or hiring process will be later.

Passive Solar:
Theory and Practice

"*The passive solar design of my house is one of its most effective and important elements. On a sunny winter day, even if the outdoor temperature is -20 degrees Celsius, there is no need to add heat to our straw bale home! However, a lot of what I was told and read about passive solar was misleading for northern climate applications. The further north you go — we're at 44 degrees north — the fewer hours of sunlight you get in the winter. Plus, winter sun is often obscured by clouds. This means that when you really want its benefits, the number of hours of passive solar gain is much lower than the number of hours of thermal loss, since heat escapes through windows at night and on cloudy days.*

Counting on passive solar gain to warm concrete floors or any other thermal mass is a mistake in northern climes, unless extreme design strategies are undertaken — windows extending to the floor and no rugs or furniture blocking access to sunlight. The thickness of bale walls means that much of the direct sunlight will fall on your window sill, not on the floor. By incorporating some thermal mass — concrete, tile, or stone — into your wide windowsills, you will gain some warming effects, but your floor and any interior walls will not see enough sun to raise their temperature appreciably.

When it is shining, the winter sun will do an excellent job of heating ▶

the air — not the mass — of your home, and it doesn't require massive south facing windows to do so. Sizing your windows too large will put you in a negative-gain situation. Standard-sized windows are quite adequate, as long as plenty of them face south.

If you shade your south windows against direct sunlight in the summertime, it does a remarkable job of keeping your home cool. However, the standard practice of using the high- and low-equinox points of the sun's angle will block the sun's heat in early spring, when you may still need it, and start letting it back in during the late fall, when you may not want it. While the static shading on our house works well, adjustable awnings would allow us to pick and choose when we wish the sun to do its remarkable job of replacing our wood stove."

— Chris Magwood ❖

REFERENCES

Aho, Arnold J. *Materials, Energies and Environmental Design.* Garland STP Press, 1981. ISBN 0- 8240-7178-6.

Alexander, Christopher, Sara Ishikawa, Murray Silverstein. *A Pattern Language.* Oxford University Press, 1977. ISBN 0-19501-919-9.

Beckstrom, Bob. *Home Plans for Solar Living.* Home Planners, Inc., 1989. ISBN 0-918894-67-0.

Broome, Jon and Brian Richardson. *The Self-Build Book: How to Enjoy Designing and Building Your Own Home.* Green Earth Books, 1995. ISBN 1-900322-00-5.

Canada Mortgage and Housing Corporation. *Tap the Sun: Passive Solar Techniques and Home Designs.* Canada Mortgage and Housing Corporation,1998. ISBN 0-660-17267-4.

Ching, Francis D.K. *Building Construction Illustrated.* Van Nostrand Reinhold, 1991. ISBN 0-442-23498-8.

Clark, Sam. *Independent Builder: Designing and Building a House Your Own Way.* Chelsea Green Publishers, 1996. ISBN 0-930031-85-7.

Cole, John N. and Charles Wing. *From the Ground Up.* Atlantic Monthly Press, 1976. ISBN 0-316-15112-2.

DiDonno, Lupe and Phyllis Sperling. *How to Design and Build Your Own House.* Alfred A. Knopf, 1987. ISBN 0-394-75200-7.

Jones, Robert T., Ed. *Authentic Small Houses of the Twenties: Illustrations and Foor Plans of 254 Characteristic Homes.* Dover Publications, 1987. ISBN 0-486-25406-2.

Kachadorian, James. *The Passive Solar House: Using Solar Design to Heat and Cool Your Home.*Chelsea Green Publishers, 1998. ISBN 0-930031-97-0.

Pearson, David. *New Natural House Book: Creating a Healthy, Harmonious and Ecologically Sound Home.* Simon and Schuster, 1998. ISBN 0-684-84733-7.

Shurcliff, William A. *Super-Solar Houses: Saunders' Low-Cost, 100% Solar Designs.* Brick House Publishing Co., 1983. ISBN 0-931790-47-6.

Todd, Nancy Jack and John Todd. *From Eco-Cities to Living Machines: Principles of Ecological Design.* North Atlantic Books, 1994. ISBN

Wade, Alex. *A Design and Construction Handbook for Energy-Saving Houses.* Rodale Press, 1980. ISBN 0-87857-274-0.

Wylde, Margaret, Adrian Baron-Robbins and Sam Clark. *Building for a Lifetime: The Design and Construction of Fully Accessible Homes.* The Taunton Press, Inc., 1994. ISBN 1-56158-036-8.

Zelov, Chris and Phil Cousineau. Design Outlaws on the Ecological Frontier: *Profiles and Interviews.* Knossus, 1997. ISBN 1–56158–036–8. Knossus Publishers, 1100 Veterans Lane, #133, Doylestown PA 18901–3412 USA.

CHAPTER 8

The Many Styles of Bale Building

Straw bale wall systems come in many different flavors. One of the key decisions you'll face is which system to use. The variation you choose will have important implications for your entire building project, and this choice must be made before any detailed planning can be completed.

Two main wall systems are used in straw bale construction, though variations and hybrids are also possible. In a load-bearing or Nebraska-style wall system, bales act both as structural components and as insulation, keeping the roof in place over your head and protecting you from the elements. In a post and beam wall system, a framework handles roof loads; bales are in-filled into the framework and act only as an insulating wall, as shown in Illustration 8.1.

Illustration 8.1
Straw bales replace the wood-frame walls common in most North American construction.

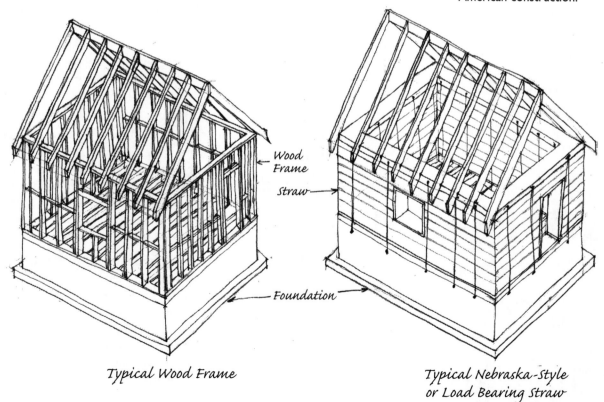

Wood Frame

Straw

Foundation

Typical Wood Frame

Typical Nebraska-Style or Load Bearing Straw

LOAD-BEARING OR NEBRASKA-STYLE WALLS

The first North American builders of straw bale homes used bales because of a lack of available lumber, stone, or suitable sod. These Nebraska pioneers saw the tight, thick, and durable bales of field hay they were harvesting — yes, they used hay! — as a solution to their housing needs. They stacked them up, built a roof, plastered, and moved in. As with other styles of pioneer buildings, Nebraska-style bale homes featured simplicity, ease of construction, and the use of local materials. These same features are the main attraction in modern load-bearing straw bale homes.

Courtesy of Ross Kembar, Architect

This large two-story home belonging to Ross and Patti Kembar of Lakefield, Ontario is a load-bearing design. It has convinced many a skeptic of the strength of this wall system.

Bales as Structural Elements

As is implied by the term 'load-bearing', a building of this style uses bale walls as structural components. The weight of the roof structure bears directly on the top of the wall, which in turn transfers the loads to the foundation. No supporting framework is used to create the wall structure, just bales and plaster. And therein lies the appeal of Nebraska-style construction. Expense, complexity, and lumber consumption can be reduced, and the skilled work of framing or creating any sort of skeleton structure is replaced by the relatively easy task of stacking bales. The walls can be built quickly and affordably with a minimum of materials, resulting in a cost saving and a less dramatic environmental impact.

Can Bales Really Support a Building?

For many people, it is a considerable leap of faith to believe in the strength of a straw bale wall that is unsupported by lumber or any other structural framework. However, as both experience and scientific testing show, load-bearing walls exhibit a strength equal to or superior to standard frame walls. But how can this be when bales are a compressible material? Shouldn't the walls sag or give?

Creating a 'Stressed Skin Panel'

If straw bale walls were left unplastered, they would continue to slowly settle and compress under roof and wind loads. However, the addition of the plaster coating to the interior and exterior of the bale wall creates a stressed skin panel. Plaster provides strength for the wall and the straw bales provide support for the plaster. Other forms of stressed skin

Courtesy of Ross Kembar, Architect

panels are commonly engineered for construction purposes; plastered straw bale walls offer similarly sound structural qualities and benefits.

Getting Rid of 'Squish'

Load-bearing walls must be stabilized. When first erected, straw bale walls have a degree of 'squishiness' to them. An immediate finishing would require the plaster to support a less stable core of bales, and cracks and failures in the plaster could occur as the straw settles. The Nebraskan pioneers addressed this issue by building the roof on unplastered walls. After allowing time for the walls to settle under the weight of the roof, they plastered the compressed bales, creating the structural 'skin' of the stressed skin panel that results in such remarkably strong and rigid buildings.

Some modern homes are still built using roof weight compression to remove the sag of load-bearing walls, but this style of building is not always appropriate, especially where snow loads, regular rains, and/or high winds can be expected. To properly allow for maximum compression to occur, you should leave bale walls unplastered for at least a week — and ideally a month — before continuing construction. This kind of waiting period is not always practical.

Pre-Compression

Modern straw builders, working to building codes and current safety practices, use a variety of systems to pre-compress their load-bearing walls. Pre-compression eliminates the need to wait for the roof to settle and allows for accurate leveling of the wall height. Builders can prepare the walls for immediate plastering, since roof loads will no longer cause the bales to give way too quickly.

Most modern pre-compression methods are low tech and use a common principle. The foundation of a building is tied to a continuous structural roof plate at regular intervals around the building, and the ties are subjected to a force that draws the roof plate down toward the foundation. Mechanical force is substituted for the weight of the roof — and for additional weights and forces to which the roof is subject — and squeezes the bales. As a testament to the compressive strength of bales, even large mechanical forces usually produce only 1–4 inches of immediate compression in a wall with seven courses of bales. Properly tensioned, the walls are remarkably strong and resistant to flex in all directions, even before plastering.

Pre-Compression Techniques

Ideal tensioning devices must be relatively inexpensive, strong, durable, and easy to work with, allowing you a simple way to add and remove tension with a minimum of hassle.

Wire or cable ties

A system of wire or cable ties can be used to pre-compress walls, as shown in Illustration 8.2. This is a fast, efficient, and cost-effective option. Heavy-gauge wire or cable is looped through the foundation and over a rigid roof plate assembly on top of the bale wall. Using a come-along or other such tensioning device, the two ends of

---

Structural Testing of Straw Bales and Straw Bale Walls

Much of the testing of straw bale walls performed to date has, unfortunately, focused on the properties of straw bales themselves, without the crucial addition of a plaster coating. While these tests show that bales have some adequate structural properties, to ignore the effects of a stressed skin panel is to miss the point of structural straw bale walls. SHB AGRA did test a plastered straw bale wall for its ability to withstand transverse loads — wind loads — with very favorable results.

"The stucco-coated panel was loaded to 50 psf [pounds per square foot, simulating a wind load of 100 mph] since there was no apparent sign of structural distress or failure. It can be seen that minimal deflections were noted, even though the load was increased to over twice the designated maximum load of the un-reinforced [unplastered] straw bales....the addition of the stucco to each face increased the rigidity of the bales substantially. Deflection of the magnitude noted for the stuccoed panels is very normal for the industry."

— from a report to the New Mexico Community Foundation's Straw Bale Construction Association by SHB AGRA, Inc. in 1993. Complete copies of these test results (which are also documented on video) can be obtained from Black Range Films, Star Rt. 2, Box 119, Kingston NM 88042 USA. ❖

the wire loop are pulled together. When the proper amount of tension has been applied, the wire is clamped to keep it from slipping.

Wire or cable can be affixed to the foundation in a variety of ways, depending on the style of the foundation. There must be a wire every 2–4 feet around the entire building, and wires at each corner should be equidistant from each other — approximately 2 feet from the outside corners. You want to avoid running wires across door and window openings. If you aren't certain where your openings will be, you can over-compensate and provide an excess of attachment points for the wires or cables, and use only those that end up being appropriate.

The wire or cable loop method can be duplicated using nylon webbing, polypropylene webbing, or metal straps in place of the wire or cable. Each option requires its own specific attachments and/or fasteners, and each will also require special tools for applying tension.

Threaded rod

Another pre-compression method uses threaded steel bars. Bars are embedded in the foundation and run through the middle of the bales to protrude through the top plate. Compression is applied by tightening a nut against the top plate.

Other pre-compression options

If you should devise your own method for pre-compressing walls, be sure to record the materials and strategies you used. If your system works, it could be a big help to future bale builders. If it doesn't work or needs improvement, it could help others avoid similar mistakes. Bale building is too young to have all the answers, so every new contribution is useful.

Obstacles to Load-Bearing Designs

Skepticism — both personal and institutional — is by far the biggest hurdle facing a builder who chooses a load-bearing design. Building a home is a large investment, and one that we hope is long-term; you definitely do not want to have doubts about the strength of your walls. If testing data and the experiences of others do not inspire a healthy trust in you, a load-bearing design may not be a suitable option for you. If you can see its numerous benefits and can make the perceptual leap, you must still convince your spouse, family, and building inspector that the idea is good. The best way to convince yourself and others is to go and see a load-bearing straw building. Its solidity, permanence, and strength will be obvious.

Even if you are convinced that a load-bearing design is for you, you still have to deal with the construction community. Many builders are concerned about obtaining

Illustration 8.3
Wire or cable ties make effective tensioning devices and can be used in a variety of simple configurations, with simple tools.

Knot or Saddle Clamp
Fence Stretcher
Gripple
Fence Stretcher

building permits for load-bearing straw bale designs. Most building inspectors are unfamiliar with the concept and may be resistant to it. However, permits have been issued for load-bearing straw homes in most American states and in several Canadian provinces. Most jurisdictions that already include straw bale construction in their building codes make provisions for load-bearing straw walls, and these existing codes can be used to support claims of methodology, strength, and soundness of construction when you meet with your building inspector.

Designing for Load-Bearing Walls

Load-bearing buildings create some challenges for builders. Walls can be relatively unsteady until pre-compressed, so builders must be able to stabilize them properly. Some building codes limit the length of a straight uninterrupted load-bearing wall; this does not indicate a lack of structural strength in the finished bale wall but rather the difficulties inherent in its construction. Support can come from buttresses, interior walls, directional changes, or from temporary bracing.

Wide window and/or door openings also pose challenges. Very stiff top plates on the wall and/or lintels over these openings must be able to transfer roof loads to the straw walls without bending or buckling.

Two-story buildings are challenging because of added structural complexity but are also quite possible. Each story is constructed as a separately compressed unit. The walls for the ground floor are built and compressed first, and then the second story walls are constructed and compressed on top of the framing for the second floor.

Most of the strategies you'll use to create sound load-bearing plans do not translate into higher costs or undue construction complexity. A well-planned, well-built, load-bearing building is cost-effective and relatively easy to construct. However, if you find yourself resisting a load-bearing design, perhaps post and beam will better suit your needs.

POST AND BEAM SYSTEMS

Post and beam construction has a long history, and many builders, architects, and building inspectors are familiar and comfortable with its application. For these reasons, it is often the design of choice for straw bale homes.

Post and beam and straw bale construction work well together. Most commonly, large-dimension lumber is used to construct the load-bearing structural framework that is fundamental to post and beam design, but concrete, metal, or combinations of these materials can also be used. By in-filling with bales, all the superior insulation capabilities of straw buildings are retained. Bales still offer an unbeatable price; walls can still be put up quickly and easily; and the character of the plastered bales will remain the dominant feature of the home. Designs are very flexible and allow for interiors that don't require a careful placement of load-bearing partitions. There is one other advantage to using a post and beam design. You can complete your framework and finish the roof before you install and plaster your bales. The roof will provide great dry storage and protect unplastered bales until they are needed.

The walls and roof of this large post and beam bungalow were completely constructed prior to the installation of the bales, as these 'before and after' pictures show.

The biggest drawbacks to using a post and beam design are cost and construction complexity. Framing materials must be purchased and additional footings for all the posts may need to be poured as part of the foundation. Time and cost factors rise, sometimes dramatically, as does the environmental impact of using more lumber, concrete, and/or steel.

Cost-saving strategies are possible. New materials are not necessarily requisite. Less expensive salvaged, reused, or home-grown framing materials can be found. Demolished barns are one source of large timber at reasonable cost. Reusable concrete block and steel may be found to suit the purpose and, of course, lumber milled from trees taken down on the construction site can also be relatively inexpensive.

Other cost-saving strategies concern the quality or quantity of your bales. Bales of slightly poorer quality — those that haven't been as tightly baled — can be used with less concern in a post and beam building. Some builders use bales laid on edge, as shown in Illustration 8.3, which reduces the total number of bales needed, but this saving in cost must be balanced against the added difficulty of having to plaster against flat straw rather than against the ends of stalks.

Building complexity is also increased in a post and beam house, both at the planning and construction stages. Builders must plan and construct carefully.

Post and Beam Variations

Timber frame

The classic timber frame can be beautiful, but it is a time-consuming and expensive option. Timber-framing, as shown in Illustration 8.4, requires the use of large-dimension lumber, which can be expensive if you have to import it. If you are cutting timber from your own property, be sure to get advice on how to mill, dry, and store the wood.

If you are building for the first time or have never tried timber-framing, you must recognize that it is a technique that requires many skills and an extensive knowledge base. It is entirely possible to learn these skills, but do not expect to erect your building quickly. If you decide to hire out, experienced timber framers can move quite quickly but usually charge in accordance with their level of experience.

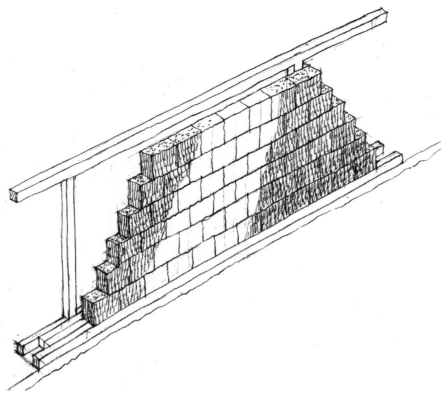

Illustration 8.3
Bales on edge take up less floor space, and fewer bales are required.

Illustration 8.4
Classic timber-framing with bale in-fill walls.

Timber-framing occupies an unusual place in many building codes. Recognizing its historical validity, many building officials will allow the use of timber-framing without requiring an engineer's approval, especially when an experienced framer is responsible for the design and/or construction.

Mechanically-connected post and beam

Mechanically-connected post and beam techniques and materials can substitute for the notched joinery and large-dimension lumber used in timber-framing. A variety of mechanical fasteners can be bought or fabricated to attach posts and beams together. Commercial brackets and fasteners are generally accepted by building officials; home-made versions may require special approval.

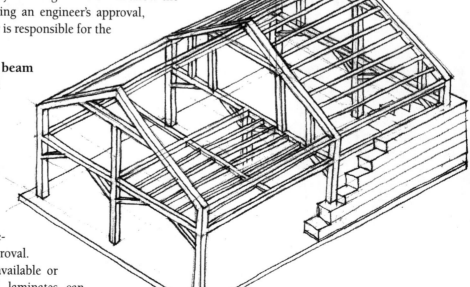

If large-dimension lumber is unavailable or too costly, site-made or commercial laminates can

Bales On Edge:
The Right Way Up?

Initial testing of unplastered bales made the point that bales 'on edge' — with the straw aligned vertically — were not as strong under compressive loads and tended to pop their strings when loaded. This testing may have wrongly discouraged builders from using straw bales on edge in load-bearing walls, as engineer Bob Platts points out.

"Can stuccoed straw bale construction play a significant role in green, sustainable housing production? Some simple changes could help. Here's a simple and easily proven 'way up' over the lumber- and labour-intensive barriers inherent in common straw building practice: place the bale on edge. Because most of the straw is now oriented vertically, the bale's much stiffer on edge, in vertical compressibility; much more stable against creep (the settling that occurs in the straw wall under load); more like wood. The bale is more precisely sized and readily built into a level-topped wall. The bale won't sleaze around on its mates or distort in its vertical plane; readjustments for those distortions are a big drain on labor. And yes, its thermal value is greater despite the thinner wall. Further, it doesn't stick thousands of straw wicks into the stucco to invite water in, and it may drain better if some water does enter. The Canadian and American technicians who so carefully tested unplastered straw bales and concluded that the on-edge orientation is not as strong as the ❯

be substituted. To create an on-site laminate, a number of pieces of standard dimension lumber are joined together using a certain nailing or bolting pattern. These laminate posts and beams may be suitable for your project and accepted by your building official.

Commercially-available laminates are also an option. They are made from glued strands of wood and are designed to equal the load-bearing capacity of large-dimension lumber. Their cost is often reasonable, especially if you must otherwise import regular lumber from a great distance. Some environmentalists praise commercial laminates because they are made from waste wood and therefore save large trees; others are less positive because of the nature of the glues used to create the laminates. If the chemical composition of the glues concerns you, be sure to do some research before inviting them into your home. Commercial laminates are often available from lumber supply yards complete with appropriate fasteners and joinery.

Manufactured joists are also an option for creating beams. These joists use 'oriented strand board' (OSB) — a product similar to plywood — sandwiched between lengths of small-dimension lumber to create strong I-beams. They can be ordered to meet your length and strength requirements, and use fewer glues overall than do full sized laminates. They are also much lighter to carry and lift into place.

Modified post and beam

Modified post and beam designs can blend the lumber-saving elements of load-bearing designs with the structural advantages of post and beam. This style uses a structural top plate, similar to that used for a load-bearing structure, as a continuous beam and transforms the strong and lumber-intensive window and door bucks used in load-bearing buildings into structural posts, as shown in Illustration 8.5.

Since a regular post and beam design would use similarly strong window and door bucks, lumber savings can be significant. The posts are rigid 'box-beams' constructed of small-dimension lumber — usually 2x4-inch — and plywood or OSB, which means that only small, reforested trees need to be harvested. The 2x4 and plywood supports can be stuffed with straw to provide nearly identical insulation values

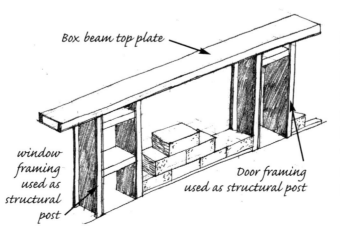

Box beam top plate

window framing used as structural post

Door framing used as structural post

Illustration 8.5
Modified post and beam designs acknowledge the strength of plastered bale walls and use less lumber by incorporating lumber window and door elements as structural components.

to the rest of the wall. Simple to construct and relatively miserly in lumber usage, this option allows for a post and beam framework that can be completely buried in the straw wall without any need to notch or cut bales. You save time and space. Until such designs become common, however, it may take an architect's or engineer's stamp for a modified post and beam design to get permit approval.

Truss systems

Truss systems are another framing option. Full truss systems are comprised of all-in-one wall and roof trusses, which are spaced at regular intervals. Bales can be placed on their ends between the trusses with either side of the bale facing out. Strapping is added between the trusses to help stabilize them, and plaster eventually gives the whole structure further stability. Trusses can be wood or steel.

Buildings of this sort can be erected very quickly, and because the trusses will be manufactured to the specifications of an in-house engineer, code approval should be relatively easy to obtain. The truss engineer will need to be aware of bale thickness and the odd spacing bales will require, but these dimensions shouldn't prove to be a problem. A truss system could be designed to allow bales to be used continuously from walls to ceiling, since truss spacing would be tailor-made for bales, anyway.

The cost of executing a truss design varies greatly, depending on the simplicity of the design. A relatively straightforward square or rectangular design will use identical trusses for the entire structure; a complicated design will require a series of varying-sized trusses that will up the cost significantly.

Concrete

Concrete columns and concrete top plates can be used together or in combination with other materials. Stacked concrete blocks or poured concrete columns can make posts or columns capable of supporting roof loads. Blocks are easily dry-stacked, and the hollow cores can be filled with cement and rebar when the column is at full height. This option requires no form work and little experience. Poured columns require either homemade or prefabricated forms to contain the wet concrete. The simplest and cheapest forming system is the Sonno-Tube, but since it creates a round column, you'll have to figure out how to blend the finished column with the bales. In either case, it is important to use adequate rebar to support the column. Check your building code or ask an experienced professional for guidance.

While concrete columns may cost less than certain lumber options and may be easier to build if you are unfamiliar with woodwork, they do have two drawbacks. First, columns built to the inside of the straw walls remain visible in the house after the walls are erected. Forms that incorporate interesting patterns, pigment in the concrete mix, or a simple surface paint job could help solve the esthetic problem of exposed concrete. Second, columns that are buried in straw walls create a thermal bridge, allowing heat to transfer outside much more quickly and lessening the overall insulation value of the wall. Styrofoam or other rigid insulation can be used to lessen this effect.

flatwise placement missed the engineering truth altogether: that aspect of bale strength has nothing whatever to do with final strength or stiffness of the stressed skin panel that is created. Shear strength (diagonal tension) and stiffness are not inherently improved by using bales on edge. And, since fewer straws run across the wall to stabilize the stucco skins against buckling under load (vertical, racking or bending load), more through-the-wall tying of mesh to mesh might be necessary. The need for ties, and their placement, can be determined analytically and/or by test, and presents little burden.

'Settling' (pre-compressing) the stacked, on-edge bales should not be necessary; one step shimming using flakes of straw under the top plate will do the fine levelling job; the top plate need only be a light lateral beam. The wall core would then be 14" rather than 18" or 24" thick. Wood usage in the top plates, window and door bucks, floors, and roofs can be reduced accordingly; headers and lintels can be designed into the bucks or set in the trusses. Looks like there's the makings of an efficient and effective SSB system here, begging for attention!"

— R. E. Platts, P.Eng. ❖

Concrete top plates and beams can also be constructed. A concrete top plate — for post and beam or load-bearing designs — can be formed on top of straw walls to replace the typical unit made of wood. Formed with lumber that would remain in place to allow for the attachment of roof framing and stucco netting, this option could be cheaper and faster to construct than a wooden unit. A concrete top plate creates a good seal against the bales and produces a level upper surface. The pour will bond with the top layer of straw and fill in any uneven surfaces along your top row of bales. For load-bearing designs, wires or cables can easily be looped over the entire unit or routed through polypropylene tubing embedded in the concrete.

Concrete beams are also an option. A concrete beam will add significantly to the dead loads your framework and/or straw walls will have to carry and reduces the allowable span between posts or the width of the openings in a load-bearing wall. Check with your building inspector before you commit to this option. At the finishing stage, concrete is easier to plaster over than wood. As with concrete posts, concrete beams create a thermal bridge at the top of your walls unless Styrofoam or another rigid insulation is used inside the wooden forms.

For both concrete top plates and beams, adequate rebar should be used to ensure that the concrete is well-reinforced against the loads they will carry. Lightweight concrete is available and could be used to lessen dead loads on the walls.

Metal frames

Metal columns and I-beams can undoubtedly create a strong, suitable frame. These components are widely used in industry and have been building code rated, giving you accurate load figures with which to work and specialized information from which to draw should you choose to build with metal. Metal components can be combined with wood and concrete in various ways — an advantage if, for example, you have found some inexpensive steel joists that could ride on wooden or concrete posts. It is quite possible to find used or surplus components at reasonable cost that can be incorporated into your design. As with concrete, you must account for the minimal insulation value of metal and plan around the esthetic effects of exposed steel in your home.

To complete a full metal frame, you will likely need to have welding skills and specialized metal-working tools. Alternatively, you can hire appropriate labor.

The Bale/Frame Connection

Plans must take into account the interface between bales and your structural framework. Frameworks can stand inside or outside the bale walls, or bales can be stacked within the framing components themselves. These options can be used exclusively or in a combination that best suits your design. Finishing details are covered in Chapter 12.

HYBRID SYSTEMS

Straw bale builders are not limited to two design choices; many successful hybrids have been constructed that take advantage of the best aspects of both load-bearing and post and beam design. Many others await creative invention. Rammed earth pillars and support walls, stone, lumber, concrete, and earth berms — all can work well in conjunction with straw. Keep in mind that hybrids combining sections of load-bearing wall with sections of framed wall must allow for their differential settling — bales squish, structural frames do not! Otherwise, the integrity of the structure is compromised, and large-scale cracking of the plaster is possible. Some examples of possible hybrids follow.

Hybrids created from a central frame with load-bearing walls use a simple structure of lumber, rammed earth, stone, brick, block, or concrete with perimeter walls of pre-compressed straw bales. The central frame is erected first, followed by construction of the bale walls. Since the roof framing will extend down from the central frame to the bale walls, compression of the walls will only change the roof pitch minimally, and bales need not be the same height as the solid material. The bales that are used to in-fill the space between the roof plate and the angled roof framing are not load-bearing, since the roof framing is designed to bear the full load.

Jack posts are adjustable steel posts. They can be used in load-bearing designs to provide support where spans within a building exceed the capacity of the straw walls to bear the entire load. The threaded end of a jack post can be adjusted to meet the height of the compressed straw wall.

Earth berm homes — sometimes called earthships — are dug into hillsides. While straw bales wouldn't be appropriate to use against the earth berm due to moisture concerns, they could be used to build walls that are not buried. Use either a load-bearing or post and beam design.

Mortared bale structures use straw bales just like concrete blocks. If you have plenty of experience with mortar and blocks, you may find this option suits your talents. Bales are set down on a thin bed of mortar, and more mortar is poured between the abutting ends. This technique can create a strong structure and does not require a framework or any pre-compression. It does require a lot of time and mortar. It also creates thermal breaks between each bale, causing the insulation rating of the entire wall to suffer because the spaces between the bales offer only the minimal R-value of concrete. Building with mortared bales eliminates one of the main advantages of straw walls — walls do not go up quickly and simply.

This load-bearing design incorporates two wooden porch posts. The height of the posts was determined after the load-bearing walls were pre-compressed. The gable end of the roof allows for a mirror image structure to be added later

HOW TO CHOOSE: LOAD-BEARING, POST AND BEAM, OR HYBRID?

The factors that weigh into the load-bearing versus post and beam debate are so many and varied that there is no hard and fast rule about which way to go. The following are some issues to consider.

Building Size and Complexity

Most modern homes do not rise higher than two full stories, making it possible to use load-bearing, post and beam, or hybrid construction styles successfully. Design choices must balance with structural and budgetary demands. Load-bearing walls are relatively untested past more than 8–9 courses of bales (9–11 feet) and probably should not be used when ceiling heights are planned that exceed these figures. However, cathedral ceilings and open lofts can be achieved using load-bearing design if high ceilings are made integral to the design.

Buildings with very wide spans — distances between opposing walls — also require some adaptation if you intend to use a load-bearing design. In a wide building, extra-strong roof trusses may be required if there is no support for roof loads in the middle of the building. You could use internal frame walls to support the roof trusses, but since the finished height of the walls won't be known until they are fully pre-compressed, framing would have to wait until the walls are completed. Adjustable jack posts could be used in such cases and so could internal straw bale walls built to the same specifications as the exterior walls. In any case, the cost of adaptations may outweigh the advantages — both monetary and environmental — of using a load-bearing design.

Buildings with many jogs and line changes work well for load-bearing designs, since each corner helps the wall brace itself. (Line changes are largely a matter of stacking in a different direction.) Any sort of post and beam design — including modified — will typically require a post at each and every corner. This adds significantly to time and cost factors during construction.

Cost

Cost is often the key factor in many building projects. Two simple formulas may help you decide which design to use. The first formula states that "More materials equal higher costs." The building that uses the least amount of materials, then, will be the least expensive to finish. Quick, simple, and reliant on inexpensive straw rather than lumber, it is difficult to beat the low cost of load-bearing or modified post and beam designs.

The second formula states that "More time equals higher costs." This formula holds especially true when you hire professionals to work for you. Straw bale walls often require more time to finish than do frame walls. If you hire a local contractor to build your walls, that crew of two to four inexperienced balers may spend a lot of time — and your money — figuring out how to stack and pre-compress your walls properly. If you and your friends and family raise, prepare, and plaster your walls, the work can be done fairly quickly and very inexpensively. You may find that architects or engineers charge less to design a post and beam home rather than a load-bearing or hybrid one. If so, it's because less research and perceived risk are involved when they design to familiar standards and practices. However, the best way to save money is to build big dreams into a modest home. Whether you choose a load-bearing or post and beam design, smaller and simpler will always be less expensive and faster to construct.

Knowledge and Experience

The acquisition of knowledge and skills is an important aspect of home-building. Don't feel that you're limited to what you already know. If you've always wanted to learn to timber frame, make that option a priority. If you're a welder, you might want a steel-framed building, but you might also want to try a load-bearing design just to see if you can do it. Load-bearing or modified post and beam structures are the best options for builders with limited skills and resources. If you decide to venture into new techniques, remember to learn first and act second. Don't ignore common building practices or advice from professionals unless you're certain you are right.

Code Approval

The building style you choose will be affected by building code conventions. Most building inspectors will be much more willing to accept a post and beam design with straw bale in-fill than an identically sized load-bearing design. Lumber, steel, and concrete are all well-tested and well-researched. Acceptable standards exist for the use of each in all building codes, even though post and beam designs often require an engineer's approval for the framework.

Load-bearing designs are entirely viable and enough documentation and examples exist to prove their worthiness. It may take longer to convince your building department to accept a load-bearing design, but consider yourself a pioneer who's helping to establish a precedent for a less expensive, more sustainable method of building.

Esthetics

Straw homes can be made to suit a wide variety of esthetic preferences. Straw will be the dominant visual theme inside and out. In the end, the esthetics of your building will have more to do with how you trim, sculpt, and finish your bales than with whether you choose a load-bearing, post and beam, or hybrid design.

Sustainability and Environmental Impact

When you are thinking about sustainability and environmental impact, consider where materials come from, how they are harvested and/or manufactured, and how much you'll need for your project. If you use local materials, you will lower the direct impact on the environment. In a lumber scarce region, timber frame buildings are not appropriate, but if you're in a region where trees can be harvested on-site, that might be the best way to build. You could calculate the resources that would be necessary to build several varieties of the same basic house design and choose the one that is least expensive environmentally.

BALES IN OTHER PARTS OF YOUR BUILDING

Straw bales have been used successfully as ceiling and floor insulation. For roof or ceiling insulation, framing must be beefed up considerably to handle the extra weight of the bales. The large dimensions of bales preclude the use of standard spacing for framing members. The installation of the bales can be a tricky and heavy procedure and can expose the bales to rainfall before the roof sheathing is installed. Unplastered bales will also be exposed to the air on the top side — as in any roof or ceiling installation — creating a home for pests and possibly creating a fire hazard. Borax and other chemical treatments have been used to lower these risks. If you plaster the open side of the bales, you add considerably more weight to the bales and create complications in the application process. However, with creative thinking and a clever use of resources — especially manufactured wooden I-beams — you may devise a suitable way to use bale insulation in the ceiling of your building.

Structural supports beneath the bales allow for this unique stepped bale roof that was covered later with steel roofing.

Eric Hart

Bales have been used as floor insulation in both concrete-slab and wood-framed floors. For slab floors, bales are placed a few inches apart in rows. Concrete is poured between the bales, creating a honeycomb of bales and concrete that is eventually covered with the top few inches of the slab. There are valid concerns about the amount of concrete a slab floor uses and about the performance of bales in the moist environment of a concrete slab-on-grade. We do not recommend the use of bales in below-grade applications.

Bales as a frame-floor insulation may make the most sense, especially where TJIs™ (wooden I-beams created with press board and narrow lumber) or open-web joists (narrow lumber joined with steel spacers) can be sized and spaced to accommodate the bales with the least amount of trimming, cutting, and use of over-sized lumber.

While many builders have met the challenges of using bales in ceilings and/or floors, the availability of other lightweight, recycled insulation materials such as cellulose fiber and spun rock-wool means you must carefully weigh the advantages and disadvantages of using bales. Be sure the costs, materials, and/or risks involved do not exceed those of other materials.

NO WRONG CHOICES

There really is no such thing as a wrong choice, only choices that are more or less appropriate for your site, budget, construction experience, local codes, and concern for the environment. No matter how you decide to build, your straw bale walls will work to your advantage.

REFERENCES

Books

Benson, Todd. *The Timber Frame Home: Design, Construction, Finishing.* The Taunton
  Press, Inc., 1993. ISBN 0-942391-60-8.

Videos

Building with Straw Series, Vol. 1–3, produced by Black Range Films,
  Star Rt. 2, Box 119, Kingston New Mexico 88042 USA.
  e-mail: resources@StrawBaleCentral.com website: www.StrawBaleCentral.com

CHAPTER 9

Design Options: Foundations and Roofs

Once you've visualized the kind of space you'd like your house to have, you need to make some technical decisions about the building itself. Foundation and roof systems must be figured into the design of your house. It's time to blend the practical with the personal.

The decisions you make about your home during the Design Game reflect your individual tastes. But to realize your design dreams, you must be able to translate them into a physical structure that can meet the demands you put on it. Foundations and roofs are important parts of that physical structure and must be considered before you move on and make up the actual plans for your building.

There are a variety of foundation and roofing systems that can be made to meet stringent building code requirements. Experimental options also exist but may be more difficult to get approved. Before you make any final decisions about your foundation or roof, be sure to research the methods that are used in your area, and talk to other builders and homeowners about what's appropriate for your region.

FOUNDATION SYSTEMS

A strong, well-built foundation is essential. It attaches your home solidly to the ground and must be able to withstand frost, winds, and roof loads. It is constructed first and becomes the template for the rest of the building. Even if you decide not to build your own, it is best to have a clear understanding of the foundation style you use.

Foundations come in three basic styles: grade foundations, perimeter wall foundations — including full basements, and pier foundations. Each style can be matched to your design requirements, and versions of all three should be allowed by your local building code.

Get to Know Your Frost

Have you ever noticed the dramatic lumps and bumps that appear on northern roads, especially in the spring? As frozen ground begins to thaw, it becomes spongy and prone to shifting and settling, causing sunken pot holes and frost heaves in the road. If you live in a northern climate where cycles of freezing and thawing are common, the same forces that wreck highways are at work in the ground around your home. You don't want your house subjected to that kind of strain. You need to build a foundation that will prevent frost from penetrating into the soil directly under your building. You will have to design with a specific regard for the soil conditions at your site and for the frost penetration depth in your region — for us, it's four feet!

Slab-on-Grade Foundations

A slab-on-grade foundation is a continuous cement pad that is designed to float on the grade surface of your site. Excavation is minimal: only the topsoil — the part that supports organic matter — needs to be removed. The thick concrete pad acts as a base and supports the walls and floors of the building, as shown in Illustration 9.1.

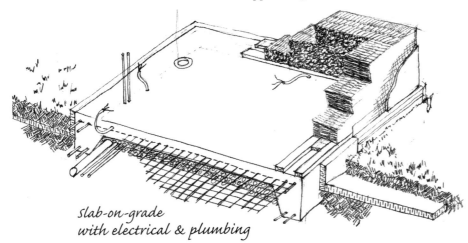

slab-on-grade
with electrical & plumbing

How floating slabs can cheat frost

Slab foundations are unique. No attempt is made to secure the foundation to soil that lies below the frost line. In climates where frost is a concern, slab foundations use an insulation blanket around the perimeter of the foundation to prevent frost penetration into the soil beneath the slab.

The insulation blanket extends out from the foundation just below grade level and remains in the ground when the soil is back-filled. For perimeter insulation, the rule of thumb is that six inches of insulation is required for every foot of frost penetration. The insulation must be specifically designed for below-grade applications.

Illustration 9.1
A typical slab-on-grade foundation incorporates thicker concrete around the perimeter and an insulation blanket to *prevent frost from penetrating the soil beneath.* Mechanical systems can be embedded directly in the slab or passed through embedded conduit.

Code issues

Check your local codes for specifics. Some building codes give specifications for slab thickness, required steel reinforcement, and insulation depths. Others require that floating slabs be designed by an engineer to ensure structural integrity. If you live in an area where slabs must be engineered, your foundation costs could rise steeply. Some engineers offer less expensive prefabricated slab plans, but if you use them, your building will have to take on the shape of the slab. Post and beam designs will require special reinforcement and extra depth in the slab where the posts bear their concentrated weight.

Cost

Slab foundations can be relatively inexpensive. The shallow excavation can be done by hand or small machine, saving the cost of a major excavation. Form work for the concrete is minimal, and even if a professional is being hired to oversee the pour, you may be able to act as an assistant to keep the labor charge minimal. Concrete should be purchased from a ready-mix service and delivered by cement truck. The strength of the slab comes from its monolithic pour, so building up a slab gradually, using small batches of site-mixed cement, is not a viable option nor would it save much money nor any time. Steel mesh and rebar used for reinforcement isn't particularly expensive — real die-hards can use salvaged steel bars, fencing, or other steel.

If you pour the slab yourself, you'll need some special tools, so purchase and/or rental costs will add to the overall price. You might be planning to us the concrete pad as your final interior floor. If so, this dual purpose foundation/floor could prove to be very economical.

Construction

In theory, slab foundations can be very simple to construct. Form work for the concrete is easy to make with a minimum of materials. The real work is in the details. They make the difference between a smooth, level pad and a lumpy disaster. Make sure you understand the processes of pouring, troweling, and finishing before you order your cement!

The bigger the pad, the harder it is to pour and finish. Finishing requires patience and experience to do well. Even professionals use many tricks and secrets to achieve smooth, level slabs. The wet cement must be troweled to the desired level and finish from the time it's poured until it finally sets. While your first-timer's slab may have some undulations and roughness, it is still quite possible to be in charge of your own pour.

Planning

You only get one chance with a slab foundation! Quite a bit of forethought is required before the cement gets poured. In northern climates, slab foundations are often insulated from below to provide a thermal break that prevents the concrete from taking on the stable but cold temperature of the earth. This is especially important if in-floor radiant heat is to be used. For all slabs, plumbing drains must be positioned and ready to be buried. Water pipes and conduits for electrical and communications wiring can be positioned, as well. If you bury these systems, it will keep them out of your straw walls and minimize the amount of time you'll spend drilling holes through wooden framing members for pipes and wires to run through ceilings and interior walls. Don't forget that you'll need to get electricity and water into the building. Plan for service entrance points — maybe in duplicate, just in case. If you overcompensate for future needs with extra plumbing and conduit, it will make life easier when changes become necessary. And keep a map of your piping and conduits for future reference.

Planning for radiant heat

Slab foundations lend themselves to radiant floor heating. They can hold pipes for hot water or ducting for hot air, producing an efficient heating system. You add a new dimension to your planning and costs, but results may be worth it.

Finishes

Slab floors can be finished in several ways. You can use bare concrete as a finished floor, especially if you color-tint the concrete during mixing or paint or stain it afterward. Tiles, linoleum, and carpets can be laid directly on the cement. If you want a wood floor, you'll have to build it on a system of spacers to keep it from direct contact with the cement. Wood floors add cost and complexity to your foundation.

Environmental impact

Slab foundations create a moderate environmental impact. They do use a lot of concrete, which has a high embodied energy, but as a trade-off, minimal excavation makes this style gentle on your site and eliminates the need for heavy machinery to be transported and operated. Also, the amount of insulation required for a slab foundation is less than that required for deeper foundations. Furthermore, if you use your slab as a heat-sink — and especially if you use radiant floor heating — it can have a dramatic effect on the amount of fuel required to heat your building, making long-term environmental benefits possible.

Perimeter Walls

Perimeter walls extend the vertical walls of your house down to a secure footing below the frost line. They are most often used to create a below-grade basement space in a building, but they can also be used to create a strong foundation without a basement, as shown in Illustration 9.2.

Illustration 9.2
Perimeter wall foundations often incorporate full basements, as shown. The same footing and wall can be used as a foundation without a basement.

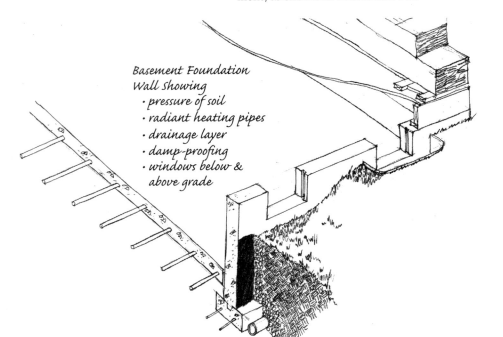

Basement Foundation
Wall showing
· pressure of soil
· radiant heating pipes
· drainage layer
· damp-proofing
· windows below &
  above grade

Code issues

Perimeter wall foundations — especially with a basement — are very common, and well-supported by building codes. Only in cases where soil depths are minimal or drainage is particularly poor will building officials question this type of foundation.

Cost

Perimeter foundations, especially those with full basements, are the most expensive foundation option. Hired digging equipment is required for the initial excavation and for back-filling when the foundation is finished. Extra materials are required for the footing, perimeter walls, and insulation, as well as the concrete and/or wooden floor systems. The payback for using a perimeter wall is its strength and the extra living and/or storage space that comes with having a basement.

Construction

Perimeter walls are generally made of poured concrete or mortared concrete block. (Early homes often used mortared or dry-stacked stone.) The outside of the perimeter wall is insulated, and provisions for drainage are made at the base of the foundation. For basements, windows and doors are built into the perimeter wall. Depending on local soil and water table conditions, basements can have problems with flooding, and your building code will have provisions for minimizing these concerns. Many basements require the use of a sump pump to keep them water-free. While it is possible for you to form your own basement walls, the materials required to make sufficient forms are expensive. The laying of concrete block requires some skill, but may be a good option for the owner/builder.

Planning

You need to consider several factors when planning. Drainage is very important for perimeter wall foundations — especially those with basements. You must check water table levels and the drainage characteristics of your soil before deciding on this option. You must make provision for services to enter through the perimeter wall and for sewage to exit.

Basements create an excellent space for mechanical systems and storage. When built with radiant floor heating, they can offer a comfortable living space as well, which may help you plan a house with a smaller footprint.

Your building code will outline practices for attaching wooden floor systems to the perimeter wall. If no basement is being built, a slab floor can be poured inside the perimeter wall, or a wooden floor can be used if code-approved ventilation and access are provided under the floor.

Finishes

Full basements can be finished like above-grade living space. Windows, doors, dividing walls, stairs, and ceiling options must be considered. A slab floor within a perimeter wall — whether above- or below-grade — can be left bare or covered with any form of flooring [see slab finishes, above]. Wooden floor systems will generally have a plywood sub-floor, on which any form of finished flooring can be laid. This can include a thin layer of concrete to support a radiant floor heating system if the wooden floor has been designed to handle the weight.

Perimeter walls and unconventional flooring options

In a house without a basement, the stable, frost-free ground can be built into a floor. If the perimeter wall is bearing the weight of the structure and preventing frost penetration, then soil cement, cob (straw and clay), concrete block, brick, natural stone, or end-cut wooden blocks can be used as an on-grade flooring system. While you won't find many of these options in your local flooring store, such floors can be created from used, found, or homemade materials and can be very beautiful when finished.

Environmental impact

Perimeter walls — again, especially those with basements — cause the most disturbance to your site. They use more materials — especially concrete and insulation — than other options. Cold, un-insulated basements are a heating nightmare, but if they are well-insulated and warmed with radiant heat, their energy consumption is lowered. In their favor, basements create a smaller overall footprint while providing the same amount of living space as a more sprawling building.

Rubble-trench perimeter wall

A cheaper and faster way to create a secure foundation below the frost line is to replace concrete perimeter walls with a rubble trench. The excavation is filled with various sized stones and compacted to avoid future settling. The outside edge of the trench is insulated, in much the same way as a concrete perimeter wall, and a concrete curb is poured on top of the stone at grade level to provide a flat surface on which to stack bales. A slab floor can be poured inside the concrete curb. A rubble trench cannot be used in conjunction with a basement. This system eliminates many of the costs of a concrete perimeter wall and produces much the same results. Rubble trench foundations are not common for houses and might not be written into your local building code. Still, the method is used in other types of construction and should be acceptable to most building inspectors.

Other Perimeter Wall Options

While the following alternative perimeter wall foundations can be strong and long-lasting, none is likely to be included on your local building code, so check with local officials before using them.

Mortared stone If your site has plenty of accessible stone, you might consider using it to create your perimeter wall. Many early builders used stone and mortar methods and their homes are still standing today. You can also use local stone in conjunction with cement. Use the sides of your dig as a form, and add stone to site-mixed or pre-mixed concrete as you pour. The stone can displace a fair bit of concrete without sacrificing strength. If you add some rebar, this option may be accepted by building officials. Perimeter foundation insulation can be used with stone foundations.

Rammed earth Where soil conditions are suitable, a stabilized rammed earth foundation might be possible. You will likely need to do a fair bit of research and experimentation before attempting a foundation, but the process could be fascinating and rewarding. Building officials may or may not approve this option.

Used tires The construction of 'earthship' homes that use old automobile tires filled with rammed, stabilized earth is a rapidly growing technique. You could use the same principle to build a perimeter wall foundation. Choose tires of the right dimension, and you could create an inexpensive perimeter wall that matches the width of your bales.

Pier Foundations

Pier foundations, as shown in Illustration 9.3, are used to raise a building above grade level. The building rests on a wooden framework supported by the piers, and the piers themselves rest on footings below the frost line.

Code issues

Most building codes accept the use of pier foundations and will have exact requirements for the sizing of the piers. The size and number of stories allowed in a building on a pier foundation may be smaller than with other foundation styles.

Cost

Pier foundations are generally the least expensive foundation option. A minimum of excavation is required, and no below-grade insulation need be provided. Little or no hired labor will be required either, and costs for materials are minimal.

Construction

A pier foundation is a very beginner-friendly option. Though they are associated with cottages and cheap housing, pier foundations can be as strong and long-lasting as other systems. Piers can be wooden posts — usually treated to protect them from ground moisture, poured concrete columns, stacked concrete blocks or, more experimentally, tire or rammed earth piers. Ready-made forms for poured concrete piers are available in many sizes. Piers should rest on wide footings, the sizing of which will be determined by your local code. The spacing of the piers will be dictated by span charts found in your building code; charts relate to the sizing of the lumber used for floor framing. Maximum and minimum height of the piers will also be dictated by local codes.

Planning

The biggest drawback to pier foundations concerns winter and water. In northern climates, your water feed pipe will be exposed to freezing temperatures in the air and in the ground. Strategies to keep water supply pipes from freezing and bursting include heated pipe wraps, drain-down systems, and pressurized bladder pipes. Check with plumbers in your area for their suggestions.

Finishes

A wooden-framed floor system, topped with a plywood subfloor is most commonly used with pier foundations and can be finished in a number of ways. You can even pour a thin concrete layer over the floor for radiant floor heating if the framing has been planned to handle the weight. The underside of your floor will need finishing to keep pests from bedding in your insulation. Thin plywood or wooden planking can be used, as can expanded metal lath or welded steel

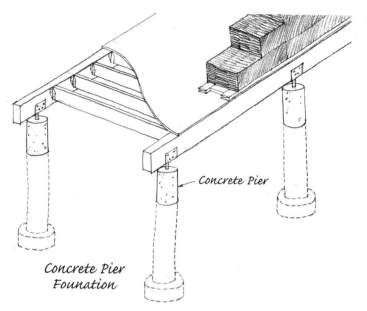

Concrete Pier

Concrete Pier Founation

Illustration 9.3
Pier foundations can use concrete piers (above) or wooden piers (below) to support a floor framework. They are simple, effective, and low-cost.

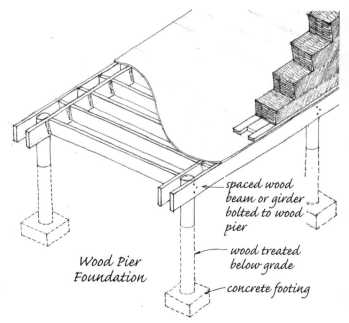

spaced wood beam or girder bolted to wood pier

wood treated below grade

concrete footing

Wood Pier Foundation

Steel Decking or Pre-Cast Concrete on Piers

"Steel decking is a common construction product and is most often used to support poured concrete roofs in industrial buildings. For homes with square or rectangular shapes, steel decking can be used to create a floor if piers and beams support it. The corrugated surface of steel decking provides natural channels for radiant heating ducts and/or pipes. Once the ducts or pipes are in place, concrete can be poured to produce a level floor surface. Such a floor system is quickly built, very efficient, and will have excellent thermal properties.

Pre-cast concrete slabs are capable of spanning long distances, making them an attractive option to lay on piers. Often, the slabs are cast with hollow tubes running through them, making them ideal for channeling heat."

— Chris Magwood ❖

mesh. Some kind of skirting between grade level and the bottom of the walls is also desirable. Options include steel mesh, wooden lattices, solid wood, bales, cob, rammed earth, or raised flower beds.

Environmental impact

Pier foundations use a minimum of materials and require the least alteration to your site. Where lumber is scarce for flooring systems, open-web joists and TJIs™ can be used, as can steel framing.

Post and beam foundations

Some post and beam designs may call for an individual pier to be constructed on its own footing for each supporting post. Where posts are placed outside the shell of the house — as for porch supports or to create wide roof overhangs — each post will definitely require its own pier.

A shallow, insulated slab-on-grade can be poured around such piers, or you could use them to support a raised, wooden floor framing system.

Foundation Combinations

You are not restricted to a single style of foundation for your house. Styles can be combined to match your needs and your site conditions, as shown in Illustration 9.4. In fact, it is possible to have the best aspects of two or more styles working together. Take time to consider how different foundations will meet and attach to one another, and how they can provide a suitable platform for the bale walls that will span their intersection.

Illustration 9.4
A building is not limited to one style of foundation. It may be appropriate to combine several styles, depending on terrain and the requirements of the design.

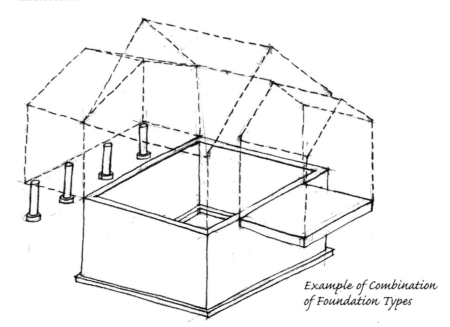

Example of Combination of Foundation Types

Foundation Considerations

Bale specifics

When you plan your building's footprint, you must consider bale dimensions. Bale walls are wider than typical frame walls, and a bale building will require a wider foundation to create an equal amount of interior space. Most importantly, bales must have a flat, well-supported base on which to rest. For load-bearing walls, the foundation must also be built to accommodate whatever system of pre-compression you decide to use [see Chapter 12, Straw Bale Construction Plans for specific suggestions].

Make sure you design a foundation that lifts the bales far enough above grade level to prevent snow and rain from seeping in at the base of the wall. In northern climates, a minimum of 8–12 inches above-grade should be considered. Building codes often specify a certain above-grade height for any plastered wall finish, so be sure to check for regulations in your area.

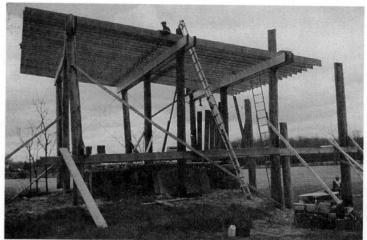

John Marrow

Be site specific

You may decide, on paper, that a certain foundation style is your best choice and realize later that it isn't suitable for your particular building site. Do some test digging. Talk to your neighbors and local builders about soil conditions and any specific techniques they use to deal with them. Soil conditions, water levels, slopes, bedrock, and erosion can all have significant impact on your foundation choice. Use whatever natural advantages your site offers, and choose a foundation style that blends well with the land. If you live in an area with permafrost conditions, be sure to adhere to local practices that deal with this unique situation.

An interesting variation of the pier foundation, this pole structure uses continuous posts from below frost level to the height of the roof, allowing the foundation and the framework to be completed in one step. In this case, old telephone poles were used, but other wooden members, concrete, or steel could also be used.

Additions

Very few houses remain unchanged over their lifespan. Adding-on is common, and if you do some early planning, you can make the job much easier for yourself — or for those who own the house after you. Consider which orientations are most suitable for expansion, taking into account site restrictions, room uses, entrance points, light conditions, roof shape, and specific plans you may have for the future — a greenhouse, office, triplets, etc.

You can provide for future foundations as you build if you fit rebar and/or anchor bolts into your foundation or leave suitable attachment points in your concrete for additional framing. If plans for an addition are fairly certain, it may be worth the extra time and money to pour the foundation. That way, you won't have to spend twice

for digging equipment and concrete delivery. Plus, you may be more likely to go ahead and build that addition if the groundwork has already been laid!

Other Kinds of Foundations

For a temporary and/or non-residential structure, you may choose to use a simpler foundation. Sheet plastic can be laid on the ground and folded up over the outside of the first course of bales, or railroad ties can be laid on a gravel bed. You can use deck supports like piers to build a structure above-grade or set wooden pallets on-grade over a gravel bed. Your comfort level and the function of your building will determine which system you use, but these foundations will definitely not meet building code requirements for residential structures.

Choose Carefully

Many structural elements can be changed once your building is erected, but a foundation is permanent, so be sure to choose the style that is right for your project. Your foundation is not the place to cut corners on cost or quality; a good one is worth the investment.

REFERENCES

Ramsey, Dan. *Builder's Guide to Foundations and Floor Framing*. McGraw-Hill, Inc., 1995. ISBN 0-07-051814-9.

Portland Cement Association. *Concrete Solutions: 1998 Catalog Supplement*. P.O. Box 726, Skokie IL 60076-0726 USA.

Steen, Athena and Bill Steen. *Earthen Floors*. The Canelo Project, HCI Box 324, Elgin AZ 85611 USA. Absteen@dakotacom.net

ROOFING OPTIONS

Roofing options are broken down into two categories. Roof framing deals with the shape and structural materials of your roofing system, and roof sheathing deals with the waterproofing membrane that covers the framing. A variety of options exist in each category, and most can be used in combination.

Roof Designs

Your roof design must integrate performance with appearance. Roofs play a very important structural role, which can't be compromised. At the same time, their size and shape affect the overall appearance of your house. Their capacity to create shade, duct rainwater, deflect winds, and blend with their environs are also important. Don't forget passive solar requirements when you design your roof. Open faces should face south and have sufficient overhangs to protect windows from summer sun. You are not restricted to a single roof style, as shown in Illustration 9.5. You can combine them, tip them, play with the pitch, and add dormers to achieve the combination of function and appearance you wish. Remember, though, that every complication — intersection, angle change, or interruption — will result in higher costs and a lengthier construction time.

Illustration 9.5
You can be creative in combining elements of different roof styles, but remember: the more complicated the shape, the more difficult and time-consuming the construction process.

Gable roofs

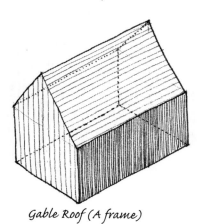

Gable Roof (A frame)

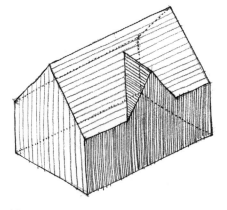

Gable Roof (A frame) with Gable Dormer

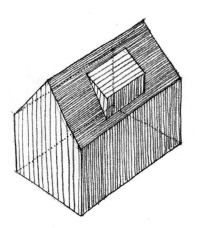

Gable with Shed Dormer

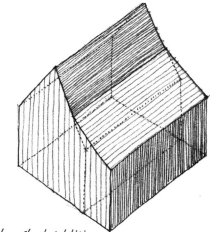

Gable with a Shed Addition

Gable roofs

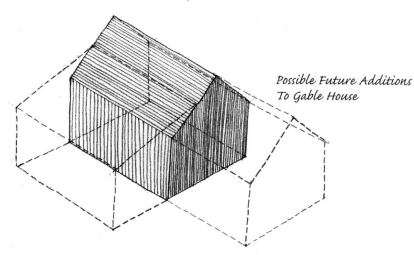

Possible Future Additions To Gable House

Gable roof

Hip roofs

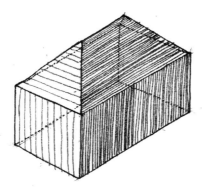

Hip Roof with Elongated Hip

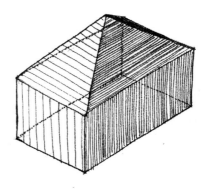

Hip Roof with Pyramidal Hip

Shed roofs

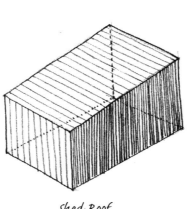

Shed Roof

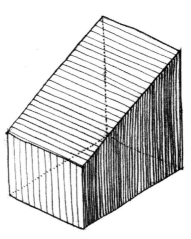

1 $\frac{1}{2}$ Storey Shed Roof

Clerestory roof

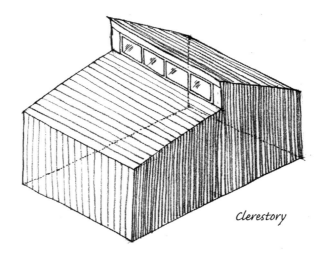

Clerestory

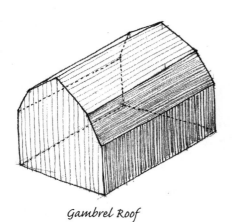

Gambrel roofs

Gambrel Roof *Gambrel Roof with a Gambrel Dormer*

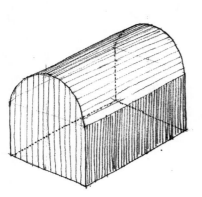
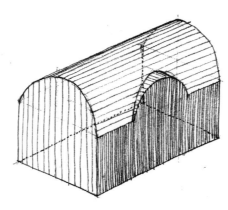

Vaults

Barrel Vaulted Roof *Barrel Vaulted Roof with Barrel Vaulted Dormer*

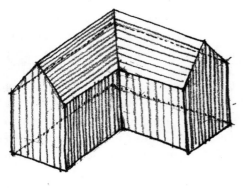
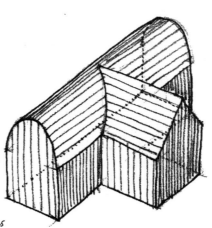

Combinations and alterations

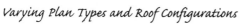

Varying Plan Types and Roof Configurations

Combinations and alterations

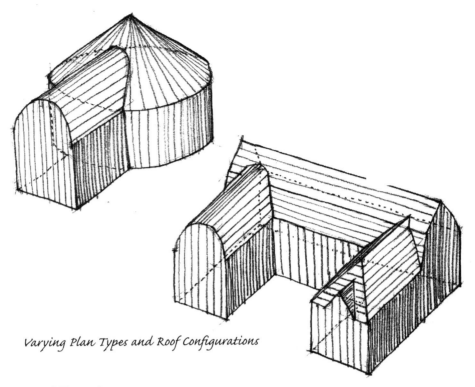

Varying Plan Types and Roof Configurations

Roof Framing

Most roof framing is done using lumber. Wooden roof frames are strong, lightweight, and easy to construct. Your local building code will contain span charts specifying the lumber dimensions — 2x6-inch, 2x8-inch, 2x10-inch, or 2x12-inch — that meet your design requirements. It's a good idea to take a look at these span charts early in your design process, since they can help guide you as you decide on overall roof dimensions. You don't want to plan a roof that is impossible or very expensive to frame and then have to change your design to suit.

Before you decide to build your own custom-framed roof, it's worthwhile to research manufactured roof truss systems. Manufactured trusses are engineered to use small-dimension lumber — 2x4-inch and occasionally 2x6-inch — to meet the load requirements specified for your region. They are engineered to fit your plans, are factory built and assembled, and delivered to your site. Their cost is often equal to or lower than the cost of the heavier lumber you'll need if you frame the roof yourself, and most populated areas have at least one truss manufacturer nearby. The truss company employs an engineer to design the trusses, so prices include the cost of having an engineer stamp your roof plan. If you are paying a carpenter for framing, manufactured trusses are likely to be a cheaper option. For complicated roofs, a combination of manufactured trusses and site-framing may be optimal. Building inspectors often prefer manufactured trusses over site-framed roofs, especially if the builder is a first-timer.

Environmentally, the small-dimension lumber used for manufactured trusses can be more sustainably harvested than the heavier lumber used for traditional framing.

Exterior Appearance and Interior Space

It is inadequate to choose a roof design merely for the sake of appearance. How you intend to use the space under the roof must play an important role in your decision-making process. Cathedral ceilings, lofts, second-story living space, or attics will all need to be figured into your roof design.

Porches

Your roof design can easily accommodate plans for a porch. Design your roof to overhang the building and create a sheltered area outside the building's shell. Wrap a porch around one or more sides of your building, or create a simple awning over an entrance way. You can even plan for an add-on. Porches provide good weather protection on the north side of your building; a screened porch can be a comfortable outside living space in areas where mosquitoes and other insects are troublesome.

Overhangs and Bale Walls

It is accepted practice (and recommended) to provide bale walls with a wider-than-average roof overhang. If you extend the roof, less rain can fall directly on the walls and snow cannot pile up against them. When planning, consider the direction of prevailing winds that will drive the rain and the availability of sun that will help with drying. There is no magic number for overhangs, but you should plan for a minimum of 18–24 inches. Wider overhangs can become a defining characteristic of your home and, used well, can add a unique visual appeal.

Other Framing Options

Though lumber is by far the most common roof framing, it is not your only option. Traditional timber-framing continues the post and beam theme into the roof structure and can provide a strong, suitable roof. If you have — or want to acquire — timber-framing skills and have access to the necessary timber, this option may be for you. If you'd rather, a qualified timber-framing company can erect your entire framework, including the roof. They are generally quite fast, but also expensive.

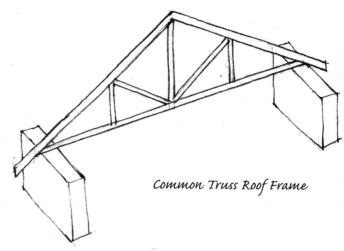

Common Truss Roof Frame

Truss roofs are built using engineered designs and smaller dimension lumber. Site-framed roofs use heavier lumber, sized according to span charts.

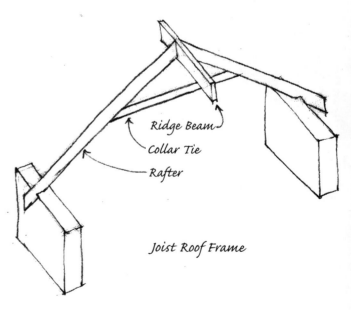

Ridge Beam
Collar Tie
Rafter

Joist Roof Frame

Though engineered metal trusses aren't very common in home construction, they are strong and not prone to the twisting or shifting that sometimes occurs with wooden roof frames.

Metal trusses will be more difficult to source and more expensive, but their capacity to span wide structures and create open interior spaces may make them an attractive option for some designs.

Bale Specifics

While roof framing for a straw bale building is very similar to that for a standard home, there is a key difference. Load-bearing and modified post and beam designs use a wide top plate, and the bearing points for the roof framing should accommodate this width. If the entire weight of the roof is allowed to bear only on the outside rail of the top plate, the force may tend to make the wall buckle — not to the point of wall failure but enough to cause cracks in the plaster. Custom-framed roofs can use wedges of lumber to equalize the downward force over the entire width of the top plate, and manufactured trusses can be designed to provide bearing points over both edges of the top plate, as long as the engineer knows their location. Roof design for post and beam buildings must take into account the location of the beams in relation to the straw bale walls. Depending on the placement of the framework, the beams may be outside, inside, or directly over the walls. Each variant will differently affect the placement of the roof framing.

Roof Sheathing Options

The framework of your roof will support some form of waterproof membrane to keep rain and snow from finding its way into your house.

Metal roofing

Sheets of galvanized steel or aluminum have a good track record as a sheathing option. They come in a wide variety of styles and colors, are relatively fast and easy to install, are very durable, and rank among the longest-lasting of the sheathing options. Snow tends to slide off rather than accumulate on metal roofs, making them a good choice if you are concerned about snow loads. The gauge, rib style, and color of the metal sheets will affect the price. Be sure to look at a wide selection before you buy.

Metal roofs are often identified with barns and rural architecture, and may be frowned upon in urban settings. They can blend with urban architecture, however. Metal roofing has been styled to look like shingles, slate, or ceramic tiles.

Anybody who has been inside a barn during a rainstorm may wonder about noise. You needn't worry. Inside your home, the roof will be separated from your living space by a substantial layer of insulation that will dampen the sound of rain to a barely audible patter. Outside, though, or under a porch roof, the sound will be loud.

Metal roofing requires plenty of resources and energy to produce — aluminum more than galvanized steel — but lasts a long time (50-80 years) and is recyclable when it is removed.

Asphalt shingles

Unfortunately, the dominance of petroleum companies in our society has led to the proliferation of asphalt shingle roofing. Relatively low in cost, shingles also have a relatively short lifespan, and when replaced can only be hauled to a landfill site. This wasteful practice is an environmental disaster, as is the energy-intensive process required to create the shingles. The shingle industry offers many color and texture choices, and qualified installation companies abound.

Asphalt shingles should not be used where rainwater is going to be collected, since the impregnated stones wear off and petro-chemicals can be transferred to your water.

Cedar shakes

Where supplies of cedar are abundant, this style of roofing is attractive and long-lasting. Cedar shakes can be purchased ready made, or can be made by hand or by machine on-site. The process is time-consuming, but the visual and environmental rewards make it a system worth considering. Cedar shakes do create a bit of a fire hazard, so check with your local building officials before going ahead with this system, especially in a densely populated area.

Ceramic tile

Tile roofs are often associated with Spanish and Latin American architectural styles. Originally made from local clays, modern tiles are mass-produced, fired, and weatherproofed.. More expensive than some options, tiles still use natural materials in their manufacture, look good with the plaster finishes common to bale homes, and provide excellent protection. Installation is slower than with some sheathing, and cutting for angles is likewise slow work. High winds have been known to damage tile roofs, so if you live in an area prone to severe wind conditions, check with your building official or other roofers before using tile.

Slate roofs

Slate is a sedimentary stone, quarried in thin, strong sheets that can be cut and nailed to the roof as shingles. The stone is heavy and the work slow. Slate roofs were once very popular, especially in areas that were close to a quarry. Often very beautiful, and ranging in color from black to green or red, a slate roof can be stunning when completed. Its natural colors and texture blend well with plaster finishes. Very durable, a slate roof will last indefinitely with some regular attention and timely replacement of loose or broken slate.

Thatch roofs

Thatch is made from bundles of grasses or reeds that are carefully arranged in thick layers and attached to the roof frame to provide protection against water. Thatch has been in use for centuries and, despite its antiquity, is still a reasonable roofing method. Appropriate natural materials are available in most regions of the world.

Although any style of roofing requires special skills, good thatching is particularly labor-intensive and dependent on knowledgeable hands. You may find it difficult, if not impossible, to find a good thatcher. A thatch roof is a perfect match for straw bale walls and is long-lasting when regularly maintained.

Living roofs

A living roof is an intriguing option. A waterproof membrane is laid down over the wooden roof sheathing to prevent leakage, and a layer of soil — which can be planted — is laid over the membrane. A living roof is very heavy and requires substantial roof framing to handle the load; you will need to do some research and design carefully if you use this option. While it makes a strong environmental statement and creates an unusual visual effect, a living roof may necessitate the use of significantly more materials than conventional roofs.

Roll roofing

A very inexpensive but unattractive way to sheath a roof, roll roofing is an asphalt-impregnated paper that is stapled to the roof in wide swaths. It is quick to install but not nearly as durable as other options. Like asphalt shingles, roll roofing is made from petro-chemicals and is not recyclable when its short life is over. Best used when you cannot afford other options, roll roofing can be overlaid with other sheathing materials at a later date.

Professional Roof Design

If you know what style of roof you want, it may be best to let an architect, engineer, or truss company complete your roof plans. Actual structural design of a roof can be quite a technical workout, even with building code span charts and reference books to help you. And, the more you stray from simple roof designs, the more reluctant your building inspector is likely to be to accept a homemade framing plan.

Leave Your Roof Open to the Future

If you think your house may grow someday, make sure your roof isn't a hindrance. As with foundation designs, it is good to think about future additions when you plan your roof. It's easy to expand in the direction of an open gable end but not so easy to expand in the direction of a sloped roof. Try to think ahead. If you have to tear up an existing roof, it will complicate your addition projects greatly!

REFERENCES

Atcheson, Daniel. *Roofing: Construction & Estimating*. Craftsman Book Company, 1995. ISBN 1-57218-007-2.

Herbert III, R.D. *Roofing: Design Criteria, Options, Selection*. R.S. Means Company, Inc.,1989. ISBN 0-87629-104-3.

Scharff, Robert. *Roofing Handbook*. McGraw-Hill, 1996. ISBN 0-07-057123-6.

West, Robert. *Thatch: A Complete Guide to the Ancient Craft of Thatching.* The Main Street Press, 1988. ISBN 1-55562-044-2.

The Slate Roof Bible: Everything You Wanted to Know About Slate Roofs, Including How to Keep Them Alive for Centuries. Jenkins Publishing, 1997. ISBN 09644258–0–7. P.O. Box 607, Grove City PA 16127 USA.

CHAPTER 10

More Design Options: Mechanical Systems

Decisions you make about the characteristics of your home's shell lead to decisions about how to provide amenities within that shell. The mechanical systems you choose will have an impact on the cost and long term performance of your house.

HEATING AND COOLING OPTIONS

It may be a surprise to see heating and cooling options included so early in the design section of this book, but we use a lot of energy to moderate the indoor temperature of our living and working spaces. Too often, our heating and cooling systems are inefficient, unimaginative, and poorly integrated into the structures they serve. The furnace has become the inexpensive standard in the home construction industry, but there are many fine options that better serve our needs and don't threaten dwindling fossil fuel supplies.

"A Candle Oughta Keep That Place Warm..."

Many people erroneously assume that the high insulation value of a straw bale wall eliminates the need to consider heating and cooling. Straw bale walls will decrease the amount of energy you require to make your living space comfortable, as will well-insulated floor and roof systems, and quality windows and doors. But significant energy savings can only be realized when you design your entire house to be energy-efficient.

Passive Solar Design

We've already talked about taking advantage of the natural heating capabilities of the sun, but we'll stress the point again. Point your house in the direction of the sun, and let its rays bathe your home during the cold months of the year, and then eliminate its access during the warm months. It's simple, it's easy, and it's one of the best energy investments you'll ever make.

Heating Air Versus Heating Mass

Heating systems can be categorized as two types. One type — a forced air system — heats the air in your building directly. Modern forced air furnaces — oil, propane, or natural gas — burn fuel to heat air, and a fan pushes the heated air around the building through ducts. Air, being of minimal mass, heats quickly. But it loses heat just as quickly — through open doors, to drafts, cold panes of glass, and cooler walls and floors. Heated air also rises, concentrating near the ceiling far from where our bodies can feel it. So, while forced air systems are the current standard in the home building industry and are relatively inexpensive to buy and install despite their comparative complexity, they are also the most inefficient and uneconomical systems available.

The second type of heating system — a radiant heat system — heats some kind of dense mass that warms air indirectly. Many homes contain a suitable mass in their concrete, stone, brick, tile, cement block, cob, or adobe floors. More efficient than a forced air system, a radiant heat system requires lower input temperatures, retains its heat for longer, and produces a steady, ambient warmth.

The continuous tubing of a radiant floor heating system is laid out and tied in place before it is buried in the concrete slab. Note how the slab will be isolated from the foundation wall by a layer of insulation.

Different Ways to Store Radiant Heat

Radiant floors
Radiant floor heating is becoming increasingly popular. Silent and hidden from sight, this system uses the entire floor area of your home as a heating device. Though they take time to bring up to temperature, radiant floors are not prone to large temperature fluctuations once they are fully operative. Because of their large surface area, a radiant floor can be maintained at a lower overall temperature than would be comfortable with another system. These floors distribute heat evenly and put it at your feet, where it is most appreciated. The price of radiant heating is dropping as more people choose this system; it's quite competitive with forced air systems. Most radiant floors use piped water as the heating medium, but air systems are also a possibility.

Radiators
Many older homes use metal radiators, through which hot water is circulated. This kind of radiator isn't manufactured much today, making them harder to find and install. Baseboard radiators that are long, low, and compact are manufactured today, and they replace the tall and bulky metal units at a fairly reasonable cost. Because their surface area is limited compared to the area they must heat, radiators operate at relatively high temperatures. Metal radiators distribute heat unevenly and take up valuable space. Still, if you have access to a supply of used or new radiators, they may be worth considering.

Sources of Heat
In addition to deciding what heating system to use, you must also choose a fuel source.

Solar heat
While passive solar gain can heat your house on sunny winter days, you will need an active solar heating system if you want to derive all or most of your home heating

from the sun. All active systems collect the sun's heat from outside the building, transfer it to another medium — water or air — and direct it to its intended destination in the home. Solar collectors can be purchased ready to install or can be built at home. Commercial vacuum-tube solar collectors — water only — are highly efficient, but also expensive. Commercial or homemade flat plate collectors — air or water — are less pricey and but still effective. In general, a fan or a pump circulates the heated medium from the hot panel to the radiator — an entire floor, a centralized mass, or a traditional radiator. The transferred heat is stored in the mass and used when the sun is not out. Solar energy can be used in conjunction with other fuels to meet your heating needs. Combination designs can eliminate some of the capacity requirements of a solar-only system, while minimizing the use of other fuels.

Solar energy is free, non-polluting, and usually abundant. In some homes in northern climates, all heating needs are met by a combination of active and passive solar, so solar-only heating is possible. The design and construction of such a home requires study, careful planning, and creative building. The rewards for going solar-only are remarkable: you will be heating for free and treading very lightly on the planet.

Planning issues for solar heat Solar heating systems don't have to be complicated, just well-planned. Solar collectors need direct, unblocked southern exposure to be effective, so if you are designing with active solar heat in mind, you must plan to have your collectors properly aligned. Collectors can be designed to act as the shades for the passive solar component of your house, combining the requirements and efficiencies of both systems.

The more integrated your solar heating system is with your house, the more efficient it will be. Keep storage mediums — hot water tanks, stone boxes, and entrance points to radiant floors — close to the panels. The cheapest systems will use convection loops that take advantage of the natural upward flow of heated air or water, without using pumps or fans. Pumps and fans increase efficiency but also add cost and complexity. Keep in mind that the house itself is often an active participant in the collection and distribution of solar heat.

At this point in its development, active solar heating is wide open to innovation and creative energy. If you want to put your mind to it, great results may follow your discoveries!

Ground-source heat pumps

Ground source heat pumps are like buried solar collectors that tap the huge reserves of solar energy stored in the earth itself. Capitalizing on the constant temperature of the earth below the frost line and using a process similar to that used by your refrigerator, long, buried pipes circulate liquid through the ground — or through a deep well or pond — and extract the small amount of available heat. This heat can then be distributed in the house via a radiant floor or forced air system.

Ground source heat pumps extract from a free heat source, but their installation requires professional assistance, and the costs of digging trenches, buying pipe, and

The Solar Convection Floor

Solar heated air and water naturally travels upward, creating a convection loop. For an ideal solar heating setup, mount solar collectors on the south side of your building so that the upper edge of the panel is even with the floor height of the building. Air can then flow through the panels, absorb heat, and rise into ducts in the concrete floor. The floor will absorb and store the heat and return the air to the bottom of the panel. A small fan will help the process along. You get maximum free heat for minimum complexity.

obtaining the heat pump are all quite high. Heavy-duty circulating pumps are required, and the electricity to power them will come at some cost. After the initial investment is made, however, ground source heat pumps are quiet, efficient, and inexpensive to operate. They are also environmentally-friendly.

Planning issues for ground source heat pumps The actual equipment required in your home for heat pumps is minimal. Most units are compact and relatively quiet and can be hooked up to traditional, radiant, or forced air distribution. You will, however, need a site that offers enough space to lay the required amount of underground piping. Bedrock, high water tables, small lots, and buried services in urban areas can all present obstacles.

Fossil fuel furnaces

Oil, propane, and natural gas furnaces are most often used with forced air systems. But they can all be used in radiant heating systems, using existing boiler technology. By applying heat to a thermal mass rather than to air alone, you can reduce the amount of fossil fuel you burn. Our culture has a century-long tradition of subsidizing fossil fuel production and distribution. While supplies last, many people will continue to rely on these sources of energy for fuel. Modern combustion technology has led to cleaner burning appliances, so be sure to research efficiency and cleanliness ratings before buying a furnace. Do think toward the future, though, and be sure that your heating system is adaptable to other heat sources, so you can switch over if supplies of fossil fuels should dwindle or escalate in price.

Planning issues for fossil fuels In general, forced air systems locate the furnace in the basement of a home, and ducting for hot air is placed under the floors. Be sure to place your ducts in appropriate places in each room — burying them under furniture only makes the system less efficient. Standardized building practices have been developed for the installation of fossil fuel heating systems. Most building codes outline common options, and many reference materials are available from the conventional housing market.

Wood Burning Devices

Most of the world's population still uses wood as a primary heat source. Four basic wood heaters are used in modern homes.

Masonry heaters

When you need good heating ideas, turning to the Scandinavians and the Russians is not a bad idea. Masonry heaters have been used in northern European homes for centuries to provide dependable radiant heat. Masonry heaters temper the boom-or-bust heat available from the more common, metal air-tight wood stoves. Its fire box does not exit directly into a metal chimney to the outdoors but into a masonry chimney that ducts exhaust gases through a labyrinth chimney before releasing them to the outside. Masonry heaters can burn at remarkably high temperatures, and initial exhaust gases — the ones that escape unburned in most wood-fueled devices — are fully combusted, generating intense heat and completely using the potential energy of the wood. The heater's thick masonry walls absorb the heat of combustion and radiate it into the house slowly and gently. Often combined with a baking oven, masonry heaters can be finished beautifully in brick, stone, stucco, tile, or ceramic and can be a visual treat.

Masonry heaters are an exciting heating option. They are virtually creosote- and pollution-free. Short, hot fires are what they require, so softwoods are a viable fuel, and the wood you use need not be cut in thick, heavy lumps. You'll burn less wood overall in a masonry heater than you would in a regular wood stove.

The sheer size of a masonry heater requires that it become an integral part of your house design. Your foundation must be able to accommodate the heater's great weight, and enough floor space must be allocated for its external dimensions.

A high level of skill is required to build an efficient masonry heater. Professionals can be hired who can provide you with an outstanding heating device, though it will come at a steep initial cost. If you want to undertake the task yourself, you should study design and construction techniques very carefully.

Wood stoves

Wood stoves produce an uneven heat — they're extremely hot when they're burning and cold when the fire is out. In a well-insulated straw bale house, even this boom-or-bust heat can be managed and used to maintain a comfortable living space. Plan to position your wood stove centrally, so heat can travel throughout your house. Heat from a wood stove rises quickly, so if you want your bedroom to be cool, don't put it above the wood stove! Bathrooms, on the other hand, make good upstairs neighbors for a wood stove.

Most older wood stoves — even those billed as air-tight — are relatively inefficient and allow much of the potential energy in a piece of wood to go up the chimney as smoke. Smoke deposits creosote inside the chimney and is the cause of dangerous chimney fires. Wood stove design is improving; many newer units burn cleaner and more efficiently than ever before, though their greater efficiency also brings higher costs. Nowadays, many building codes require that you install expensive, insulated chimneys if you intend to heat with a wood stove.

Fireplaces

Set into an exterior wall, traditional fireplaces — even those with heat-recovery equipment in the chimney — have a largely esthetic value and should not be relied upon as a central heating source unless the climate is quite moderate.

Outdoor furnaces

Located outside the shell of the house, prefabricated outdoor furnaces burn wood to heat water that is piped into the house for heating and domestic use. Many of these

John Marrow

This masonry heater takes on a decorative role as well as heating a large straw bale home.

systems burn very efficiently and safely and can burn softwoods or fuel sources other than wood — corn husks, sawdust, etc. They are expensive but eliminate the need for an indoor chimney system. You won't need to create space inside to accommodate a heating unit, consider details of style, or worry about the smells or oxygen consumption associated with an indoor stove. Though you'll not have to haul wood into the house, you will have to go outside to stoke your furnace.

Planning issues for wood burning devices

Indoor wood heaters require central placement in your house and as straight a chimney as is possible. Plan for a fresh air vent that can provide an oxygen source for a wood-fueled heater. If you have an indoor wood stove, a brick or stone shroud behind and/or around it will temper extreme temperature variations and retain some heat long after the stove has cooled. Be sure you make it easy to move and store wood inside. The less time you have to spend moving your wood, the happier you'll be!

Trees are a valuable and dwindling resource. Large-scale and indiscriminate burning of fine hardwoods is not sustainable, especially if wood is cut elsewhere and transported to your home. Still, if you have access to a suitable wood lot and manage its resources well, wood burning can be a relatively inexpensive heating option once you've made the initial investment for equipment.

Don't Squander Your Heat!

No matter how you heat your home, you can always find ways to prevent heat waste. Create sheltered entries so doors don't open directly outside. Mud rooms, boot rooms, and closed porches are more than just practical; they save on energy costs, too. Inside the house, match heat distribution to activity. An office, where you sit for long periods, will likely require more heat than a kitchen, where you are moving about or creating heat with the oven. Finally, be moderate with your temperature settings, and treat your heat like the valuable resource it is.

Heat Recovery Ventilators

Modern air-tight construction can lead to air quality problems in the home, especially if indoor combustion is used to provide heat. Many jurisdictions now mandate the use of heat recovery vents (HRVs) that exchange stale inside air for fresh outside air, with a minimum of heat loss. These units can be expensive, and installation usually requires a trained professional. Heating systems that do not feature indoor combustion may not need an HRV.

Cooling

The principles that apply to heating also apply to cooling. It is not as effective or efficient to cool air as it is to cool a mass. Radiant floor systems can help keep your house comfortably cool in the summertime. Hot indoor air will be moderated by the floor, which, even when fully heated, does not exceed 72–74 degrees Fahrenheit (21–23 degrees Celsius). Ground source heat pumps also act as cooling devices in the summer, since ground temperatures are likely to be consistently cooler than air temperatures.

Don't stop with flooring when you think about cooling. Shade your south-facing windows from the summer sun; it is the most effective step you can take to keep your house cool. Plan for adequate ventilation. Take into account the usual direction of summer breezes, and allow for cross-ventilation from one side of the house to the other. One of the best ways to beat the heat is to plan for an enclosed porch area on the north side of your house. Constantly shaded, this space can provide cool outdoor living quarters that are naturally air-conditioned!

REFERENCES

Montgomery, Richard H. *The Solar Decision Book: A Guide to Heating Your Home with Solar Energy*. John Wiley & Sons, 1978. ISBN 0-471-05652-9.

Siegenthaler, John P.E. *Modern Hydronic Heating*. Delmar Publishers, 1995. ISBN 0-8273-6595-0.

Canada Mortgage and Housing Corporation. *A Guide to Residential Wood Heating*, 1995.

Lyle, David. *The Book of Masonry Stoves: Rediscovering an Old Way of Warming*. Chelsea Green Publishers, 1996. ISBN 0-931790-57-3.

Fine Homebuilding Great Houses: Energy-Efficient Houses. The Taunton Press, 1993. ISBN 1-56158-059-7.

WATER AND SEWAGE OPTIONS

Water System Options

Water collection methods vary by region. Standard procedure in one locale is often an impossibility in another. If you are new to your area, ask neighbors and local officials about standard practices, and keep in mind that the standard option is not necessarily the only option.

Municipal service

If it's available, a municipal water supply offers you easy access to water. Guidelines and costs will be outlined by the municipality.

Drilled well

A drilled well is a narrow shaft that has been drilled by machine to access underground water supplies. Wells can range in depth from 15–20 feet to 200 feet; the depth of the drill determines their cost. The deeper the well, the stronger the pump you will need to lift water to your home.

Dug well

An older version of the drilled well, a dug well is dug by hand and/or back-hoe to access a water supply. Well tiles — usually made of pre-cast concrete — are inserted into the hole to prevent cave-ins. Dug wells are usually less deep than a drilled well.

Lake, river, or stream collection

Water can be drawn from a natural body of water. Fast-moving water is likely to be of better quality, but it is rarely possible anymore to find safe drinking water from a surface source.

Reservoirs

Rainwater can be collected and stored in above-grade or below-grade holding tanks. If you will be collecting rainwater as a central part of your water system, plan carefully to position the storage tank close to your house. Choose roofing that will not contaminate rainwater, and plan for a roof that has quality eavestroughs that can duct water to the storage tank. Even in areas without heavy rainfall, efficient methods can collect and store abundant quantities of water. Collection methods, storage methods, and proximity to sources of airborne pollution will all determine whether or not the rainwater will be drinkable.

Water Pumping Options

Regardless of where your water comes from, you will need a delivery system to bring it to your taps.

Electric pumps

Electric pumps are the standard. In either a submersible or non-submersible form, an electric pump will pull water from the source and push it into your house. Many pump options are available, including models designed for independent power systems.

Wind pumps

It takes much less wind power to pump water than to generate electricity, making wind pumps a suitable option in many regions. Because the pump will move water only when there is wind, such systems require a storage tank for calm periods.

Hand or foot pumps

If your well or reservoir is close to the house and is not overly deep, a hand or foot pump is quite viable. Manual pumps can be used to supply water on demand or to fill raised tanks for gravity feed systems. Old-fashioned hand pumps are often easy to find and inexpensive to restore to working condition. Modern hand pumps and foot pumps are more efficient, though similar in design.

Gas pumps

A noisy, inconvenient solution, gas pumps move large quantities of water very quickly. If you have to move water a great distance or have no access to electricity or wind, gas pumps can be used to fill reservoir tanks.

Gravity feed systems

Gravity feed from raised storage allows you to pump water when it's convenient — by hand, or with wind, electric, and/or gas pumps — and provides quiet distribution on demand. Raised water storage can be created inside or outside your house.

Interior storage requires additional planning for weight loads and the installation of trustworthy tanks. Exterior storage requires protection from winter freezing.

Sewage Options

Municipal sewage treatment

Municipal waste treatment facilities vary tremendously in their approaches to treating waste before it is released back into the environment. If you are concerned about treatment methods in your area, talk to municipal officials, or visit the waste treatment plant. Pressure the government if you feel waste is being handled poorly or irresponsibly. It is possible to use alternative waste treatment methods even within a city, but you will probably face a struggle to receive approval to do so.

Septic systems

Septic systems are the most common sewage treatment option for rural residences. These systems use a large, buried storage tank into which liquid and solid wastes are deposited. Weeping tiles then siphon off the top layer of liquid and distribute it into the ground. Because septic systems release untreated liquids directly into the environment, the success of the system depends on what's being put into the tank. Conscientious use of a septic system can be gentle on the environment, but thoughtless use can deposit dangerous chemicals in your soil and groundwater. Septic installation is expensive, especially where problematic soil conditions exist. Approval is generally required before building can proceed.

Composting toilets

Composting toilets change human waste into usable compost, offering you a degree of self-sufficiency in waste management. Many brands of composting toilets are available, as are instructions on how to make your own. Not all brands are created equal, and there are many capacities and styles to choose from. Installation often requires a storage unit below the toilet itself, so if you choose this system, be sure to plan your house appropriately. Composting toilets do not handle gray water, so they must be used in combination with a separate gray water treatment system.

Outhouses and leaching pits

A well-constructed outhouse can be pleasant, long-lasting and relatively odor free. It is a reasonable option if you are willing to travel from your house to your facilities. It can also function as a back-up for your main sewage system, and you can use it to lighten the load on other systems during the warm months when you are outdoors anyway.

Easy to construct, a leaching pit or French drain is basically a hole in the ground into which waste water — gray water, not sewage — can be ducted. From the leaching pit, bath and sink water can filter back into the soil. Again, what goes into a leaching pit comes out in your water table. A leaching pit may not be allowed by local officials.

Other waste alternatives

A lot of study and research has gone into new ways to treat waste. Many experimental systems exist and have proven to be very effective. Constructed wetlands use aquatic plants to feed on waste. This system often resembles a small canal system in which each stage is populated by different species of waste-loving plants. A biological filter systems uses a pump to spray black water — sewage — over containers of foam cubes that harbor sewage-eating bacteria. A gray water recycling system can be a simple arrangement that stores water to irrigate a garden or a complex system akin to greenhouse hydroponics. These alternatives to standard methods of waste treatment are worthy of your research and support.

REFERENCES

Del Porto, David and Carol Steinfeld. *The Composting Toilet System Book: A practical guide to choosing, planning and maintaining composting toilet systems.* Chelsea Green Publishers, 1999. ISBN 0-966678-30-3.

Wehrman, Robert. *Basic Plumbing Techniques.* The Solaris Group, 1993. ISBN 0-89721-250-9.

ELECTRICITY OPTIONS

Humans have survived, often quite comfortably, for thousands of years without electricity. Indeed, much of the world's population still gets by without easy household access to electrical power. In this spirit, we include electricity options!

Grid Power

Modern homes are designed with grid power in mind. Little in the way of special planning is required for it during your design process. Grid power is convenient, relatively abundant, and reasonably priced. Many of the appliances considered normal in a home require grid power to function.

The majority of new homes are built to be supplied with power from a utility company. You may be offered a choice between underground delivery or pole delivery. The choice is largely an esthetic one. There are many good reasons to hook up to the grid, but we won't elaborate on them here. Instead, we will provide a reminder that convenient electrical power comes at a cost, both to the environment and to consumers. If you choose to evaluate those costs, you will perhaps be persuaded to consider other options.

Independent Power

There are many ways to generate your own power cleanly and safely. Independent power production methods take several forms and, unlike grid power, produce varying quantities of power. Photo-voltaics — solar panels — and wind or water turbines are well-tested, viable, and affordable. As prices for grid power rise, independent power generation is becoming an increasingly popular choice.

You will need to assess your building plans and budget. Most modern homes are built close to the road because of the cost of extending utility service any great distance. When you sever the electric umbilical cord, you are free to build in areas that would otherwise be impracticable.

At the planning stage, you will want to integrate your generating system into your home. Most independent systems use large batteries for storage of electrical power, and they require venting to the outside. Batteries should be kept cool but not exposed to freezing. Placement of photo-voltaic panels can be integrated into your design on the south face of your house and can double as a shading porch roof or window awning. If you will be using wind or water power, don't build too far away from your source, since costs for transporting the power will rise.

Check with your local utility company about hook-up fees and services. The money you don't spend for grid power could be used to purchase a small and serviceable independent system that you can upgrade or add to as time and finances allow. Switching to independent power is a big commitment, but there are many excellent sources of information available to you and experienced people willing to help you out. Think about it.

With both photo-voltaics and thermal collector aimed at the sun, this house is energy independent.

No Electricity

It is possible to lead a relatively comfortable life with no electrical power at all. This choice involves greater adjustments than the move to independent power, but you can't beat the cost!

Kerosene or propane for lighting, wind- or hand-pumps for water, solar heating for hot water, wind-up radios — the choices exist. If you plan to build for no electricity, it is not a bad idea to include some provisions for wiring should you decide to add a few solar panels or go onto the grid at a later time. Conduit through the floors, walls, and ceilings that you put in now will allow you to add wiring later without you having to tear your house apart.

REFERENCES

George, Steve and John Lowe. *Basic Wiring Techniques*. The Solaris Group, 1993. ISBN 0-89721-251-7.

Gipe, Paul. *Wind Power for Home and Business*. Chelsea Green Publishers, 1996. ISBN 0-930031-64-4.

Jeffrey, Kevin. *Independent Energy Guide: Electrical Power for Home, Boat and RV*. Orwell Cove Press, 1995. ISBN 0-9644112-0-2.

Potts, Michael. *The Independent Home: Living Well with Power from the Sun, Wind and Water*. Chelsea Green Publishers, 1993. ISBN 0-930031-65-2.

Schaeffer, John and Doug Pratt. *The Solar Living Sourcebook: The Complete Guide to Renewable Energy Technologies and Sustainable Living.* Chelsea Green Publishers, 1998. ISBN 0-930031-82-2.

Tickell, Joshua. *How to Make Cheap, Clean Fuel from Free Vegetable Oil.* Greenteach Publishing, 1998. ISBN 0-9664616-0-6.

Home Power: The Hands-on Journal of Home-made Power. P.O. Box 520, Ashland, OR, 97520, USA.

Canadian Renewable Energy News: Practical Information Exchange for Energy Independence. P.O. Box 14, Pink Mountain BC V0C 2B0 Canada.

INTERIOR PARTITION OPTIONS

Most people assume that 2x4 studs and drywall will form the interior partitions of their building. There are other options, and you can mix and match them to create different partitions in different rooms. Most of these options are not suitable for load-bearing partition walls.

Studs and Drywall

Wooden 2x4-inch studs clad with drywall — Gyproc — are most commonly used for partition walls. Quick and efficient, they are made using standard framing principles. Steel studs can be used at a comparable cost, and sheathing for stud walls doesn't have to be drywall. Straw panels, paneling, wood — weathered barn board is attractive and recycled, and other options exist.

Straw Bales

In general, bales take up too much space to be used as interior walls. In places where you want an effective sound barrier, bales laid on edge can be used, or you can cut them in half lengthwise to minimize the floor space they occupy.

Cob

Cob is a straw/clay mixture that is sometimes used to build entire homes. It can be hand-formed or poured into wooden forms to create interior partitions that are thinner than bales and that blend well with exterior bale walls. Cob is easily sculpted to create bench seats and other interior elements.

Woven Twigs

Studs of any sort — including saplings — can have long, thin sticks or saplings woven between them. The partition wall can be left with the sticks exposed or can be plastered over with gypsum, cob, or any other plaster.

Bricks and Concrete Block

Bricks and/or block make attractive partitions and function especially well if they can be used as 'heat sinks' behind wood stoves or in the path of direct sunlight. If the partition is not load-bearing, you can be creative with your brick and block laying and incorporate protrusions, built-in shelving, and other arrangements.

Other Mortared Materials

Mortared bottles, cordwood, or other common recycled materials can make interesting walls at minimal cost.

Screen Dividers

Removable, changeable, and rearrangeable room dividers may be all that's necessary to mark out space and provide a bit of privacy. From homemade versions to expensive, traditional Japanese varieties, screen dividers can be beautiful and effective. Even if they are not a permanent solution, they can allow you to experiment with different room layouts before you commit to more solid walls.

Mix and Match

No option has to exist on its own. A straw bale base can be topped with woven twigs; bricks can be placed below studs; or you can create other variations. Wall materials can be divided in non-horizontal fashion as well. Be creative!

CHAPTER 11

From Designer to Draftsperson

As you approach final decisions about the size, shape, and features of your house, it's time to put pencil to paper and create some drawings.

DESIGN VERSUS PLANS

The terms 'design' and 'plans' are often used interchangeably. They refer to two different kinds of drawings, however, and understanding the distinction can be important. Design is a spatial concept. It can refer to a floor plan, an elevation, and/or a model. In the design stage, dimensions and proportions only define the building's appearance and attributes. A design alone will not receive a building permit. Plans are the technical drawings that make the execution of a design possible. Plans include specific instructions for structural components, are fully scaled, and include all relevant dimensions. A good set of plans is literally an instruction book for the creation of the building.

DESIGN STRATEGIES

There are many different strategies for overcoming blank page phobia. If you have already created cut-outs of your rooms, you can start by translating them into individual forms on graph paper that in turn can be cut out and arranged like a puzzle. Alternatively, you may have a strong sense of the size and shape of the footprint of your house. If so, you can translate your outline onto graph paper and sketch in your interior rooms, hallways, etc.. Perhaps you are very clear about the size, shape, and placement of one or two particular rooms. Draw these first, and add the rest in relation to the first. If you know how you want your house to appear from the outside, draw it from all four directions, to scale. The dimensions of these drawings can be translated into an outline for the floor plan.

It's Like Lego!

The proportions of a typical block of Lego are very similar to that of a two-string bale. So, a return to your Lego-building days can result in accurate scale models of your home design! In addition to acquiring a good, three-dimensional understanding of your design, you'll be familiarizing yourself with many of the key rules for stacking bales. When it comes time to build the real thing, your Lego experience will serve you well!

If you've always wanted a particular kind of room or space in your home, make it part of your design.

John Marrow

Disposable Drawings

Designing can be fun and frustrating. Draw and redraw. If something isn't working, change the perspective and work from a different approach. Don't be afraid to take a break. Designing is a long process, so allow yourself time to create something you're happy with. Think of your initial drawings as disposable, and start over whenever you feel lost. Don't throw your drawings away, though. Save them in a file, and go back to them every so often. Sometimes you'll surprise yourself with how right you were back when you first started, and you may be able to work those older elements into your newer drawings.

Add Detail Gradually

Your first drawings don't have to be accurate or beautiful. As you create a design that meets your needs and pleases you, you can gradually add detail. Make your outline reflect the width of your bale walls, and draw doorways and windows to scale. Add thickness to interior dividing walls. Consider the direction in which doors will open. Sketch in permanent fixtures like sinks, baths, and toilets, and add in counters, built-in shelving, closets, beds, desks, and tables. Think about where you can place items like stereos, televisions, or computers. In two-story designs, draw in your stairs and landings. Don't forget mechanical systems. Consider plumbing routes, heating devices, and passive solar features.

John Marrow

Fixtures like sinks, ranges, and appliances will determine how a kitchen functions.

Dimensions

As you start to work with more accurate dimensions, you might want to carry a tape measure around with you. By measuring existing rooms, you can build a realistic understanding of what dimensions work best for you. Most people tend to overestimate the amount of room they will need. Only by knowing how your numbers translate into real-world space can you avoid over- or under-sizing. Consider how space will be used, not just the amount of space that's available.

The Building Code and Dimensions

Your local building code may have particular space requirements. Minimum and maximum square footage, ceiling heights, door widths and heights,

John Marrow

minimum number of windows and their window surface, and hallway and stair widths may be included in the building code. Become familiar with these requirements; you'll have to work within them. Design for efficiency. Try to arrange rooms to limit the number of hallways and the amount of space they use. Interlock closets and storage spaces. Build in shelving, cupboards, and counters. Observe how these elements have been incorporated in other buildings and other designs.

Don't Strain to Be Original

If you understand what you want from your house, a unique form will necessarily follow. You don't have to come up with your own design from scratch. By copying and slightly altering an existing design that has many of the features you want, you can create a highly personalized living space. Two houses built from identical plans by different people can each look remarkably original. So, don't shy away from plan books; rather, make those plans your own. The building techniques you use and the choices you make about finishing and interior detailing will be as integral to the creation of a unique living space as the floor plan and elevations.

John Marrow

Large features, such as these windows, require large spaces and can be marvelous centerpieces in your home.

The simple addition of a uniquely-sized set of windows can transform a wall — and the space behind it — into something individual and personal.

FROM DESIGN TO PLANS

At some point, you will create or find a design that suits you. That design needs to be translated into plans. Plans have their own language, a collection of symbols and drawing conventions that allow builders to understand plans from any designer, architect, or engineer. Typical elements include a scaled floorplan, elevations (exterior views), a foundation plan and details, floor framing and details, wall section and details, and roof framing and details. The floorplan and the elevations will be marked for 'cut lines', through which the house will be 'sliced' to show cross sections of the various elements. Cross sections are shown for areas that are

Courtesy of Ross Kembar, Architect

typical of the construction method to be used. Special exceptions are also shown in detail. It is important to become familiar with these symbols and conventions if you intend to draw your own plans or build yourself.

Do-It-Yourself Plans

If you intend to perform your own translation from design to finished plans, it is crucial to have a copy of your local building code. If straw bale is included in your code, homemade plans should be acceptable; currently, most other jurisdictions will not accept them. You may, however, draw up your own plans before approaching an architect.

Everything in your plans should be drawn to an exact and consistent scale. Try to avoid incorporating odd dimensions that will require excessive trimming of each piece of plywood or lumber. Sheet materials — plywood and drywall — usually come in 4x8-foot sheets. Lumber usually comes in 8-, 10-, 12-, 14-, 16-, or 20-foot lengths. Access to a drafting table or computer drafting program can be useful and could speed up the planning process.

If you have previous building experience, some knowledge of drafting, or a lot of time and patience to acquire these skills, it is entirely feasible to draw your own plans. If you don't, it may be better to hire a professional to do the work for you.

Purchasing Plans

Prefabricated plans for straw bale homes are not yet common, though some architectural firms are producing them. Most commercially-produced plans will need to be adapted for bale homes. A professional may be able to make adjustments for you, or you may be able to adapt them yourself. If plans are altered, approval by the original architect or engineer will no longer apply, unless you work directly with that person.

Architects

Architects perform a unique set of tasks ranging from the artistic to the scientific. Primarily, they visualize and create plans for a built environment. An architect can take you from the early design stage to finished, approved plans that will meet code requirements and still provide you with a building that is original in its concept and design. A good architect can save you time and money and relieve your building inspector of the burden of approval, since liability for the home shifts from the municipality to the architect for plans bearing a professional's stamp.

Architects are licensed by a self-regulating professional body in their particular state or province.

An architect can help you envision a space that wouldn't have occurred to you. A startling architectural feature can also have practical benefits — here, it's the movement of heat from the wood stove to the second floor

Courtesy of Ross Kembar, Architect

Once registered, an architect agrees to work within the established guidelines of that body and is insured by it. His or her stamp is recognized by building officials as a sign that the architect assumes legal responsibility for the plans in question.

Your area may support several architectural firms and individual practices; each will have its own specialty, fee structure, and style. You can set up an initial consultation with an architect — it should be free of charge — to discuss ideas, fees, and scheduling and to determine mutual compatibility.

Take your ideas and questions to the meeting. Even if you intend to use a professional to design and plan for you, it is worthwhile to play the Design Game before you make an appointment. Anything you take into the office will help you communicate your vision and goals.

It helps if you know why you have chosen certain options and not others. If you feel strongly about some aspects of your design — or even certain design concepts — be sure to let the architect know. He or she might be able to tell you about options that make sense to you that you didn't even know existed. On the other hand, you might meet with strong disagreement. If so, you may want to work with someone else.

Ask to see pictures of buildings the architect has designed or planned; it may be possible to tour one or two. Remember, you are hiring someone to help you achieve your goals. As long as your demands are reasonable, you should expect them to be met. Consult with several architects, and take time to evaluate them before choosing one.

Good referrals are the best way to find good architects. You may want to talk to some previous clients to get their opinions on the quality of work and level of service that was provided by the architect you're considering. Check with a contractor or builder who has worked with that architect's design. He or she can tell you whether or not the plans were practical and economically feasible.

Regardless of the architect you choose — and it is perfectly valid and common to hire a professional — be sure you proceed at a pace that allows you to feel comfortable with the important decisions you'll have to make.

Budget, fees, and services You should be satisfied with the agreement you make with your architect regarding your budget and his or her professional fees and services. Most architects know how to create plans to fit a budget. If you have doubts that the design can be completed within budget, be sure to raise the issue and make sure you are convinced that the response you get is reasonable.

Determine how you will be billed, when you are expected to pay, and what services the fee covers. Know what you are purchasing. If you want finished plans, make sure you will receive all the relevant drawings and references your building inspector and financiers require. Also, make sure that you can understand them. If you cannot follow the drawings or feel that certain details have not been adequately addressed, request clarification.

Be clear about how changes and modifications will be handled and billed. Building inspectors, hired carpenters, or even your own eagle eye may spot problems with the plans that will require changes; if your professional is not available to make or approve changes you can experience long delays and incur extra expense.

Finally, you should be comfortable with the amount of support your architect offers. From site inspections and meetings with building officials to advice on materials and finishes, you should both be clear about the amount of involvement your architect will have in the project.

Engineers

Engineers most often work from completed plans, performing calculations to ensure that the plans, as drawn, are feasible and meet code and safety requirements. As with architects, the stamp of a structural engineer can circumvent the concerns of a building official and allow you to get approval for your straw bale building plans. If you have drawn your own plans or purchased prefabricated plans that require adaptations or minor changes, it may be better to take them to an engineer rather than to an architect.

Professional draftsperson

A competent draftsperson has the training and knowledge to assist you with your design and your plans, but he or she does not have the stamping powers of an architect or engineer. A good draftsperson can be a valuable partner and will often work for much less money than a registered professional, while still turning out excellent, high-quality plans.

The Thrill of a 'Paper House'

It is exciting to see your house go from an idea in your head to a detailed drawing on paper. You can finally show off pictures! The project will take on an air of reality that may have been lacking during the planning stages.

Let your house rest in its paper state for a while. Show it to people you trust and get their input. Start making some preliminary cost estimates. If you will be hiring professional builders, begin to set up meetings and use a draft version of the plans for your consultations. Your straw bale house will require construction details unfamiliar to many architects and builders. Before you call your plans finished, be sure that everyone involved understands how the bales are to be used, integrated with other structural elements, detailed, and finished. When all seems right, make up enough sets of the finished plans so that each key person involved in the project can have his or her own set.

CHAPTER 12

Straw Bale Construction Plans

For your construction plans to be ready to use, they must be well-detailed and thoroughly checked. Bale details will be especially important.

Construction plans for straw bale buildings must be detailed, accurate, and reliable. It should be obvious from your detail drawings that your building will be structurally sound, impervious or resistant to accumulations of rainwater and snow, and practicable to execute with a minimum of materials and time-consuming fussing. We suggest that you consider using several details that will address key aspects of your straw bale wall.

BALE DETAILS

Bale Curb

Real-world bale widths rarely match the nominal dimensions used in drawings. It is best to know the actual width of the bales you will be using and/or to plan for slightly wider curb rails. An 18 inch curb will often end up tucked underneath the bales, making it difficult to attach stucco mesh or to achieve a smooth plaster finish, as shown in Illustration 12.1 Figure 1. A flush curb allows a straight plaster finish to extend right to the floor, as shown in Figure 2. A curb with rails set slightly wider than the bales would allow the plaster to end on top of the curb, leaving a nailing strip available for trim. While 2x4-inch curbs are most common, lumber misers could easily get away with 2x3-inch or maybe even 2x2-inch curbs. In general, rigid insulation or drain board is used between the rails of the curb.

Illustration 12.1 Bale curbs

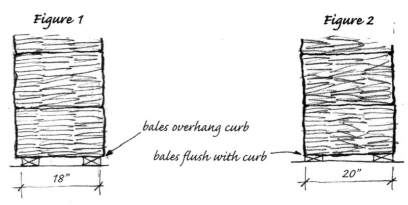

Figure 1

Figure 2

bales overhang curb

bales flush with curb

18"

20"

Corners

To maintain a strong 'running bond' at the corners of a bale wall, your plans must allow a minimum of 1½ bale lengths between corners and windows or doors. Otherwise, there is little to stop the bales from bowing out, especially under compression in a load-bearing design, as shown in Illustration 12.2.

Foundation/Bale Junction

There are many ways to successfully create a good junction between your foundation and your bales. In all cases, care should be taken to isolate the bales from the foundation — especially a concrete foundation. One layer of tar paper, or paintable asphalt-based foundation coating should be laid under the curb and another placed over the curb upon which the bales will rest.

Illustration 12.2

Figure 1. Improper running bond and resulting problems

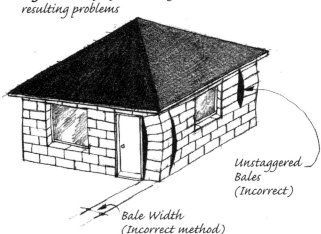

Bale Width
(Incorrect method)

Unstaggered
Bales
(Incorrect)

Figure 2. Proper running bond

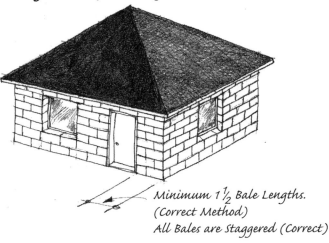

Minimum 1½ Bale Lengths.
(Correct Method)
All Bales are Staggered (Correct)

Illustration 12.3 Figures 1–4 show a variety of methods you can use for placing bales on a concrete slab foundation. In Figures 1 and 2, pre-compression wires have been routed through conduit that has been cast into the slab at the time of the pour. This method requires the most forethought and preparation but provides a strong anchor, and the smooth curve of the conduit eases the threading and tightening of the wires.

Figure 3 shows eye bolts that have been cast into the slab. The eye bolts must be at least 3/8-inch stock and should have welded eyes to prevent opening under the tension of the wires. Eye bolts can be expensive and must be placed during the pour.

Figure 4 shows pre-compression wire that has been run directly under the curb. If a lot of pre-compression is required, the wires may cut deeply into the wooden curb, so care must be taken to fasten the curb securely to prevent wires from twisting the curb from the foundation. Right-angled metal protectors placed between the wire and the wood can remedy the situation. This method allows you to place wires anywhere, without prior planning. While anchor bolts are shown to be fastening the curb in each drawing, pre-drilled concrete nails or screws can also be used.

Figure 5 shows the routing of pre-compression wires when a wooden-framed floor system is being used — either a basement/perimeter wall or a pier foundation. When the joists are perpendicular to the bale wall, a U-shaped block of wood made from a joist off-cut can be attached and the wires run underneath it. The wire could also be looped around the rim joist and a piece of solid blocking located under the inside of the curb. The wires are easily looped around the doubled joists running parallel to the curb, requiring no additional steps for preparation.

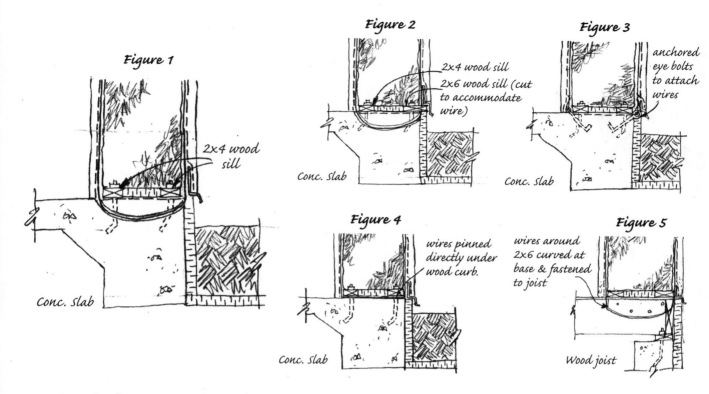

Figure 1

2x4 wood sill

Conc. slab

Figure 2

2x4 wood sill
2x6 wood sill (cut to accommodate wire)

Conc. slab

Figure 3

anchored eye bolts to attach wires

Conc. slab

Figure 4

wires pinned directly under wood curb.

Conc. slab

Figure 5

wires around 2x6 curved at base & fastened to joist

Wood joist

A wooden floor system can be cantilevered past the edge of the foundation wall so that the bales are centered over the foundation wall. This allows for a bit more room on the floor of the house without requiring a larger foundation footprint. Note the use of a metal flashing at the base of the wall in each drawing. Extending up the bale wall a few inches, covered with stucco mesh, and then plastered over, the flashing prevents water from seeping under the curb and accumulating under the wall. The flashing is an important detail, especially on walls that will be exposed to rain. For post and beam designs, the need to route the pre-compression wires is eliminated.

Rebar Foundation Pins

Rebar foundation pins were used in early straw bale buildings to impale the first course of bales. We discourage their use. A wall that is built without pins will not differ appreciably in stability or structural strength from a wall with pins.

Rebar pins are a nuisance to place during foundation construction and often end up being poorly embedded and floppy. They unfailingly do damage to knees and shins and pose a serious safety hazard should someone fall on top of them. They also make the important task of sealing the foundation from

Illustration 12.3
Foundation Bale junctions

Two volunteers fall victim to sharp rebar and clutch their shins in pain!

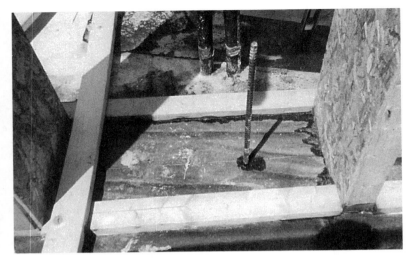

The dark patch at the base of the rebar pin shows the serious accumulation of moisture that a pin can allow into the bale wall. It is next to impossible to seal the wall effectively against rising moisture around the pins.

the bales virtually impossible and may provide a place for migrating moisture to condense inside your bale walls. By eliminating the pins, you'll save time, money, and eliminate a high embodied energy material that is simply not necessary.

If you live in an area where the use of pins is prescribed, you may want to express your disapproval, but chances are you'll need to abide by the code until it is changed. Make sure you seal any pins you do use with a generous amount of tar or asphalt at the base.

Door and Window Bucks

The rough frame bucks installed in the bale wall will provide a place to attach the actual windows and doors. Design and construction of the rough frame bucks are open to a certain amount of improvisation by the builder as long as certain principles are adhered to. The bucks must be strong enough to bear the weight of the straw and the roof without distorting, and the design must be able to accommodate the finish you want.

Illustration 12.4 Figures 1 and 2 show two rough buck designs that can handle significant loads. The box beam lintel is the same width as the buck itself, simplifying its placement in the bale wall. The steel angle lintel can be equally as strong but requires welding skills to create. The width of the opening, the strength of the top plate above the opening, and the amount of straw bearing on the buck will determine the strength required of the lintel.

Figure 1

Figure 2

Illustration 12.4
Rough buck designs

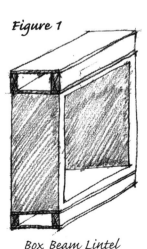

Box Beam Lintel

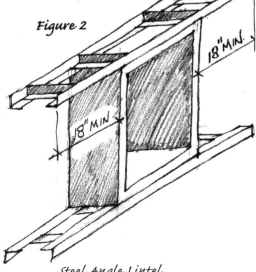

18" MIN.

18" MIN.

Steel Angle Lintel

A variety of window buck designs can be used. All bucks should be designed for appropriate strength and to create the desired finish. Bucks can be made from solid, unbraced lumber, like the odd-shaped small buck being leveled during a workshop, shown in photo at top; from 2x4-braced OSB, like the non-floating bucks that sit on the floor and have a bottom sill placed later, shown in centre photo; or from 2x4-braced solid lumber bucks, like the bucks that have been made with notched corners for extra strength, shown in photo below.

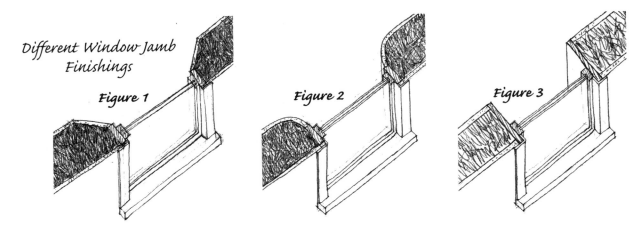

Different Window Jamb Finishings

Figure 1

Figure 2

Figure 3

Illustration 12.5
You can choose the wide bevel shown in Figure 1, the curved bevel shown in Figure 2, or the square sides shown in Figure 3, or any variation thereof.

The design of the rough bucks will determine the kind of finish you can achieve around your windows and doors. Different sizes of lumber used at the sides, top, and bottom of the buck will create different curved openings, as seen in Illustration 12.5 Figures 1–3.

Illustration 12.6 Figures 1 and 2 and the photos on the following page show different ways of finishing window sills and the top edge of your windows, based on the rough buck design. The wide sill shown in Illustration 12.6 Figure 2 can be an integral part of the buck or can be added in afterward.

Illustration 12.6 also shows two key finishing details for windows in bale walls. At the top of the window, a metal drip-edge flashing directs water away from the window. At the bottom edge, a flashing or sill with a drip kerf prevents water from being drawn into the wall through capillary action — gravity is doing its job here. As an extra precaution, the joints of the rough buck frame can be caulked when being assembled. To protect against water that is blown in through an open window, place ice and water shield — a rubbery roof product — over the sill of the rough buck, drape it over the bales inside and out, and bury it under the plaster.

Once you have chosen your rough buck design, you must consider how you will finish the plaster at the door and window openings. Illustration 12.7 Figures 1 and 2 on pg. 112 show a variety of finishing methods that range from a simple plastering over of the frames to the installation of J-molds that provide a clean finished contact edge for plaster. If you

Illustration 12.6
Finishing details for windows and sills

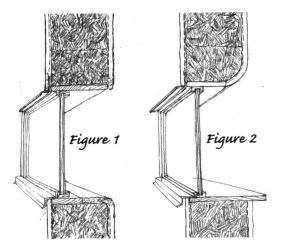

Figure 1

Figure 2

John Marrow

Partial curves

Full depth curves

Courtesy of Ross Kembar, Architect

John Marrow

Square finish

want to finish the plaster directly to the buck — or the finished window frame — set the buck and/or frame to protrude about an inch from the bale walls so that the plaster will sit flush when its three coats have been applied. This will allow trim to be fastened to the window after plastering.

In northern climates or where heavy rains are normal, windows should always be set to the outside face of the wall. The wide, exterior sill or a deep-set window is very difficult to seal effectively against the rain and snow that will inevitably accumulate. Where porch overhangs provide protection, windows can safely be set to the inside.

Bale heights

Bale heights are an important consideration at the planning stage. Obviously, they will determine the overall height of the finished walls. But bale heights should also be taken into account when you are designing window and door openings. Rough bucks that correspond to bale heights will help solve annoying stacking difficulties.

Illustration 12.7
Plaster finishes

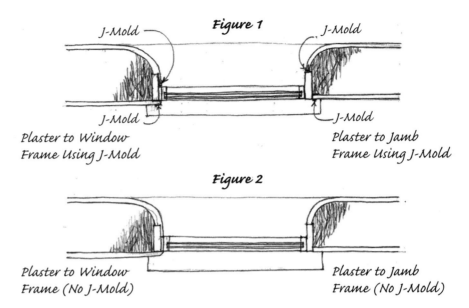

Plaster to Window
Frame Using J-Mold

Plaster to Jamb
Frame Using J-Mold

Plaster to Window
Frame (No J-Mold)

Plaster to Jamb
Frame (No J-Mold)

Illustration 12.8
Roof plates

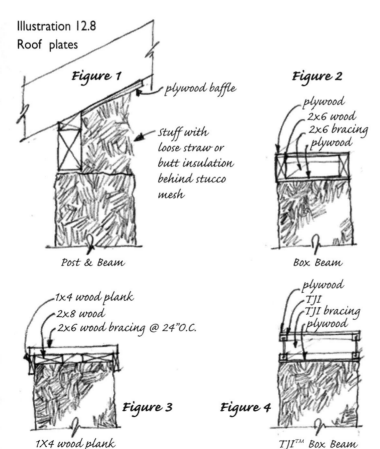

ROOF PLATES

For post and beam designs, the roof plate is simply a plywood baffle or barrier under which the top course of bales comes to rest. It provides protection against pests and moisture — from possible roof leakage — and provides a point of attachment for stucco mesh.

Illustration 12.8 Figure 1 shows a plywood top plate set against the roof joists. Horizontal top plates are also commonly attached to the underside of ceiling joists or trusses, eliminating the need to stuff loose straw into angled spaces. As with any top plate for a straw bale design, tar paper or vapor barrier should be placed under the plywood to protect the bales in case of an eventual roof leak.

The top plate plays an important role in load-bearing designs, acting as a lintel over window and door openings and providing the stiffness required to transfer the loads of pre-compression evenly over the top of the wall. Many different roof plate designs have been used successfully, and improvements are always being made.

Illustration 12.8 Figures 2–4 show a variety of ways to create a top plate. A simple timber — 4x6-inch or larger — placed over plywood would be effective, but many methods using conventional lumber to reduce the consumption of large-dimension lumber have been devised. For the design shown in Figure 2, a pair of 2x6s — or larger if the spans dictate — is sandwiched between plywood to form a box beam. The box beam is blocked with 2x4s, over which the pre-compression wires are run. Depending on how you choose to finish your plaster, the box beam could be encased in plaster or left exposed as a nailing surface for trim. It must be filled with insulation — either straw or regular batt insulation.

For the design shown in Figure 3, flat planks are used; 1x4s are attached on either side to provide additional stiffness and a nailer strip for stucco mesh or trim. Two-by-six braces bridge the planks where wires and/or roof trusses will be placed. This method is not as rigid as a box beam and may require the use of additional lintels for window and door bucks that are wide. This roof plate also leaves the tops of the bales exposed and susceptible to the infiltration of moisture, air, and pests, so some provision must be made to seal the openings.

Manufactured wooden I-beams can be used to create a very strong and lightweight box beam roof plate, as shown in Figure 4. Wooden I-beams can be purchased in your required lengths and eliminate the need to splice joints.

Illustration 12.9 shows how solid corners can be created in a plywood base — and top, for a box beam application. A corner formed from a single piece of plywood provides extra strength and is an asset when you are trying to square the top plate once it has been lifted on top of the wall.

A concrete top plate is formed in place on top of the bale wall. Wooden forms remain in place to provide an attachment point for stucco mesh and/or trim. Rebar is used and the thickness of the roof plate is determined according to the openings it is required to span. A concrete roof plate provides a tight seal against the top of the bale wall. Its weight consumes some of the dead load capacity of the wall.

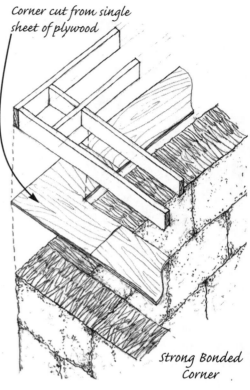

Corner cut from single sheet of plywood

Strong Bonded Corner

Illustration 12.9
Corners

A box beam roof plate assembly is lifted into place. Note the tar paper fastened to the bottom side as protection against moisture. (The tar paper could have been wrapped over the rails of the roof plate, too, eliminating the need to apply it separately before plastering.)

Heide Bateman

The guts of a 2x6 box beam are visible and the pre-compression wires are running over the 2x4 blocking. The joints at the corner are staggered, and the two intersecting top plate units are firmly bolted together.

Illustration 12.10
Variations of post and beam
in-fill walls

POST AND BEAM DETAILS

Post and beam designs must be carefully adapted for use with straw bales to ensure that the two elements integrate well. The first decision to be made is where to place the framework. As shown in Illustration 12.10, the framework can be set interior to the bale walls (Figure 1), buried in them (Figure 2), or set exterior to them (Figure 3). Internal frames are left exposed, which can add to or detract from the finished appearance of your home depending on the materials you've used. Internal frames require extra thought when you plan for roof overhangs and require knee walls and/or beams to be cantilevered out through the straw walls.

Figure 1

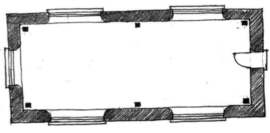

Columns Inside Building

Figure 2

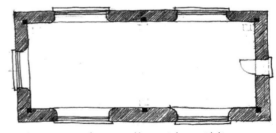

Columns Within Wall, Inside Building

Figure 3

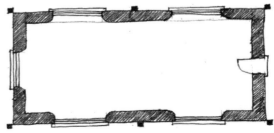

Columns Outside Building

Buried frames allow for a seamless plaster finish inside the house but can require the time-consuming and often inaccurate notching of bales to accommodate the frame members within the wall. If the bales can be placed such that notching is minimized or eliminated, a great deal of time and effort will be saved.

Frames built outside the wall envelope make for simpler roof construction, but the foundation of the building must be larger to accommodate the frame, or individual piers must be poured for the posts. Careful detailing of the foundation is required to prevent rainwater from pooling and running underneath the bales. Exterior posts will be exposed to the elements, and may require treatment to prevent early decay.

Builders of post and beam straw bale buildings must ensure that the junction between posts, beams, and straw is well detailed.

Illustration 12.11 Figures 1–5 shows different ways of finishing plaster to posts and beams. If the framework rests a minimum of 3–4 inches away from the straw wall, then the plaster finish does not have to meet the frame, as shown in Figure 1. It is very common to have the post facing the interior of the structure and for it to be flush with the interior face of the bales. Figure 2 shows that the plaster must then make a seam with the post. Because the plaster won't make an air-tight seal where it meets the post — due to shrinkage during curing — a vapor barrier is attached to the back side of the post and extended 2–4 inches beyond it before the straw is installed. The vapor barrier is thus keyed into the plaster and creates a continuous air barrier. The same procedure can be used to tie the ceiling vapor barrier into the wall around the beams. Some caulking applied after the second coat of plaster has cured will help to minimize air leakage at the post/plaster seam.

The flush post and the buried post shown in Figures 3 and 4 respectively will require time-consuming notching of the bales. If this is the final finish you want, the vapor barrier treatment described above is also recommended here, since the junction may be prone to some plaster cracking.

If your framework is buried in the straw, as is shown in Figure 5, you will likely have some spaces on either side of the framing member that will need to be stuffed with loose straw and held in with plaster lath or diamond lath. A vapor barrier is not required, since the plaster will be continuous and not prone to cracking where loose straw is behind the lath.

Illustration 12.11
Finishing plaster to posts and beams

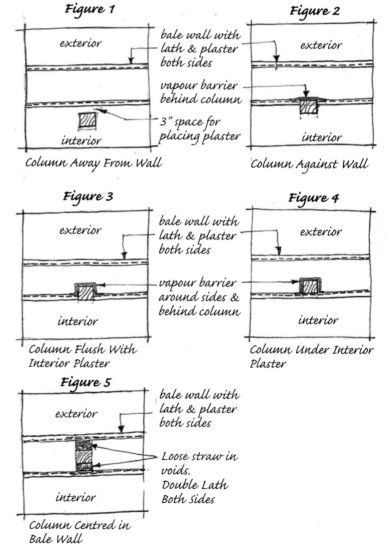

Figure 1

exterior

interior

Column Away From Wall

bale wall with lath & plaster both sides

vapour barrier behind column

3" space for placing plaster

Figure 2

exterior

interior

Column Against Wall

Figure 3

exterior

interior

Column Flush With Interior Plaster

bale wall with lath & plaster both sides

vapour barrier around sides & behind column

Figure 4

exterior

interior

Column Under Interior Plaster

Figure 5

exterior

interior

Column Centred in Bale Wall

bale wall with lath & plaster both sides

Loose straw in voids.
Double Lath Both Sides

PRE-COMPRESSION DETAILS

Whatever system of pre-compression you use for a load-bearing structure, it will take some planning to ensure that the placement of attachment points is accurate and useful. Always plan to have pre-compression points within 1–2 feet of every inside corner, and keep the spacing to approximately 2–4 feet between points. Where wide openings are planned — sliding doors, large windows — pre-compression points should be located as close to the opening as possible, without interfering with the buck frame or the plastering finish.

You want to avoid pre-compression points that run through a window or door opening. You can plan for more attachment points than are necessary and then choose the ones that are appropriate once the walls have been constructed and doors and windows have been placed.

PLASTER FINISHING CONSIDERATIONS

Illustration 12.12

Finishing plaster at ceilings and floors

At the planning stage, it's a good idea to give some thought to the kind of finishing details you want for the plaster. Illustration 12.12 Figures 1–5 shows some of the ways plaster can be finished where it intersects the ceiling and the floor. Bullnose finishes (Figure 1) require no pre-planning, but the 1-inch nailer strips (Figure 2) and the wider base on the top plate (Figure 3) must be accounted for during the planning stage. The finish at the floor (Figures 4 and 5) can likewise be affected by your choices of curb design — plaster can end on the floor/foundation or on the curb itself.

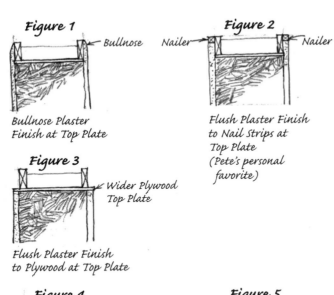

Figure 1
— Bullnose

Bullnose Plaster
Finish at Top Plate

Figure 2
Nailer — — Nailer

Flush Plaster Finish
to Nail Strips at
Top Plate
(Pete's personal
favorite)

Figure 3
— Wider Plywood
Top Plate

Flush Plaster Finish
to Plywood at Top Plate

CEILING AND FLOOR INSULATION

Regardless of the type of insulation you choose for your ceiling and floors — bales, batts, loose-blown, or rigid — don't skimp on quantity. Your ceiling insulation should at least match the R-value of your bale walls — R-40 or more. Your floor should be insulated adequately for your climate and foundation style — heat does radiate downward, too — otherwise, the benefits of your highly insulating straw bale walls will be lessened.

ASKING QUESTIONS OF YOUR PLANS

It is a good idea to ask yourself a series of questions as you scrutinize your plans. The world's best authors have editors and proofreaders; your plans will benefit from a similar third-party reading. Friends and family may be able to help a little, but someone with building experience will be most helpful. It may even be worth it to pay a professional builder to review your plans. If you can find someone who has had some experience building with bales, all the better.

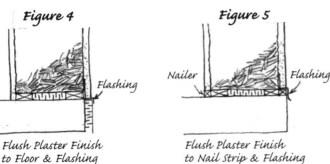

Figure 4
Flashing

Flush Plaster Finish
to Floor & Flashing

Figure 5
Nailer — — Flashing

Flush Plaster Finish
to Nail Strip & Flashing

Run your plans through a philosophical checklist to be sure they fulfill your original intentions. Is the house the right size? Does it contain the kinds of rooms you wanted? Does its appearance suit your esthetic sense and the landscape it will occupy? On a more practical note, do some budget estimates. By this point, you'll be able to do an accurate tally of all required components, including lumber, doors, windows, roofing, concrete, and interior finishing. Give your plans to professionals who can generate estimates for you for materials and labor.

Check your plans for build-ability. Do all your measurements pan out? Will the intersections of different components be possible to construct as drawn? Do measurements make sense — lengths, widths, and spans? Where there are interruptions in wall or roof directions, can the transitions be achieved without undue hassle? Will

Illustration 12.13
Straw bale wall details

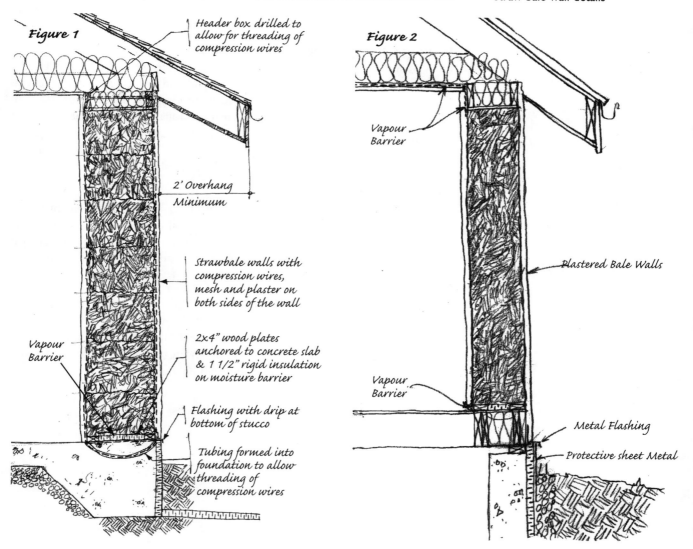

Figure 1

Header box drilled to allow for threading of compression wires

2' Overhang Minimum

Strawbale walls with compression wires, mesh and plaster on both sides of the wall

Vapour Barrier

2x4" wood plates anchored to concrete slab & 1 1/2" rigid insulation on moisture barrier

Flashing with drip at bottom of stucco

Tubing formed into foundation to allow threading of compression wires

Figure 2

Vapour Barrier

Plastered Bale Walls

Vapour Barrier

Metal Flashing

Protective sheet Metal

your finishing components — plaster, drywall, wood, etc. — be well-detailed, with accurate starting, finishing, and attachment points? Have you planned adequately for the use of bale walls? Sufficient roof overhangs, raised curbs, and flashing? Does the height of your walls correspond to even bale heights? Do you understand how you will achieve directional changes with your top plate? Do your window and door bucks correspond with bale heights and your desired finish?

Illustration 12.13 show two well-detailed cross sections of straw bale walls. While detailing can vary, depending on your construction style and the design of the roof plate, roof framing, curb, and foundation, both drawings include important details. Note the base flashing at the bottom of the exterior wall, vapor barriers tied in to the plaster at the ceiling, and the routing of pre-compression wires for load-bearing designs. With drawings of this caliber, your trouble-shooting scrutinizing process can begin in earnest.

Making Changes Can Make Problems

Changes and corrections made to plans must be executed carefully. Every alteration can have implications that affect the whole building, so if you change or correct one dimension you must follow through and make sure that the rest of your plans are adapted to this change. Consider how changes you make will affect the spacing of framing members, the dimensions of rooms, the foundation, and the roof. If you've spent time trying to make the most effective use of materials, don't forget that changes to your plans may result in odd sizing for lumber and sheet materials.

The Detail That Got Away

Most plans are bound to contain some contradictions, problems, and minor inconsistencies. A thorough study can help to reveal most of these errors. What details escape notice will have to be dealt with during construction. When you are satisfied that you are ready and able to begin construction, it's time to submit your plans for approval. Or, if you don't require approval, it's time to start building!

HAVE A PARTY!

Finished and approved plans call for a celebration! You will be poised on the brink of your building adventure, and you'll have made it through the long and often difficult planning process. Blow off some steam and regenerate your excitement and enthusiasm before you grab your tools and start building!

CHAPTER 13

Do-It-Yourself (DIY) and Building Professionals

Your role in the creation of your straw bale home can vary from the purely administrative to a hands-on creation of the entire building. How you choose to employ yourself and others in the building process requires careful consideration.

Some people know for certain that they want to build their own home. Others are equally certain that they want no part in the hands-on building. Still others take a middle path and hire professionals for particular aspects of the work or act as their own general contractor.

DIY

Most able-bodied people can acquire the skills and learn to perform the tasks required for building their own houses. Even unappealing tasks can be undertaken if you are motivated by necessity, desire, or ambition! Books, manuals, and codes are readily available that address every aspect of house-building, and you can use them as reference material. Choose sources that reflect your perspectives and values. There is no point in following a guidebook written in a spirit that conflicts with yours.

For any given aspect of construction, you must understand why you are performing a task; to follow instructions without comprehending their purpose is a recipe for error. If you can grasp the theory, its specific application in your building will follow much more easily. You do not have to cram an encyclopedic amount of information into your head at once — no one can absorb and retain that much new information. Learn enough about each stage to know what specific planning is required, then set about each task individually and in the order in which you need to perform it. Don't be afraid to tackle a job you're unsure about. Often it is only when you get your hands on the materials that you will understand what's required. You might make a mistake or two before it all comes clear, but if you wait until your theoretical understanding is flawless, you may never get your house built.

Professional Advice and DIYers

Often, the best way to learn how to do a particular task is to seek advice from an experienced professional. Many professionals have spent decades learning the hard way, and the information they'll be able to give you is valuable While some professionals may be willing to share their knowledge freely, you should never expect them to do so. Offer to pay for consulting time, and take them your plans and a list of specific questions. During your consultation, take notes, make drawings, and ask for clarification when you don't understand. Try to spend more time listening than talking, and avoid getting into arguments on points where you disagree. By keeping the consultation positive and focused on an exchange of information, you will get the best possible return on your investment.

While time and money spent in consultation may seem to be a waste at first, a few big mistakes made solo can cost you much more in the end. Even if you strongly disagree with the advice you are given, contradiction can pave the way to clearer understanding. If a professional advises against a given practice or idea, it is usually because he or she has had a bad experience with it and is trying to help you avoid a similar pitfall. You are always free to seek more than one opinion if you find yourself unconvinced or still unsure.

TASK HIRING

Some specialized tasks may be better left to professionals. While we encourage you to attempt as much of your project as you want, if you feel like you're in over your head, it may make sense to hire. Specific experience and proper equipment often allow professionals to do a job faster, more efficiently, and with fewer errors than you can, and you may find the cost is less than you expect. Let your own interests, skills, and budget determine if you want to hire or not.

Building professionals cover the spectrum from highly skilled, enthusiastic practitioners to scam artists. Your hiring decisions will be based on a combination of factors, including the personality of the person you are considering. Do you get along with this person? Does he or she seem easy to talk with, open, honest, and forthright? If you are bringing particular values to the project — ecological awareness, attention to detail, or esthetics — does this person share or respect your values? Is he or she easy to reach, organized, and punctual? If a gut feeling attracts you to a particular professional or warns you away, listen to your instincts.

Experience is another important factor you will need to consider before you hire anyone. Someone with experience usually makes fewer errors, works faster, and uses materials effectively. But not always. On specialty projects like straw bale homes, someone who has performed the same set of standardized tasks hundreds of times may not be who you need. You need someone who can think, plan, and act to achieve particular goals. So, ask to see pictures of the professional's work, or go and visit projects he or she has completed. Make sure you understand what kind of experience he or she has had and that it meets your needs.

Cost is another factor to consider if you intend to hire out for certain tasks. You should obtain a written estimate from whoever you hire and a clear commitment from them that they will meet it. If the estimate is not guaranteed, reach a clear agreement on how increases are to be handled. You should be notified as soon as a cost overrun is suspected and should receive another written estimate covering the new or unforeseen expenses. Payment terms should be clear. If you plan to use materials other than standard building-supply yard fare — for cost or environmental reasons — be sure to let the professional know before he or she submits an estimate, so that pricing can be done accurately. Don't let cost alone determine your hiring decisions, since quality of work, timeliness of completion, warranty, and the accuracy of estimates can all affect the price you'll pay in the end.

Beyond cost, you will likely want to consider warranty, references, and scheduling. Will the professional guarantee his or her work? For how long? Has he or she made a commitment to return and fix problems? If you can, talk to others who have employed the professional you're considering. You'll get a better idea of his or her on-the-job performance. Time is important. Can the professional meet your scheduling requirements? How will delays be handled? Make sure you allow yourself an option that released you from the contract if the work cannot be performed on time. Be prepared to meet with many people before you make a hiring decision. The people you hire will help to keep your project on time and on budget.

The owner gives instructions; the hired builders do the work.

OWNER GENERAL CONTRACTING

If you are going to hire all or most of the labor for your project, you will be fulfilling the role of general contractor' In commercial construction, general contractors oversee entire projects, for which they hire other individuals or companies to complete particular tasks.

General contracting can demand as much of your time as a full-time job. You must juggle the needs and schedules of many different professionals and are responsible for seeing that all work is done correctly and on time. It takes organizational skills, planning, and crisis control abilities to keep a project running smoothly. The process can be rewarding, however, and allows you to be closely involved without requiring that you actually undertake the construction yourself.

Organize a project meeting; it will allow all parties concerned to meet and discuss your project. You will likely have to pay for the time the meeting takes, but the benefits to your project can far outweigh the costs. Plans can be reviewed and issues raised and solved with input from all relevant sources. If the foundation builder understands what the carpenter needs, and the carpenter the bale raiser, etc., a much better project will result. It may surprise you to find out that professionals often don't meet or confer on-site, but simply pick up where the other person left off. The meeting, therefore, will give everyone a chance to confer, make sketches, and form a more complete understanding of the project. If an architect or engineer helped draw up the plans, be sure to invite him or her to the meeting.

*General Contracting
a Straw Bale Home*

Anne-Marie Warburton acted as general contractor for her family's two-story, 2,500-square-foot post and beam home (featured on the cover) in the Hockley Valley, Ontario, Canada. The house was built by professionals, and the bale walls were raised by volunteers. The project was completed with a conventional bank mortgage and received regular home insurance.

"Basically, I think general contractors earn their money. General contracting is hard work, and you need lots of time to be able to do a good job. It was important to me that everybody I hired to work on the project was totally aligned with our goals ▶

and ideals. If a tradesperson wasn't supportive, I didn't want them on the project. You have to find people whose attitudes match your own. If any crews are resentful or aren't getting along with you, it can make it unpleasant to be at the building site. But you can't stay away, it's your house! So a good working relationship is a must. Right from the quoting process, you can tell if you're dealing with someone who's going to be thrilled to be involved. You can tell by the questions they ask and their language and attitude. It's not just the price to be watching for. We have a friend who is Cree, and he taught us that you leave your energy in anything you do. So make sure you like a person's energy before you hire them, because they're going to leave it behind in your house. The guys who did our post and beam frame always gave us updates and let us know their needs and schedules. You need that kind of relationship or you could really screw up. When it works, it's very exciting.

I had prior knowledge of other building types, having self-contracted a conventional home. But that didn't prepare me for the specifics of putting up the bales. I'd read a book and seen a video, but had no hands-on experience. As a result, I missed entire aspects of the process. Quilting the stucco mesh was a process I didn't even have in my schedule, and it took as much time as raising the bales. If you have the time to do it yourself and learn as you go, that's fine. But if you have a tight schedule, it's good ▶

If you are incorporating non-standard materials in your project, be sure everybody knows what materials are to be used, where they can be sourced, and how they function in the building. Otherwise, most professionals will price, source, and buy materials based on their own experience and habits.

Try to work out an actual schedule, and make written lists of what each professional requires of the other. Keep the meeting short and focused, and be sure everybody leaves with what they need to know.

Building professionals usually work on a first-come, first-served basis; make sure you book your work early. In areas with harsh winters, building projects are crammed into a short, frantic season, so trying to hire somebody mid-season can be difficult and frustrating.

Hiring a General Contractor

A general contractor's job is to provide you with a finished home that meets your expectations and demands. General contractors hire the appropriate professionals to build your house, on schedule and according to a determined budget. It is up to you to be sure your general contractor understands the requirements of your straw bale building. While you will be consulted during the construction process, contractor-built homes are a 'hands-off' option. Because the job involves a great deal trust and responsibility, you want to select your contractor carefully.

WORKING WITH PROFESSIONALS

Even the most enthusiastic professional is, at the end of the day, working for you to make money. While your project is of the utmost importance to you, a professional cannot be expected to always match your enthusiasm and eagerness. Other people who are similarly enthusiastic and eager to have their projects completed are likely to be in line for your professional's services, and their needs are being balanced against your own. You need to have realistic expectations about hours of work, breaks, and responsibilities.

Many professionals rely on work from large contracting firms for most of their income. Your project may not take precedence over a contractor's. You are unlikely to build again — in the near future, anyway! — while a contractor will be hiring continuously, year in and year out. You shouldn't be given compromised service, but the reality is that you might be.

Be clear from the start about your expectations. Arrange to inspect or receive regular reports on the progress of any work being done for you. If you are unhappy with the quality of work or the pace at which it is proceeding — or not proceeding — make your displeasure known and try to work out a solution. Your hired help should be told how to deal with unforeseen needs for changes. Make sure you can be reached if you are not on-site to make critical decisions, or give someone the authority to make decisions on your behalf.

Building Professionals and Snowflakes

Every single builder has specific beliefs, methodologies, and materials by which they will swear. (This may be doubly true for straw bale builders!) In order to stay sane and keep your own goals intact, listen to the advice you are given, but don't feel you need to defer to it all. It's better to have a plumber mutter about your being crazy than to be talked out of a system you are convinced is right for you! Keep an open mind but a firm one. The opinions of a professional are like snowflakes — every one is unique, and every one will eventually disappear. Be sure you have what you want before they go away!

LOOSE ENDS, DEADLINES, AND CONSTRUCTION MADNESS

Even if you are remarkably well-prepared at the outset of your project, the construction process is fraught with unforeseen obstacles. Expect a strange kind of chaos, complete with noise, debris, and time warps galore!

Adapt yourself to the pace of building. Sometimes, weeks can go by and it will seem as though nothing has changed. Other times, work will progress so quickly it will make your head spin. Schedules shift, expectations need to be modified, budgets get challenged. All of this is normal. Your only defense is to try to remain calm and focused. At the end of all the madness, you will have a house to live in. When it all gets to be too much, remind yourself why you started this process, and remember what you can expect once it is completed!

John Marrow

The Warburton Home

to have someone knowledgeable to oversee the bale-raising process, even if you're using volunteers. I also wasn't prepared for how much time it would take to call and arrange volunteers. Phoning and asking for help is not something I'm good at, and it was hard to do.

There is always the problem of running out of money. Don't forget to add in taxes when doing your budgeting! That extra percentage makes a big difference. Wood prices can change, too. Wood went up almost 40 percent in the six months between the quotes we got and delivery. You've got to manage your money well, and know when to hold back and when to pay in full. You don't want to pay for a job that isn't done right.

When you're building a unique house, you've got to expect that something's going to happen that you didn't expect. You'll have to make decisions on the fly. I was always trying to visualize what was coming next, and anticipating what would be needed. Mistakes can often be turned into design opportunities and decorative bonuses.

It's a great feeling to be so involved in the building of your own home, making decisions and knowing where things are and why. In the end, I'm thrilled to have this house." ❖

CHAPTER 14

Budgeting

While budget considerations have been central factor throughout the planning process, once your plans are complete, you can attempt to assess your actual costs.

HITTING A MOVING TARGET

There is never a single point during the planning process when you can fix an exact budget for your project. Once your plans near completion, however, you have a chance to use them as a guide for estimating both materials and labor costs.

If you find you have missed your budget target by a significant amount, you will have to go back to your plans and start making adjustments. This can be disheartening, but it is better to catch such a problem early than to run out of money before there's a roof over your head! You may be able to adjust costs without changing your plans, if you commit yourself to finding cheaper materials and hiring less labor. If you do change your plans to reduce costs, don't forget to work in planning that will allow you to bring your building back to its originally planned size later.

You may discover that you have apparently created plans that will allow you to build for less than what you budgeted. Congratulations! This is every homebuilder's dream. Don't change your plans, however. When the project is over, you'll be able to spend a bit more on detailing, furnishing, and landscaping.

IT ALWAYS COSTS MORE THAN YOU THINK

The building project that is completed without going over-budget is rare. Your plans will allow you to create a budget estimate, but there will always be unforeseen costs, delays, and problems that will require extra cash to solve. Leave yourself with plenty of budgetary breathing room so you can deal with the inevitable. Try to reserve at least 10 percent of your total calculated budget to cover unforeseen costs.

Pre-construction Costs

The pre-construction costs of your project will not be evident from your plans. They include the price of property, interest on your property payments, building permit fees, driveway allowances, access roads, septic permits, service and utility hook-up, and municipal development fees and taxes. Depending on where you are building, these fees can total several thousand dollars and take quite a bite out of your actual construction budget. Wells, septic systems, service entrances, and the excavation of your foundation must all be completed before you actually begin construction and will take another bite out of your budget.

Other Hidden Costs

Before you start taking count of the dollars needed for materials and labor, don't forget to consider other hidden costs you may need to cover. The purchase and/or rental of tools can add up to a significant budget factor. Working without the right tools is frustrating and slow, so think your way through the construction process and make a list of what you'll need. From shovels and picks for digging to carpentry tools and plastering trowels, the list will be extensive and expensive. Keep a bit of your budget set aside for unforeseen specialty tools you'll need to buy or rent.

Any building project can involve lots of 'tarping up' to cover materials from the elements. This can be especially true for straw bale projects. Invest in enough good quality tarps to cover the walls of the building and the mounds of straw.

Depending on the availability of grid power at your site, you may require a generator for your power needs. Check the costs of purchase and rental.

If you are building yourself, you might find it beneficial to own a truck, van, or trailer that can be used to pick up and move materials. Such vehicles can be sold when you no longer require them, but you will need money to purchase, license, insure, and service them.

Unless you are building in a well-serviced area, you will need some sort of on-site toilet. You can rent serviced units, or you can build an outhouse. Rental toilets are convenient and are removed when you are finished with them. They can also be expensive if the project is a long one. An outhouse requires an early outlay of time and money, but you get some building practice, and an outhouse is not a bad back-up facility to have in case of plumbing disasters in the future.

You will need proper clothing. Buy good safety boots — spend extra for comfortable, well-fitting boots, gloves, and maybe a hard hat. If you are working in an inclement climate, warm and/or waterproof clothes will make a big difference to your ability to work efficiently. Construction will wreak havoc on your clothing, so buy quality clothes or plenty of cheap, second hand stuff.

Construction insurance covers your project in case of mishaps. Rates can vary tremendously, so get a number of quotes, and be sure you are covered for the risks that concern you most — fire, accident, damage from wind, rain, etc..

Don't forget the tax man. Sales taxes can add a significant percentage to both material and labor costs. Don't just total up pre-tax costs!

If you are doing your own building, don't forget to include your cost of living for while you are building. Rent and food must be covered, as will all your regular bills. If you are taking time off work to build, these expenses can take quite a bite out of your budget.

MATERIALS

Cost of materials is likely to be your single highest budget entry. It is best to base estimates on average prices for new materials. You might, in fact, come in under budget if you find used materials or materials at bargain prices, but your figures will be realistic in case you don't.

Most building supply yards will have a catalog that you can use to help you with your materials estimates. These catalogs do not usually include prices for supplies — like lumber — whose costs fluctuate. You will have to get a quote on such items in person or over the phone. Remember that lumber prices can vary, so don't assume the price you are quoted will be in effect when you are ready to purchase.

Labor Estimates

You ought to obtain an estimate from every professional you hire. Ideally, those estimates will be guaranteed and not subject to increase. However, in the real world of building — and in the sometimes shady world of estimating — oversights are made and problems can occur that will change the price. It is highly unlikely that the price you are quoted will decrease, so leave room in the budget for each and every quote to go up.

Be suspicious of especially low quotes. There is a good chance that suspect numbers are being used to secure the job and that the price will rise later to reflect real costs.

A well-negotiated labor arrangement will include provisions for dealing with cost overruns and can help you plan for a contingency fund. You can always change your labor budget — simply take on the tasks yourself that you had intended to hire out, or find friends with special skills who may be willing to help you out.

Labor Costs versus Tool and Equipment Costs

For specialized tasks — plumbing, wiring, heating, roofing, concrete form work, etc. — weigh the cost of acquiring or renting the appropriate tools and equipment against the costs of hiring labor. It may be more economical to hire labor.

To Finish or Not to Finish

Many owner-built homes never see completion — at least in the first decade! Money and/or time often run out first. If you think you can handle living with bare ceilings, no trim, unfinished counters, or other uncompleted elements, this may not be a problem. If you find this thought abhorrent, then be sure to leave plenty of money in reserve to ensure that you will not run out before completion.

Know What You Can and Cannot Live Without

Apportion your spending so that key elements of your home can be finished even if the project stalls. Plan to stay warm and to have working plumbing and heating. It's no fun to have to boil water in your well-appointed kitchen in order to take a bath! Know your priorities and make sure you buy what's required to achieve them before spending elsewhere.

AN INEXACT SCIENCE

Unfortunately, budgeting is an inexact science. It is impossible to account for every contingency and glitch that may arise. The further afield you move from conventional construction, the more variables enter your budgeting equations. The only certain advice is spend plenty of time figuring out your budget, and leave lots of room for error.

Dahl Atin's Budget

Dahl Atin acted as her own General Contractor for the building of one of the first code-approved straw bale homes in Ontario. She kept close track of the costs of building the 1444-square-foot post and beam house. Her complete budget is presented here in order to show proportions in one particular budget, not as a model on which to base your own. This information can be helpful for assessing and extrapolating the relative costs of materials and labor for various phases of construction. Where could you save money? Where will you have to pay more? Only you can answer these questions.

Cost Summary for Atin's Straw Bale House	*May 1997*

House Details	
	Two story, four bedrooms, two bathrooms
	Eleven rooms, no basement
	1444 square feet
	Propane gas heating (high efficiency furnace)
	Propane water heater (50 US gallons)
	R-35 insulation in walls (plastered straw bales)
	R-40 insulation in ceiling (cellulose)

Permits and Approvals **$1,519.70**	
Engineer's Fee	*642.00*
Septic System Fee	*160.50*
Building Permit Fee	*717.20*

Site Preparation **$3,274.34**	
Remove topsoil, excavate for footings, backfill inside and out, pond	*2,770.53*
Water lines, house to well	*503.81*

Septic System **$8,346.00***

Foundations		*$8,465.00*
	Footings, 4 ft. frost walls, rebar, wire mesh, concrete floor, polish	8,053.87
	Custom-made post shoes	411.13
Framing and roof		*$15,225.77*
	Cedar posts	522.73
	Lumber to frame walls	4,134.78
	Labor to frame walls and roof	3,400.00
	Truss and steel roof material	4,801.26
	Replace leaking vent cap	135.00
	Soffit, fascia, more vents	2,232.00
Straw Bale Walls		*$5,121.16*
	Straw Bales, 570 (used 550)	1,185.00
	3 ft. rebars, 1000 (used only half)	957.38
	Labor to stack bales	1,050.00
	Expanded metal lath	710.13
	Plastic, nails, supplies	183.85
	Scaffolding rental	94.30
	Labor to secure lath	682.50
	Pine strapping for securing shelves, electrical	258.00
Plastering		*$11,500.00**
	Exterior, three coats	5,500.00
	Interior, three coats	6,000.00
Custom Windows (16)		*$2,592.34*
	Glass	878.95
	Cedar Lumber	449.23
	Labor to build and install	954.00
	Materials for vents	310.16
Doors		*$2,736.49*
	Exterior (2) and installation	433.50
	Interior upstairs (7) and installation	971.29

Interior main floor (3) and installation	1,331.70
Interior Finishing **$11,219.62**	
Lumber	434.47
Vapor barriers for ceiling, lumber	264.54
Spruce window trim	84.35
Drywall and supplies	1,453.10
Drywall ceiling	350.00
Tape and mud drywall second floor	1,021.89
Strapping	61.53
Drywall main floor	1,498.00
Tape and mud drywall main floor	2,485.45
Custom stairs, railing, installation	2,362.54
Ceiling insulation R-60 (16")	1,203.75
Mechanicals **$11,265.95**	
Roughed-in plumbing, bath	1,769.29
Finish plumbing	642.32
Electrical box and wiring	2,619.74
Finish electrical	796.93
Chandelier and chain	79.95
Ceiling, wall, exterior fixtures	104.25
Telephone jacks	187.00
Furnace ducting and installation	2,071.61
Propane supply, hot water heater	805.38
Submersible pump in well	1,600.16
Vacuum system	37.50
Pedestal sink and toilet	182.75
Install washing machine	117.13
Main floor toilet	91.97
Outdoor faucet	159.98

Kitchen $5,081.50

        Custom counters and cupboards   4,780.00

        Range hood   60.00

        Used plywood   241.50

Decorating $3,198.35

        Paint and supplies   930.74

        Floor sander and rental   221.76

        Bathtub tile, installation, rod and curtain   444.88

        Shelving and hardware   102.12

        Tongue and groove pine panelling   214.85

        House plants   84.00

        Carpet (to be installed)   1,200.00

Landscaping $757.70

        Finish grading   224.70

        Perennial plants, hanging baskets   73.00

        Gravel driveway   150.00

        Topsoil, grass seed   310.00

Total Cost, including septic system, landscaping, interior finishing and mechanical systems $90,303.92

cost per square foot $62.54

*Notes

- Labor costs represent a high proportion of the total budget. This makes evident the savings to be made by doing the building yourself. But don't simply delete these costs if you are building for yourself, because your time has value as well, and you must continue to pay for accommodation and food (at the very least) while you are building.

- Dahl required an expensive, raised-bed septic system consuming almost one tenth of her total budget.

- Even with hired labor, the straw bale walls represented a low percentage of the overall building cost.

- Plastering costs are not broken down into labor and materials, but the materials being relatively inexpensive, labor represents the majority of the cost.

All figures are in Canadian dollars.

CHAPTER 15

Going Shopping: Materials

Your finished plans will enable you to make a shopping list for all the materials you'll need to build your house. As with any kind of shopping, prices and quality will vary widely. Good decisions about materials purchases will help you create a building of excellent quality that's within your price range.

Some people collect building supplies for years before they actually construct a house. Others go and place a giant, single order just before they're about to build. It all depends on your budget and personal style.

BARGAIN PRICED MATERIALS

If you have adequate storage for all your bargain buys, it is possible to shop first and design later, allowing your existing materials list to shape the house you will build. If you shop first, you may be able to realize some significant savings, since you can take advantage of low seasonal prices and spread out your investment over an extended period of time. There are many sources for bargain building supplies.

Scavenging

It is remarkable how many excellent building materials get thrown away. Dumpsters, construction sites, demolition sites, and neighborhood trash collection sites can be full of useful stuff. You can probably find lumber or plywood, doors, windows, toilets, sinks, furniture, and just about anything else that goes into a house, though your scavenged items may need a little repair or come in odd sizes or shapes. A clever scavenger will make note of piles of materials sitting in people's yards and garages and offer to clean up in exchange for keeping the materials. This kind of activity can net you large quantities of good materials. Municipal dumps and landfill sites often have special areas set up for construction waste, much of which can be salvaged.

When scavenging lumber, remember that in many jurisdictions you will be required to use 'grade-stamped' lumber for structural elements. Much scavenged lumber will not be grade-stamped and will only be usable as non-structural elements in your house.

A patient collector can assemble a goodly number of building supplies, though it would take a long time to scavenge enough material to build an entire house. Still, every item you find for free is one you won't have to buy later on. Whether you save a few hundred dollars or several thousand, the effort may well be worth it. Ecologically, scavenging building materials is a double benefit, because you reduce the demand for more new material and save old materials from filling up landfill sites.

Garage Sales and Flea Markets

Some people enjoy making regular rounds of local flea markets and garage sales. It is often possible to find excellent used and new building supplies in such places. At garage sales, quantities will usually be small and consist of leftovers from other people's building projects. Prices are often low, since people want to get rid of these bulky and useless items.

Larger flea market vendors are usually aware of market values and don't often offer outstanding bargains for building supplies. Still, materials will be cheaper than if you buy new. If you develop a friendly relationship with vendors, they may start filling your requests and/or sourcing items they know you need. Give these vendors a good list of what you want; over time they might find most of what you need.

Classified Ads

Classified ads can net you all kinds of useful supplies. Do your hunting the same day the paper is released; otherwise, you'll miss out on the best of what's available. Advertised materials are often new or in very good shape and in sufficient quantities to make the ad worth placing for the vendor. Many classified ads have a 'Building Materials' section, but don't limit your reading to these ads only. You don't have to just read the Classified section, either. Place your own want ad with a list of the supplies you require; it can bring a flood of calls and lots of good materials. People who respond may not have considered selling their goods before, and their prices might be great. If you keep a rotating list in the 'Wanted' section, you might get regular finders calling you with materials.

Used Building Supplies Stores

The sharp climb in the cost of building materials over the last decade has given rise to many used building supplies stores. Often working in cooperation with demolition companies and/or using the same scavenging methods outlined above, these stores stock a wide range of useful materials. Items that are easily removed from old buildings are always in stock at such stores. Lighting and plumbing fixtures, windows, doors, trim, and hardware can all be found in good shape at good prices. You are unlikely to find any remarkable bargains, but you will find good used stuff at about half the price of new materials. Used supplies warehouses will often take lists of your needs and let you know when they have found certain items. The more frequently you buy from a particular store, the better are your chances of getting first pick of newly arrived materials.

Building Supply Yards

Most building supply yards are members of a particular chain that offers one-stop shopping for building materials. It can be worthwhile to treat them like other bargain centers. Sales can net you some excellent finds, as can spring and fall clear-out specials. Chain stores are usually quite competitive. Their advertising flyers can alert you to good prices on common building supplies.

Remember that building supply yards stock items required by mainstream builders. If you are looking for environmentally-friendly options or anything slightly outside the norm, you probably won't find it at a typical building supply yard. Advice, too, will tend to pertain to conventional building practices.

Building supply yards do offer convenience for contractors and builders. They stock full inventories of common products and will deliver to your site for any sizable order. You can take your finished plans to a single outlet and place your order for everything you need — except for bales! Quite often, you will be offered a discount for a large purchase, and you may be able to arrange for credit directly from the supply yard. Some yards have knowledgeable staff who may be able to advise you on purchases and construction techniques. Most supply yards charge higher prices than do comparable specialty shops. Item for item, it is usually possible to find lower prices in other places but not under one roof. For some builders, the one-stop convenience of a building supply yard is worth the extra money they spend.

Lumber Mills

Small-scale lumber mills are experiencing a widespread resurgence as affordable milling technology develops and the clear-cutting techniques of giant lumber companies become unsustainable. Portable mills can be brought to your site if you have sufficient trees; quite often, you can trade milled lumber for your project for additional lumber from your property that the operator can sell later. There is a good chance that you will find several small mill operators within a reasonable distance of your site. Prices from small operators are almost always lower than from building supply yards, and you can question the operator about his or her harvesting techniques if you are concerned about sustainable forestry.

Lumber quality can vary greatly, depending on the operator. In areas where grade-stamped lumber is required for construction, the operator can hire an independent lumber inspector to approve and stamp your wood. In general, small operators take quite a bit of pride in the quality of their lumber and mill better wood than larger companies. Be sure that lumber purchased this way is dry enough to use before you start construction; otherwise it may shrink, warp, and twist once you have it in place.

Specialty Shops

A specialty shop exists for almost every construction need. It will likely stock a wider selection than a building supply yard can, and sales staff will probably give more detailed and knowledgeable advice. Watch for sales and remaindered items at these shops. Some stores may also sell used items or factory seconds, so be sure to ask about their availability. Prices at specialty stores will vary; most will undersell the building supply yards, and some will price higher. Often, the higher prices will get you a higher quality product and better service. Specialty shops are frequently independent and locally-owned, so more of the money you spend there will stay in your community.

Farm Supply Stores

Farm supply stores and/or cooperatives can be a very good source for many building supplies at good prices. They tend to specialize in products useful to farmers and will likely stock framing materials, steel roofing and siding, sheathing, plumbing, wiring, and tools. Many of the bale-specific supplies you will need are most easily sourced at farm supply stores.

If you join the cooperative, you will receive a discount on your purchases. If you become a member or even a regular customer, you'll be able to get plenty of good advice for finding items you need or the names of professionals worth hiring. Farm supply stores can provide a welcome relief from glitzy showrooms and high-pressure sales techniques.

Look Around Before You Buy

Regardless of where you decide to buy, take some time to become familiar with the pricing of certain items. You can't recognize a bargain unless you are aware of a base-line price for comparison. Read widely through flyers, catalogs, and classified ads, and visit several different building store outlets. After a while, your ability to assess quality and price will allow you to make better decisions.

There's Always a Better Price

Even after the most thorough research and dedicated shopping, you are likely to find a better bargain after you've already made a purchase. Don't despair. It happens all the time. You can only choose the best combination of quality and price available to you at the time of purchase. If you calculate the savings you could have made, it will only drive you crazy!

NEW VERSUS RECYCLED MATERIALS

For cash outlay, recycled materials always win out over new. However, lower prices often come with other costs attached. You may have to spend more time locating, assessing, and picking up used materials. Many used items will need a little resuscitation — or maybe a lot! — before they are ready to use. Sanding, straightening, repairing, refinishing, de-nailing — all of these can add time or money to your project. This may not matter to you if you are not under a strict deadline or if you are able to do all your repairs prior to actual construction.

When you buy used materials, you forego any warranty. If you feel better with a guarantee, it may be worth it to 'buy new' for items that will be subjected to heavy use or play a critical role in your house. Consider your willingness and ability to provide service and repair to your home when you are deciding what to buy new or used.

COST VERSUS QUALITY

It is not always best to choose materials by cost alone. Cheap but inferior materials may end up costing more in the long run. A mid-price item may split the difference between quality and price in a satisfactory way. Consider the relative importance of each item and its strength, durability, reputation, and warranty before you buy.

Critical items like windows are worth a significant investment. Windows will help with heat retention for as long as your house stands, giving you a good return on your investment — heightened efficiency and lower operating costs. Consider, too, the costs and ease of replacement or upgrade for any item in your home. Professionals can guide you in your decisions, but your own satisfaction is what counts in the end.

TOOLS

Proper tools can make a big difference to your project, affecting not only the speed at which you can work but the quality of your finished product. Buy quality for tools that you'll use a lot — hammer, tape measure, tri-square, handsaw, power saw, drill, screwdriver, and pliers. For other tools, assess how useful they will be after construction before you buy. Buy or rent larger tools as your budget determines; used tools are also an option. You may need specialty tools for some aspects of construction. Decide which tasks you intend to perform yourself, and try to locate the necessary tools and equipment before it's time to start. Valuable days can be lost if you don't. Like anything else, tools are of differing quality and come from a variety of sources and at different prices.

SHOPPING FOR BALES

To find bales, you can approach farmers directly, inquire at or order from a farm supply store or cooperative, or place a want ad in a rural newspaper. Average prices can vary from Can$1–4 per bale. Chapter 2 gives advice on sourcing bales.

BALE BUILDING SUPPLIES

Some of the bale-specific materials and tools you'll need will require non-traditional sourcing.

Stucco Meshes

Chicken wire is a popular choice for wire reinforcement mesh. It can be purchased in rolls of varying widths and with different-sized holes and gauges of wire. You must use galvanized wire, preferably with 1-inch holes and in the heaviest gauge you can afford. Common 22-gauge wire is too flimsy and difficult to work with; 20-gauge is suitable and 18-gauge ideal. Wider rolls — (4–6) feet — will require less time to hang, but it may be helpful to have some narrower 2-foot ones on hand too. Building supply stores probably stock chicken wire, but the price can be high. Check a farm supply outlet or a gardening center for price comparisons.

Expanded metal lath — or diamond lath — is heavier than chicken wire, and comes in flat sheets rather than rolls. It is more expensive and can be more difficult to work with, but its extra strength is useful in corners and other bumpy locations. It can be sourced through building supply yards or stucco specialty shops.

Welded fencing uses much heavier gauge wire but often costs little or no more than good quality chicken wire. The use of welded fencing can save a lot of labor time because less stitching or quilting of the mesh is required. Welded fencing with 2x2- or 2x3-inch holes will work well.

Staples

In order to attach your stucco mesh, you will need thousands of staples and some good quality staple guns. Buy your staples in case lots, rather than by single boxes.

Pre-compression Materials

If you are building a load-bearing structure, your pre-compression system will require materials. Wire systems use 9-gauge galvanized fencing wire — also known as merchant wire — available in bulk at farm supply outlets. The saddle clamps you'll need are also available at farm stores or hardware stores. Depending on the system you use, you will need tools to perform the pre-compression of your bales. Wire methods use 'fence stretchers' — purchased from a farm supply outlet or fencing specialist or borrowed from a farmer — and a 'come-along,' available at most hardware or farm stores. Load-binders — from an automotive or trucking supply outlet — can do the same job as a come-along.

Baling Twine or Wire

Polypropylene twine can be used for re-tying bales and stitching or quilting stucco mesh. Twine can be purchased in large rolls at farm supply stores. Sisal/ binder twine is not recommended, as it is prone to rotting. In areas where baling wire is in common use, it is a good option. Specialty wire-twisting pliers can speed up bale wire re-tying.

Bale Needles

Used to re-tie bales and sew on stucco mesh, bale needles are a homemade item. You can use your own ingenuity to source the materials and create the design. Needles should be several inches longer than your bales are wide and have a hole or a notch capable of routing twine through the bale, as shown in Illustration 15.1.

Line Trimmer

The most efficient way to trim and shape your bale walls is to use a gas- or electric-powered line trimmer or weed-whacker. Standard nylon string will work, but you will go through a lot of it. Plastic blades or metal chain attachments, intended for heavier brush, work better.

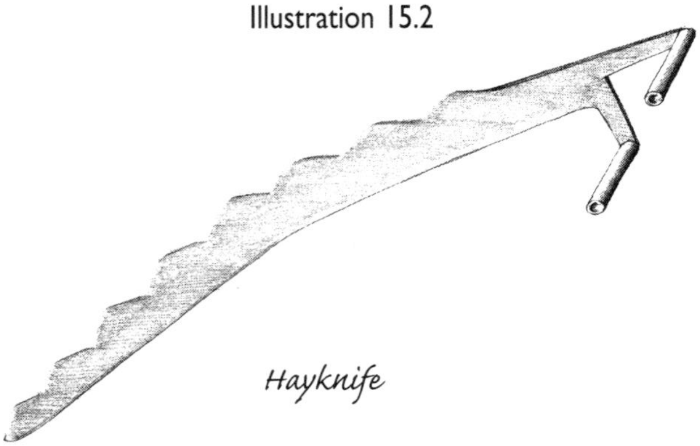

Clippers and Hay Knives

Regular garden shears are useful for trimming and shaping walls, especially where weed-whackers have a hard time reaching. If you can find and sharpen an old hay knife, as shown in Illustration 15.2, it may be handy for these purposes too.

Plastering Supplies

Depending where you live, stuccoed homes may be popular or rare. The availability of plastering supplies in your area will vary with the popularity of the finish. A specialty outlet catering to masons

Illustration 15.1
Bale needles can be made from ¼-inch stainless round bar. One end is pounded flat and drilled with a hole.

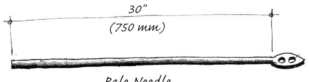

30"
(750 mm)

Bale Needle

Illustration 15.2

Hayknife

will stock the tools and supplies you'll need to plaster your house. High quality cements, clays, and limes are critical to a good finish. Ask about favorite choices at a specialty store. You can also get advice on mixtures and application techniques from active practitioners. Be sure the ingredients you are buying are meant for stucco, and not just for poured concrete or mortar.

A wide range of stucco stops, edgings, moldings, and meshes are available. While it is possible to plaster a bale home without any of these products, you can choose the ones that suit the style of finish you want.

Quality plastering tools ease the effort required for this considerable job, so invest wisely.

Trowels for applying and smoothing plasters come in a galaxy of shapes and sizes. Choose the ones that fit your application needs and are comfortable to use. Those with a die-hard, do-it-yourself ethic may want to fashion their own plastering tools.

Bale Beaters
Usually homemade, a bale beater is used to help align and straighten bale walls after they are erected. Any hammer-shaped object on a handle will suffice, as long as you are capable of swinging it and it applies its force over a reasonable surface area.

Bale Tarps
Farmers use heavy-duty, UV resistant tarps — usually silver in color — to cover outdoor hay mounds. These tarps make the best covering for your walls and your straw mound, too. More pricey than other tarps, they are designed to be rugged and long-lasting, and can more than pay for themselves when the first wind and rainstorm batters your building site.

Big or small, just about anything can be used as a bale beater!

BUYING RESPONSIBLY
While you are bound to give a lot of thought to price, quality, and convenience when you are shopping for materials, don't forget to consider other significant factors.

Sustainable Options
You can choose to support products and manufacturers that make an effort to reduce environmental impacts. From sustainably harvested lumber to natural paints and

stains, almost every product you will use is also available in a greener format. You may want to research your product choices and the production methods used to create them; often, the cheapest products come with nasty environmental side effects. Green products are often more expensive than their less sustainable counterparts, due mostly to economies of scale. Your purchase of green products helps ensure their continued production and increases the possibility of a more competitive pricing in the future.

Allergies and Toxins

Many of the manufactured products that go into standard home construction contain chemicals and toxins that have undetermined effects on human health. Treated and glued wood products — pressure treated wood, laminates, plywood, and particle board — are of particular concern. Many finishing products, including paints, stains, carpets, and floorings are also suspect. Research these purchases if you are concerned about their potentially harmful effects.

Local Economies

The money you spend on your home can have a significant impact on your local economy. If you buy from local suppliers and hire local labor, you will strengthen your local economy, which in turn will help you to thrive. Some regions have local economic trading systems, better known as barter economies. Whether formally organized or entirely spontaneous, this kind of trading can lower the cash costs of your building and encourage the development of stronger communities. Remember that barter tends to undermine government taxation, so you may want to keep records and claim income and expenses incurred through barter transactions.

YOUR PROJECT IS UNDERWAY

With the first materials purchases you make and the first labor contracts you sign, your building project will truly be underway. It is both exciting and scary to start spending money on your future home. Now, you're ready to build!

REFERENCES

Canada Mortgage and Housing Corporation. *Building Materials for the Environmentally Hypersensitive.* Canada Mortgage and Housing Corporation, 1995. ISBN 0-662-21107-3.

Chapell, Steve. *The Alternative Building Sourcebook: Traditional, Natural and Sustainable Building Products and Services.* Fox Maple Press, 1998. ISBN: 1-889269-01-8.

Hermannsson, John. *Green Building Resource Guide.* The Taunton Press, 1997. ISBN 1-56158-219-0.

Pearson, David. *The Natural House Catalogue: Everything You Need to Create an Environmentally Friendly Home.* Simon and Schuster, 1996. ISBN 0-684-80198-1.

CHAPTER 16

Construction: Before the Bales

Before you even touch a straw bale, your foundation must be built. And, if you are building a post and beam design, the framework must be raised and a roof assembled. If you keep several basic ideas in mind as you build, it will help avoid problems when it's time to install the bales.

What follows is not a complete construction guide for building your home. Depending on your design choices, the process of readying your project for the installation of straw bales may be quite fast, as for load-bearing walls on a simple pier foundation or quite lengthy, as for a multi-story post and beam frame with a full basement. There are so many variables — design options, climatic and geographical considerations, and building code variations — that hard-and-fast guidelines governing the completion of the non-bale aspects of construction are impossible. Accurate information, experience, advice, and common sense will help to ensure a smooth transition before you build your bale walls.

FOUNDATIONS

Sealing Foundations

You must seal your foundation. Concrete can act as a wick, pulling moisture up from the ground and passing it on to wall elements. Wherever wood or straw will come into contact with concrete, 'gaskets' made of tar, tar paper, plastic, or foam should be used. For post and beam construction, spacers made from horizontally sliced hockey pucks make an excellent and inexpensive barrier between wood and concrete! Even when you have taken steps to seal the foundation, it is important to include a second moisture-proof barrier between the foundation curb and the first course of bales.

Curbs

Raised wooden curbs must be firmly attached to the foundation. Anchor bolts must be embedded in the wet concrete in accurate locations. Concrete nails and screws can also be used, but will require drilling with special masonry bits. Curbs built on wooden-framed decks should be built on top of the sub-floor. If it is running parallel to framing members, the curb should be placed directly over top of joists to support the weight of the wall and provide adequate attachment points. This will affect the on-center spacing of the joists, and may require doubling of the affected joist, as shown in Illustration 16.1. Where the curb runs perpendicular to floor joists, solid blocking should be used under it, as shown in Illustration 16.2.

Illustration 16.1
The bale curb is placed directly over a pair of doubled joists that run parallel to the bale wall.

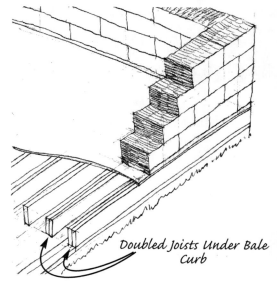

Doubled Joists Under Bale Curb

Illustration 16.2
When the joists are perpendicular to the wall, doubled blocking provides an attachment point for the curb and will be strong enough to handle the loads of the pre-compression wire for load-bearing walls.

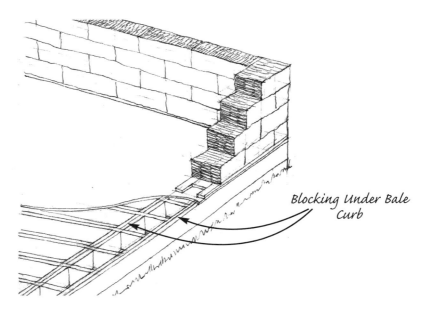

Blocking Under Bale
Curb

Not the right size!
This flashing should completely cover the insulation.

Flashing

A properly designed flashing will prevent water that is running down the walls from seeping under the bales or under the curb. If your foundation has exterior insulation, the flashing may also be used to protect the insulation from damage. Check your building supply yard for prefabricated designs that may suit your purposes before you order custom-bent flashing.

Vapor barriers and caulking

Vapor barriers and caulking prevent air and moisture migration. If your floor and/or foundation design incorporate a vapor barrier, you will want to continue that barrier so it blends into the plaster on your bales. The barrier can be folded up and stapled to the wooden curb. Stucco mesh and plaster can be applied over top of this vapor barrier to create a seamless joint. It is a good idea to caulk the joint between the foundation and/or floor and the wooden curb with high quality caulking. This will help prevent air and moisture migration at a vulnerable point.

Your house will also have a vapor barrier between the ceiling and the roof insulation. This should also be cut to finish under the wall plaster. If you are building a post and beam design, be sure to have the vapor barrier continue from the ceiling behind the beam and into the plaster. Vapor barriers around your window and door bucks should also be positioned to create a continuous seam with the plaster.

PLASTERING CONSIDERATIONS

Mesh Connection

The use of some form of metal reinforcement for your plaster is often mandated by the building code and is recommended for many kinds of plaster. If you are going to be using stucco mesh — chicken wire, diamond lath, etc. — be sure your curb and top plate design easily accommodates its attachment. Staples are usually the attachment method of choice, so be sure your stapler can be used easily and that enough material exists for the staples to grip properly.

Plaster Finishing

Most bale builders are not professional plasterers and may not think about how to finish the plaster at the top and bottom of walls and around window and door openings. The most important thing to remember is that the plaster is approximately an inch thick on both sides when the wall is completed. You want this thick coating to create a seam with the floor, the ceiling and/or beams, posts, doors, and windows. Always ask yourself, "How will my plaster finish to this edge? What kind of look do I want to achieve? How can I achieve a leak-free seal?"

POST AND BEAM CONSIDERATIONS

Reality Checks

In Chapter 12, different ways of finishing bales, posts, and beams were detailed. When you are constructing your framework, be sure real-world conditions are consistent with your intended finish. Check that the meeting points between bales and posts are really going to work when the bales are put in place. Note how any brackets you use will affect the plaster and its ability to seal the wall against air leaks.

Cross-Bracing

Plastered straw bales offer a great deal of stability to your post and beam frame, but before the bale walls are finished — including one coat of plaster — your framework will have to stand against wind loads without the help of the bales. A finished roof acts like a giant sail on top of your frame. Proper cross-bracing is essential. Cross-bracing can either be a permanent feature of your frame or it can be temporary. Be sure it will not directly interfere with the placement of the bale walls. Cross-bracing should be added as each new part of the framework is built, not once the frame is standing. Never underestimate the power of the wind to topple well-fastened frame members if they are not adequately braced.

This post and beam frame did not incorporate any permanent cross-bracing, so it was heavily braced with 2x4s before the bales were installed and plastered. Once plastered bale walls are finished, they will provide more than adequate cross-bracing.

DOOR AND WINDOW BUCKS

Pre-building all your door and window bucks will save you a lot of time when you begin installing the bales. The joints in the box frame of your bucks can benefit from caulking when you assemble them. Be sure to build bucks with strength in mind and use long screws rather than nails. Brace your bucks to keep them square. Scraps of lumber and/or plywood can be used to make adequate braces. You can keep the braces in place until you are ready to plaster. It's a good idea to clearly label the bucks as you build them. That way, there will be no question of which buck goes where. If you are working with a crew — or have a bad memory — it is worth noting the direction of installation with some simple arrows drawn right on the buck. You don't want to have to pull down a straw wall to get a buck turned right side up!

TOP PLATES

For load-bearing designs, a strong top plate is a must. You will already have determined the size and style of top plate you will be using, but when building it, you must ensure that the corners will meet in a strong bond and that any joints in the lumber are offset to avoid creating weak spots in the structure. Cut out plywood corners can help to strengthen corners and ensure that they are as square as possible. Top plates can be constructed on the foundation, before the walls are built. By using the foundation as a template, you assure a perfect match between the top and bottom of the wall. Be sure to label the top plate sections with directional arrows — N, S, E, and W — so that installation is simplified.

TARPS

You may have to install tarps to cover and protect your bale walls in poor weather. For load-bearing designs, this may mean building a tent over your walls. This is no small feat, and advance planning can mean the difference between wet walls and dry. You must be able to erect the tarps quickly and they must be well-fastened against the wind. It's not a bad idea to drape the walls inside the tent, just for added protection. Post and beam builders will have the advantage of a finished roof to protect the tops of their walls. However, the sides will still be vulnerable to driving rains, and provisions to cover the sides of the building should be in place in advance. In either case, make sure you have an adequate number of tarps on hand.

DON'T RUSH THE JOB

You may find yourself frustrated by the amount of work you need to do before you can install your bales. And you will probably encounter delays, problems, and oversights that can dishearten you. Don't let problems force you into making rash decisions. It is better to miss deadlines and fall behind schedule than to compromise the integrity of your project just to speed things along.

Peanut Butter Problems

When construction problems arise, take a break and think about them. Ask for advice, make lots of sketches, or hold discussions with co-workers until the best plan of action has been devised. A good friend calls these problems 'peanut butter problems' because she finds that the time it takes her to stop and chew a peanut butter sandwich allows her to come up with solutions that work!

Sometimes there is a simple solution to your problems, sometimes only a complete dismantling and rebuilding will do. Always keep your overall objectives in mind, and be sure that your solutions are in keeping with your goals. Ask yourself what the problem element is meant to achieve and what role it has in your building. Often, when you are clear about what needs to be achieved, a solution comes clear, too. Someday, your construction problems will become stories you tell for a laugh. Construction flaws that go uncorrected, however, can be an ongoing source of concern and expense.

REFERENCES

Allen, Edward. *Fundamentals of Building Construction: Materials and Methods.* John Wiley & Sons, 1990. ISBN 0-471-50911-6.

Canada Mortgage and Housing Corporation. *Canadian Wood Frame House Construction*, 1995.

Ching, Francis D.K. *Building Construction Illustrated.* Van Nostrand Reinhold, 1991. ISBN 0-442-23498-8.

DeCristoforo, R.J. *Housebuilding: A Do-It-Yourself Guide.* Sterling Publishing Co., Inc., 1987. ISBN 0-8069-6512-6.

Fine Homebuilding. The Taunton Press, 63 S. Main St., P.O. Box 5506, Newtown CT 06470-5506 USA.

Leger, Eugene. *Complete Building Construction.* Maxwell Macmillan Canada, 1993. ISBN 0-02-517882-2.

CHAPTER 17

Raising Bale Walls

This is the moment that most of us have been waiting for: it's time to put the straw in place. As with any construction technique, there are some strategies that will help you to achieve the results you want.

The act of creating a straw bale wall is a joyous and celebratory one, and we have yet to be present at a wall-raising where wide smiles are not the order of the day. Often, there are many people on hand, and the atmosphere is that of an old-style barn-raising. Everything about straw bale lends itself to fun, creativity, and ingenuity. Each new building goes up in a slightly different way and can add to our collective knowledge of techniques and approaches. There are few hard-and-fast rules for stacking bale walls, only some common concerns that need to be addressed.

When you raise your bale walls, it is important to think clearly about what you want to achieve and how you can best accomplish your goals. You will very likely come up with your own variations and/or innovations as you start moving and placing bales. This is precisely what makes building with bales so much fun! And it's even more fun if you share your insights and knowledge with others....

Smiles are infectious at a bale wall-raising.

Nine courses high and still maintaining running bond! These windows on the down-wind side suck out hot air at the ceiling. You can't strike a match in the top windows even on a calm day.

THE GOLDEN PRINCIPLES OF BALE STACKING

Some aspects of building a bale wall will benefit from common construction practices. These in no way inhibit your creativity but rather ensure that you will have structurally sound walls.

Stack the Bales in 'Running Bond'

Treat your bales as though they were bricks or blocks, making sure that the joints on the lower course are overlapped with solid bale on the following course. If joints run parallel up the wall, you will be sacrificing structural integrity. Bales are not consistent in length like bricks or blocks, so perfect running bond is not really a practical pursuit; keep running bond as a guiding principle, not absolute law.

Start Each Course From the Corners and the Buck Frames

You will find it easier to achieve running bond if you begin each course at the corners and frames and work your way toward the center of the wall. This can lower the number of custom bales needed, since you'll use only one in the middle of each course, rather than one at each end. Too many half-bales above one another can form a 'fault line' in your wall by creating a poor running bond. Stagger bales at the corners so a strong overlap is created. Once a pattern is established, running bond will be simpler to maintain.

Don't Over-Pack or Overstuff the Walls

Your bales should fit comfortably against one another. Pushing them too tightly together or jamming in the last bale in a course will cause undue stress on your window and door bucks, forcing them out of square. You will also end up with a case of bulging corners, as shown in Illustration 17.1. It is a slow, time-consuming process to fix bulging corners, so avoidance is your best defense.

Illustration 17.1
Bales stuffed too tightly will inevitably bulge at the corners. The only way to prevent bulging corners is to avoid overly tight fits between bales. If you need to push a bale down to get it in place, it's too long for the space.

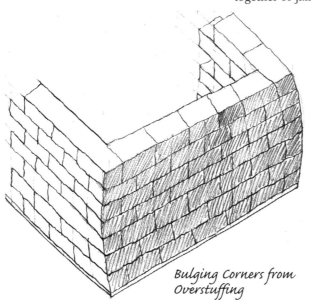

Bulging Corners from Overstuffing

Have a Cover-Up Plan for the End of the Day or In Case of Rain

Have plenty of waterproof coverings available to completely protect your walls. Putting up tarps can take you quite a bit of time, so don't leave it until the end of the day when you're really tired and the sun is setting! You'll want to securely fasten your tarps to prevent them from disappearing in the wind. Such a broad expanse of material will act just like a sail unless it is properly fastened.

Be Aware of Fire Hazards

We can't emphasize enough the importance of fire precautions at a straw bale work site.

It is inevitable that your site will get covered in loose straw. This straw is extremely susceptible to fire. Keep smokers well back from the site, and provide sand-filled buckets for butts. Keep spark-producing activities like welding and grinding far from loose straw. Be sure to rake whenever loose straw gets overly abundant, and create a mound or two some distance from the walls. Always maintain a straw-free space between the walls and the loose stuff on the ground.

In case of an accidental fire, make sure you have adequate water on hand, as well as proper fire extinguishers. If running water isn't available, strategically-placed drums and buckets will have to do.

Take Your Time

Bale walls go up very quickly. Because the work is fun and energetic, the tendency is to go fast and keep stacking. Do your best to temper your enthusiasm! Frequent checks to ensure you are progressing correctly will help ensure straight walls, square corners, and properly placed windows and doors. It is all too easy to build a solid wall where a window should have been!

CHRIS AND PETE'S HIGHLY UNPATENTED BALE STACKING METHODOLOGY: CONDENSED VERSION

With the above advice firmly in mind, it's time to take the following steps:

Inspect carpentry Check your foundation, top plate, buck frames, and all other elements that will interact with the straw. Be sure everything's ready.

Prepare corner guides Corner guides are constructed, fastened, and rechecked for plumb — vertical straightness — as shown in Illustration 17.2.

Mark and place bucks Door bucks can be attached to the curb/foundation in advance. Positioning for window bucks can be marked on the foundation or the side of the curb and the appropriate bucks placed close at hand. Make note of the course number on which the buck should be installed. If full-height bucks are being used for windows, they can be attached to the curb/foundation in advance as well.

Uncover and distribute bales Distribute bales evenly around the site to minimize the need for travel time. Only distribute enough bales to suffice for a partial day's work, so you don't have to re-store them at the end of the day.

Ceremonial first bale Make a big deal out of laying the first bale — at a corner, of course. Take pictures, open champagne, kiss your spouse. Yell! Shout! Celebrate!

Complete the first course
Lay the entire first course. Make whatever custom bales are required to fill odd spaces. Fill narrow gaps with untied flakes. Then do an inspection. Fuss and fiddle until everything is just right. We often try to place the cleaner, cut side of the bales toward the inside of the building to minimize indoor trimming later on.

Corner Guides

Illustration 17.2
Corner guides help to ensure straight walls and can be constructed on the outside or the inside of the bale curb.

A ceremonial first bale is laid in place.

Lay out an entire course of bales before going higher.

Continuous 'course meetings' keep the pace manageable and allow you to spot and deal with problems.

Place appropriate bucks
Where needed, place the buck frames onto the straw. Brace them to the ground and/or the curb and/or the post and beam frame where necessary. Double check that they are oriented in the right direction!

Continue stacking, one course at a time
Keep placing bales in running bond. If you limit yourself to one course at a time, it will enable you to monitor your progress. 'Course meetings' can bring everyone together, give you a rest, and allow you to make sure all plans for the next course are implemented, including service entrances and attachment points.

Pin, where necessary Whatever style and quantity of pinning you are using — see 'Pinning Bales' on page 154 — drive the pins at the appropriate courses. Be sure the walls are relatively straight before pinning.

Complete walls to full height Top your walls with the final course of bales. Stuff holes and crevices with loose straw. Celebrate again.

Place top plate and compress (load-bearing designs only) Once your walls are full-height and you are happy with their attitude, install the top plate on the bales. Make solid connections at the corners. Affix your compression ties and apply force until walls are compressed and level. If you are concerned about weather and exposed bales, you can pre-cut your roof framing before attempting pre-compression. Even partially completed, the roof framing will give you an easy, secure way to cover your walls with tarps in case of inclement weather.

Trim, carve, and straighten With all bales in place, you can now trim the walls to give a good surface for plastering. Your window openings can be cut and curved, shelves notched in, and the walls fine-tuned so they appear as you want them to be.

Install flashing and stucco mesh Wherever you are using flashing — above windows, under windows, at the bottom of the wall — they can now be fastened. Whatever form of stucco mesh you are using can also be attached.

Stitching or quilting stucco mesh Your mesh can now be pulled toward the walls close to the surface of the straw without touching, using bale needles and twine to stitch through the walls and tighten the mesh.

Cover up and celebrate This whole process may take only a single day, or it may be spread out over a week or more. When you're finished, you'll have beautiful straw walls that are ready to be plastered. Cover up the walls so there's no concern about rain soaking them, then it's relaxation time. Have a celebratory meal — keep your bonfire a safe distance from the walls, stand back and admire your work, then get a good sleep. (You'll need it before plastering!)

AND NOW, IN MORE DETAIL

Corner Guides and Straight Walls

For structural reasons — especially for load-bearing designs — you want to create reasonably straight, square corners with your walls. The simplest way to achieve this is to build corner guides before the bales go into place.

Quilting stucco mesh with a bale needle. Chicken wire takes longer to quilt than does welded steel fencing.

Corner guides have been plumbed and braced and are ready for bale stacking.

Corner guides are being raised to ensure straight walls. The two door bucks have also been attached to the deck.

Using any straight pieces of lumber, make a 90-degree 'L' the approximate height of the finished wall. Nail or screw the corner guide to the bale curb. Then, using a level to determine exact positioning, fix some braces to the corner guide and bale curb to prevent it from being knocked out of position. Corner guides will be removed once the walls are raised, so the lumber can be reused.

Check the corner guides occasionally during bale stacking to be sure they are still standing straight. If your bales push hard against the corner guides, they will knock them out of position. Bales that are tight against a corner guide will tend to push out when the guide is removed. Allow for a loose fit against the guide. If you can still put your hand between the guide and the bales, you're on the right track. It is better to err on the side of extra space than to overstuff. 'The bulge' can only be avoided if you leave sufficient space in the corners.

Similar guides can be built to help ensure that long sections of wall go up straight. These can be braced to the ground or to the inside of the building, as shown in Illustration 17.3. You can also build a 'wow checker' by using a long, straight piece of lumber with a carpenter's level strapped to it, as shown in Illustration 17.4. Make frequent rounds of the building with this tool and make adjustments to the walls as necessary. The earlier you catch problems, the easier they are to fix.

Illustration 17.3
Wall braces can be constructed to keep long, straight sections of the wall plumb until the first coat of exterior plaster has begun to cure.

90°

wall brace

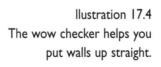

llustration 17.4
The wow checker helps you put walls up straight.

"wow" checker

Distributing Bales

A lot of time and effort can be saved if you place your bales in well-planned stacks around the site. Each wall should have its own stack near at hand, so that stacking need not be accompanied by long walks to a faraway mound.

The bales arrive at the site and must be unloaded so that walking time is minimized. If you have your bales arrive on the hay wagon on the day of construction, it simplifies the handling of bales. This 'bale slide' works very well.

Bales are all unique. The better the selection at hand, the better the chance you will find the right bale. It will be the perfect length or have just the right curve. Be choosy about your bales. If you think a bale feels or smells damp, don't use it. If the strings seem improperly tied, use that bale to cut open and use as flake.

Custom-Sized Bales

Within a few minutes of starting your first course of bales, you'll recognize the need for plenty of custom-sized bales to fill odd spaces in the wall. Re-tying bales to custom lengths is as big a job as actually stacking the bales. The wall can only rise at the speed of the re-tying, so as many 'custom re-tiers' will be needed as 'stackers.'

Measurements for custom-sized bales should be a bit on the short side rather than the exact size of the opening.

Two bale stackers wait while a 'custom tie-er' makes the short bale they need. A straw bale site needs at least as many custom balers as it does stackers!

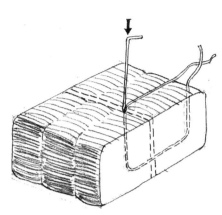

Illustration 17.5
A bale needle runs string through a bale before it is tied off and the old strings are cut.

Custom lengths can be achieved in a couple of ways. The simplest is to cut the strings, remove excess flakes until the bale is approximately the right length, and then re-tie the strings. Create a loop in one end of the string, and feed the other end through this loop. Press down on the bale with your knee, and cinch the string tightly before tying it off. Repeat for the second and — where appropriate — third strings. The leftover flakes can be used to fill small spaces in the walls, or re-tied with new string to make more short bales.

Bale needles can also be used to re-tie bales to custom lengths, as shown in Illustration 17.5. With the original strings still in place, thread the bale needle and insert it through the bale at the appropriate length, just inside the original string. You will now have a string coming out both sides of the bale. Remove the needle and, using a cinch knot, tie the new string tightly. Repeat the process once for two-string bales, twice for a three-string bale. Then cut the old strings and you'll have a new, shorter bale. By feeding two strings through the bale each time you insert the needle, it is possible to tie off two shorter bales if the strings are tied on opposite ends of the bale. You must be sure that the two strings don't cross over one another inside the bale, or your two custom bales will be bound together!

Bale presses, as shown in Illustration 17.6, have been built to compact bales during re-tying. Simple to make and operate, these big levers allow lots of force to be applied and ensure tight custom bales. For two-string bales, the time and effort required to make each bale in the press is overkill, but it may be appropriate for three-string bales.

Pinning Bales

'Pinning' helps to stabilize a bale wall while it is under construction. While the width of your bales and the considerable amount of friction that exists between the wide, rough surfaces gives your walls a fair bit of inherent stability, driving pins down through several courses of bales can improve that stability. This is especially the case in corners.

Metal rebar is commonly used as a pinning material, but its small surface area gives it little purchase on the inside of the bales and lends almost no stability to the wall. If you do use rebar pins, you can have them cut to length for you at the point of purchase. It will be helpful to make some caps in order to provide a wider whacking target when you are driving the rebar through the bales.

Rebar is more effective as a stabilizer if it is used externally. Eight-foot lengths, placed vertically against the wall directly opposite each other inside and outside

Illustration 17.6
A homemade bale press for three-string bales.

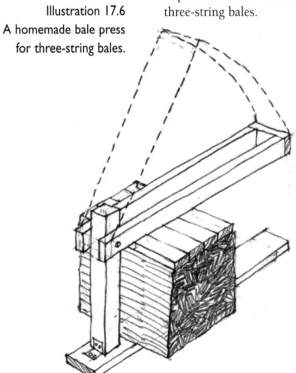

the wall, can be stitched to each other through the wall with bale needles and twine. Large fence staples can fasten rebar to the curb on the inside but may interfere with flashing on the outside

Wooden stakes or bamboo make very good bale pins, creating more friction against the bales. Many garden supply outlets carry pre-sharpened, 1x2-inch wooden stakes which make excellent pins. You could also cut your own 1x2 with a 45-degree angle to create a point. If you drive the 1x2 into the bales with the width aligned against the grain of the straw — yes, the hard way! — it gives the wood extra purchase on the straw. If you use bamboo, it should be about 1-inch in diameter. Both wood and bamboo will benefit from some sort of cap to prevent splitting when they are being driven into the bales.

Where straw bale construction is covered in building codes, there are carefully prescribed requirements for the pinning of bales, one course to the next. Be sure to follow any applicable pinning arrangements.

One common pinning technique is to use 4-foot lengths of pinning material and drive them through the third, fifth, and seventh courses of bales. This way, each layer of pinning shares a common bale. Using one pin per bale is good rule of thumb, though you should let your own judgment dictate where more or fewer pins may be needed. Be sure to check the walls for straightness before pinning. Though you will be able to adjust bales right up until the first coat of plaster is applied, a pinned bale is more difficult to realign.

While there is some speculation about the beneficial role of pins in bale walls during seismic activity, the main purpose of the pins is to stabilize the unfinished wall while you are constructing it. It is quite possible to build a wall without any pins at all, or one that has been pinned only where necessary. Unless prescribed by code, let your best judgment determine how much pinning you do.

Metal rebar is forced through the bales but offers only minimal purchase on the bales.

Driving a wooden corner stake with a homemade 'bale beater.'

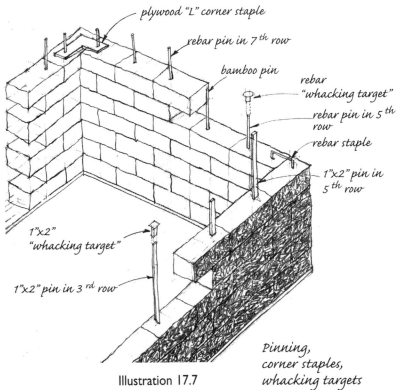

plywood "L" corner staple

rebar pin in 7th row

bamboo pin

rebar "whacking target"

rebar pin in 5th row

rebar staple

1"x2" pin in 5th row

1"x2" "whacking target"

1"x2" pin in 3rd row

Pinning, corner staples, whacking targets

Illustration 17.7
A variety of different pinning methods and materials are shown, including rebar, bamboo, and 1x2-inch lumber. Buildings have also been raised quite successfully with no pinning whatsoever, so unless your building code dictates the use of pins, you can leave pinning decisions to your own judgment.

Illustration: 17.8
A folded piece of diamond lath helps secure bales to buck frames.

Pinning Corners

Some builders may want more than a single pin driven into the corners to hold them together. Several clever means of providing extra corner support have been devised, as shown in Illustration 17.7. The first uses L-shaped plates, commonly made from plywood, that are laid over the adjoining bales in the corner and pegged through pre-drilled holes. The second uses rebar 'staples', which are bent so that the ends can be driven into two bales, drawing them together and holding them in place. If you feel your corners would benefit from this extra stability, try one of these methods, or devise your own.

No Pinning At All

Many bale buildings have been successfully raised with no pinning whatsoever. Not pinning eliminates another time-consuming step in the process. Straightening of walls is easier to achieve without pins in place, and once the top plate has been installed, even unpinned walls are stable enough to walk atop. Once the bale walls are plastered, the pins play no structural role; if walls can be stacked without them, you can save time and money.

Attaching Bales to Buck Frames

If you are concerned about stability where bales meet wooden buck frames, there are several strategies you can use to provide extra stability. The first uses sections of diamond lath that are cut to the width of the buck and pinned to the surface of a bale adjacent to a buck frame, as shown in Illustration 17.22. The sheet of lath is then bent to the wooden frame and nailed or stapled in place.

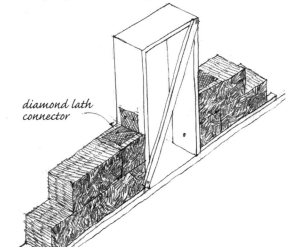

diamond lath connector

Bucks can also be stabilized if you drive sharpened dowels through drilled holes and into the bales, as shown in Illustration 17.9. The number of dowels is determined by the size of the frame being secured. Dowels can be used top and bottom as well as on the sides of the frame.

Attaching to Post and Beam Frames

Depending on your choice of post and beam system, you may be able to use the diamond lath system previously outlined to secure the bales to the structural frame. Another option is to use doweling or small-dimension lumber that attaches to the framework and extends into the bales. Supports can stop inside the bale walls and be supported by a stake driven through an eye bolt or drilled hole, or they can extend to the far side of the bale wall and be secured by a thin square of plywood, as shown in Illustration 17.10. It is also possible to tie bales to the posts temporarily, using baling twine that can be cut after the first coat of plaster has hardened.

Creative Bale Stacking

As you are putting up your bale walls, you can experiment with some creative bale placement, as shown in Illustration 17.11. In general, it is best to pre-plan any creative stacking, but there's nothing wrong with some on-site experimentation as long as the structural integrity of the building is not being sacrificed. Post and beam designs allow for more creative stacking than do load-bearing designs.

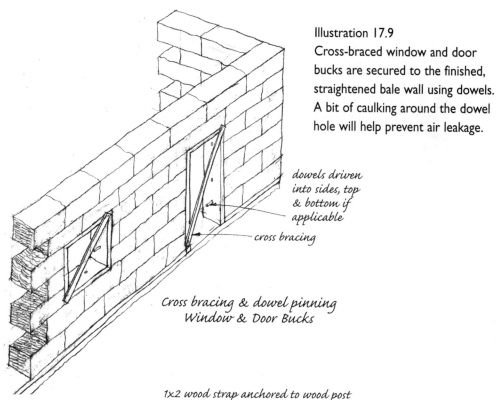

Illustration 17.9
Cross-braced window and door bucks are secured to the finished, straightened bale wall using dowels. A bit of caulking around the dowel hole will help prevent air leakage.

dowels driven into sides, top & bottom if applicable

cross bracing

Cross bracing & dowel pinning Window & Door Bucks

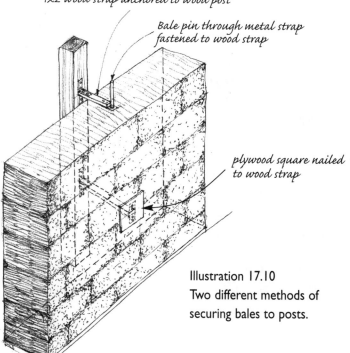

1x2 wood strap anchored to wood post

Bale pin through metal strap fastened to wood strap

plywood square nailed to wood strap

Illustration 17.10
Two different methods of securing bales to posts.

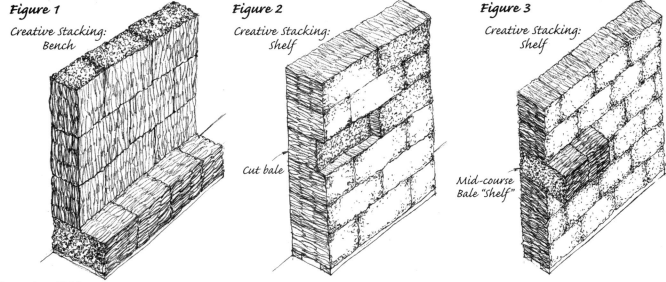

Figure 1
*Creative Stacking:
Bench*

Figure 2
*Creative Stacking:
Shelf*

Cut bale

Figure 3
*Creative Stacking:
Shelf*

Mid-course
Bale "Shelf"

Illustration 17.11
Bales do not have to make
perfectly straight, uniform walls.
Some experimentation
can produce wonderful results.

Fastening Points

Most bale walls will require some attachment points, service entrances, and electrical boxes. Many good methods have been devised for creating attachments to bale walls, as shown in Illustration 17.12.

Illustration 17.12
Pegs made of 2x2s can be hammered
into bale walls at regular intervals to
provide nailing points for cupboards
and shelving. The pegs can be buried
in the plaster or have a 1x4-inch
nailing strip fastened across them
that is either flush with the plaster
or buried just under the plaster surface. Pegs can go right through the
bale wall and attach to a plywood
square for a very stable mounting
point, as shown in Figure 1.

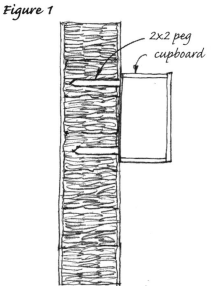

Figure 1

2x2 peg
cupboard

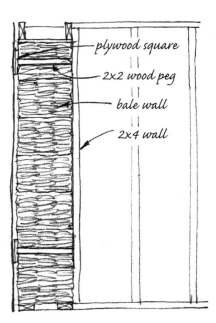

plywood square

2x2 wood peg

bale wall

2x4 wall

Figure 2

Wooden ladder &
electrical box

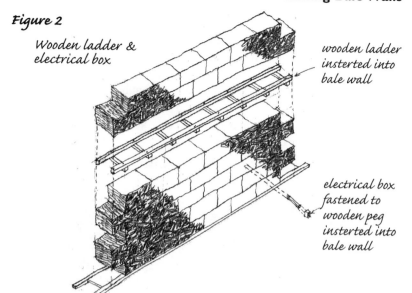

wooden ladder
insterted into
bale wall

electrical box
fastened to
wooden peg
insterted into
bale wall

A wooden ladder can be
laid between an appropriate course
of bales, as shown in Figure 2.

Figure 3

Conduit or plywood box
through wall

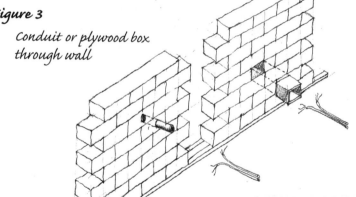

Wires and plumbing can go through
walls in conduit or, for larger service
entrances, through a plywood box
built similarly to a window buck, as
shown in Figure 3.

A ladder-type assembly
is secured between
courses of bales, ready for
mounting cupboards.

Stuffing Holes and Crevices

Your walls will inevitably have some gaps that need filling. Filling can be done course by course as the walls go up. You never want to stuff too much material into too small a space. A handful of straw folded over on itself can be pushed into the gaps between bales, leaving the folded edge exposed so it won't be pulled out by trimming devices. Take a close look at places where bales meet wood — foundation curb, bucks, or top plate — and do your best to fill the gaps at these junctions.

Load-Bearing Walls

Roof plates can be lifted into place one section at a time. Be sure to attach intersecting pieces firmly, using bolts rather than nails or screws in the splices to ensure a strong connection. Joints along the length of any section should be minimized. Where necessary, stagger the joints of the side rails of the roof plate to avoid creating weak spots.

Load-bearing walls are particularly susceptible to rainy weather, since they must be built before any roof can be put in place. Unless rain is rare and predictable in your area, it is important to erect some or all of the roof framing immediately after installing the roof plate. Even a few rafters or trusses will allow you to better hang tarps to protect the walls while you complete the pre-compression process and the placement of stucco mesh.

The Squeeze

Chapter 12 outlines several different systems of pre-compression for load-bearing walls. All the elements required for your pre-compression system should already be in place, including the right kind of top plate, and fastening points or conduit through the foundation.

Route all your wires, cables, straps, or other tensioning devices, and fasten them appropriately. Adequate pre-compression cannot usually be achieved with a single application of force at each point. Your first round of the building will be used to lightly draw down the top plate to stabilize the building and locate the top plate accurately. While achieving level is not the goal of this first round of tensioning, be sure that you are not drawing the building out of shape by applying too much force on one particular side. Leveling by eye is fine at this first stage. Use your wow checker to ensure that the walls remain straight.

Volunteers raise a roof plate on a load-bearing wall.

A load-bearing building is draped under a large bale tarp. Only a few trusses or rafters are necessary to secure a good rain-ready tarp.

Wire is passed through the foundation and over the top plate.

A loop is created in the upper end of the wire with a saddle clamp.

A come-along is clipped to a fence-stretcher in readiness for pre-compession.

The steel bar method is fast and low tech. Note the clamped loop in the top wire.

A downward force is applied to the bar or come-along drawing the top plate down.

Merchant Wire Pre-Compression

In our ongoing search for good pre-compression methods, the key factors we consider are cost, efficiency, availability of suitable materials, effectiveness, and user-friendliness. Here's our favorite system, to date.

"For pre-compressing, we've found 9-gauge galvanized fencing wire — sometimes called brace wire or merchant wire — to be the simplest and least expensive to use. We route a wire through the foundation and top plate to create a loop around the wall. Where the two ends of the wire meet, we create a closed loop on the top wire, securing it with a saddle clamp. (A farmer who attended one of our workshops could tie a knot in the wire that also worked effectively.) The lower wire is fed through this loop and pulled back down on itself.

The beauty of this system is that the wire is strong enough, once bent through the tied loop, to maintain its position even without clamping. This allows us to move quickly from wire to wire around the building without having to clamp and unclamp for each adjustment. When the roof plate is level, a saddle clamp is added to the adjusting wire to ensure that it holds its position when we're finished."

— Chris Magwood and Peter Mack ❖

Pre-compression, regardless of the method used, is an attempt to create a stable, level roof plate; you needn't squish the bales within an inch of their lives! Careful, balanced tensioning will yield the best results.

Round one of pre-compression gives you a chance to assess the performance of all elements in your chosen system and to familiarize yourself with your tensioning devices and fasteners. You want to check for any binding of your strapping materials and for places where the strapping is showing signs of early fatigue. If you can arrange for pre-compression to occur at two points on the building simultaneously, the overall time required for pre-compression will be halved, and it will be easier to apply offsetting forces on opposite sides of the building. Before beginning round two of pre-compression, measure the height of the roof plate at several spots around your building; the shortest measurement will be your target for round two.

During the second round, you can apply most of the compressive force to the walls. You may not be able to apply maximum force at each point immediately. Each strap may need to be visited two or three times in order to reach maximum compression. Defining maximum compression is difficult. Prescriptive standards do not exist in current straw bale building codes, and due to the variable nature of straw bales, it would be impossible to pre-determine an exact compression figure that would apply to all structures. Variables such as bale quality, wall height, expected live and dead loads, size of openings in the wall, and system of pre-compression will all create unique conditions and requirements.

It is important to remember that the point of pre-compressing your walls is not to squeeze every last bit of squish out of the bales but only to ensure that minimal settling will continue to occur before the plaster is applied. Pre-compression is not a matter of brute strength; balance and equilibrium are what is important.

You may find anywhere from 1–4 inches of easy compression in your walls. This compression can be achieved with relatively little effort with a mechanical device. Apply force until the wall offers enough resistance to make any further application of force difficult. Continue around the entire building, then check for any loose straps or obvious problems with the level of the top plate. If you have a spot where the top plate is significantly lower than the rest of the building, you may have to release your compression and add some flakes of straw as 'spacers' in these areas. Tighten again until all the straps are loaded and the roof plate is close to level.

Round three will allow you to achieve a completely level top plate if you tweak your straps in various locations to bring the top plate into alignment. This process can range from a few quick adjustments to a long and involved process of compensating adjustments around the whole building. When you are satisfied with the level of your top plate, fasten your straps securely to prevent slippage, and trim any loose ends or major protrusions that might interfere with plastering. Once your building is pre-compressed, it is a good idea to add some additional, diagonal straps to provide cross-bracing, as shown in Illustration 17.13, especially if you are building in areas with seismic activity or extremely high winds.

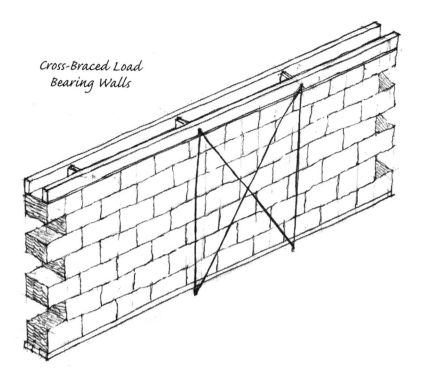

Cross-Braced Load
Bearing Walls

Illustration 17.13
Cross-bracing is run
diagonally between the holes
for the pre-compression
wires. All the wires will be
buried under the plaster.

Straightening and Tweaking Bale Walls

Your bale walls will continue to be adjustable right up until you apply the first coat
of plaster. Homemade 'persuaders' of many shapes and sizes have been employed in
this task, as have feet, knees, arms, and hands. It's a good idea to work with a partner on opposite sides of the wall when you're straightening. By mutual consultation,
you can arrive at the straightest possible wall. Anybody who's ever had the pleasure
of thumping a bale wall with a giant sledge will attest to the fun that can be had at
this stage of the process!

Trimming and Carving Bale Walls

It is very important that your bale walls be well-trimmed before they are plastered.
Loose, uneven ends of straw will make plastering very difficult, so aim for as smooth
a surface as possible. You can use several tools for trimming. A line trimmer or weed-
whacker works well. The more powerful the whacker, the faster the job will go.
Either gas or electric models will do, but exhaust fumes can be bothersome when
working on the inside of the walls. Regular trimming cord can be used, but be prepared to go through several spools of cord, since straw is much more resilient than
the grass for which it was intended. A plastic blade or metal chain attachment is better than cord, though you will have to be more careful about using blades or chain
close to wooden or metal elements in your wall. These attachments can also be used

> ### The Cut Side and Folded Side of a Bale
>
> *"Each bale has one cut side, where
> the straw has been sliced by the
> blades of the baling machine, and one
> folded side where the straw has been
> bent over. We try to arrange our bales
> so the cut side always faces to the
> inside of the building. We find this
> minimizes the amount of messy, noisy
> indoor trimming that's required and
> allows us to get as straight an interi-
> or wall as possible. It may have the
> additional benefit of leaving fewer
> wicks for moisture on the outside face
> of the wall, since folded ends do not
> expose a 'drinking-straw' stalk end
> to the plaster."*
>
> — Chris Magwood and Peter Mack ❖

A line trimmer, especially with plastic blades installed, makes an effective wall trimmer.

to carve curved window openings and perform other sculpting chores. In hard-to-reach places, or to trim close to wood and metal, hand-shears are useful. A well-sharpened set can quickly and effectively do the job.

You can also use many different tools to sculpt your bales. An old-fashioned hay saw is the low tech option. Well-sharpened, it can be used effectively to cut deep into a bale wall.

A chain-saw can be used carefully to make big cuts for rounded window openings or to create channels for plumbing drains or other embedded elements. Be aware that chain saws can create sparks around loose straw. Use with caution, and keep a fire extinguisher handy. A hand grinder with a cutting wheel or stiff wire wheel can also be used to carve into bales to create rounded openings, niches, and channels.

Remember to wear appropriate safety gear when trimming and carving bales. Proper respirators are important, since a good deal of lung-damaging dust will be created. Eye protection is important, since flying chips of straw are every bit as dangerous as chips of wood or metal.

Bale Wall Esthetics

Bale walls can be beautifully adapted to many esthetic tastes. Whether they are intentionally bumpy, gently undulating, or perfectly straight, your bale walls will create a unique home. Even someone who builds with the exact same set of plans won't end up with a building that looks like yours.

Finishing can be individualized, too. Some people adopt a 'take-it-as-it-is-built' approach to finishing their walls; others carefully craft a particular texture and shape. You can adopt different strategies for the interior and exterior of the house or vary the finish from room to room. Your walls should please your esthetic sense before you install the stucco mesh. You will be able to continue shifting bales once the mesh is hung, but it is easier if you do any rearranging while the bales are still exposed and uncovered.

Flashing

A good, moisture-resistant design will incorporate flashing at areas of critical importance for water shedding, including the base of your foundation and the top edges of windows where walls are likely to be exposed to direct rainfall. Prefabricated flashing can be purchased, or you can have them custom-bent to suit your design. Attach them securely to your wooden foundation curb or window buck. Be sure that the drip edge will be clear of the walls once the plaster has been applied. Never rely on caulking alone to seal out water; gravity and flashing must work in concert to shed water effectively. Consider caulking only as insurance.

Stucco Mesh

Metal mesh embedded in the plaster offers strength and adhesion to the plaster. In the days before metal reinforcement, plasters and cements were strengthened by the addition of chopped straw, horse hair, and other natural fibers. The straw served the same function as metal mesh, enabling plastered finishes to last longer and be stronger.

Given the symbiotic nature of the straw/plaster relationship, the application of plaster to a straw bale wall is quite different than its more common application over brick, block, or wooden walls. The ends of straw provide excellent grip for plaster and create a strong bond both during application and over the lifetime of the wall.

While chicken wire has been the straw bale standard, the welded wire fencing seen at right is easier to apply, requires less stitching and labor, and is no more expensive.

Chicken wire is unrolled vertically onto bale walls and stapled at the top plate and curb.

It is quite possible to apply your plaster directly to the bales without any mesh reinforcement, and to skip the process of hanging and fastening mesh altogether. If this is the option you choose, you will still need to provide mesh where your bales intersect wooden, metal, or cement elements. Cracking and flaking of the plaster can be expected on these surfaces if they are not reinforced. You may also want to place mesh at the corners of the building, since the ends of bales do not hold plaster nearly as well as the end grains.

This wall is completely meshed with 20-gauge chicken wire.

Most current building code requirements for plaster application do not take into account the interaction between straw bales and plaster. Your building official may require that you meet all the plastering provisions in the local building code or that you at least use some kind of mesh reinforcement. The most commonly used reinforcing mesh is 20-gauge chicken wire. It is lightweight, relatively inexpensive, and provides effective reinforcement. Expanded metal lath or diamond lath is specified in most codes for stucco reinforcement and is heavier and more costly than chicken wire. Welded steel fencing mesh is available in a range of sizes, and is both cost- and time-effective. Other options include landscaping mesh or manufactured air barrier/stucco mesh.

Regardless of which kind of mesh you use, it will need to be securely fastened to your top plate, foundation curb, and window and door bucks. To fasten the mesh, start at the top of the wall and work down. Mesh can be stapled or hung from

For this tall building, welded steel fencing was installed before the bales, providing a form against which to place the bales. The wire was pulled taut with a crowbar and fastened with fencing staples or U-nails.

nails that have been driven at angle into the top plate at six to 12-inch intervals. Once attached, the mesh can be pulled taut at the bottom of the wall and fastened securely.

Mesh must also be secured to window and door bucks, and over top of your flashing. If you are using a light mesh, you will need to double it over top of wooden, metal, and concrete elements, or else fasten heavier diamond lath over the lighter mesh. Be sure you allow the doubled or heavier mesh to extend into the straw wall by six inches or so. Heavier or doubled mesh can be useful in places where you expect the wall to take some punishment, such as around doorways and exposed corners and where cracking is most likely, such as at the corners of windows and doors.

A Stitch *and* Time

Once you have secured your mesh to the inside and outside faces of the wall, you will need to anchor it to the straw. If you don't, it will have a tendency to sag and poke through the plaster. The most common method of anchoring mesh is to sew it onto the wall using bale needles and twine. With one person working on either side of the wall, a bale needle can be passed back and forth and the stitches drawn tight to prevent the mesh from sagging or riding too far from the surface of the wall. Don't worry about placing stitches at even intervals; rather, focus on placing them where they're required. You will quickly develop a pattern with your co-stitcher that will allow you to pass the needle while the previous stitch is being pulled tight.

Stitching is quiet, meditative work and can go quite slowly if the mesh was initially applied very loosely or if only a few people are stitching. It can take as long to hang and stitch the mesh as it did to build the bale walls, so be sure to plan for this extra time.

You may be able to avoid doing a lot of stitching if your mesh is tightly stretched between the top and bottom of the wall. Occasional loose spots can be pinned down using homemade bale staples shaped from galvanized fencing wire. Pushed into the bales over the mesh, these staples can add localized tension. Use all the wooden attachment points you've located in the bale wall to help secure the wire; 2x2-inch pegs can be driven into the bales to provide extra anchoring points, if needed.

A bale needle is passed through a straw wall to begin stitching the mesh — in this case chicken wire — to the wall. Stitches are used only where necessary to bring the mesh close to the bale surface for plastering.

Covering Up

Bale structures must be kept dry. The best possible protection for your bale walls is a completed roof. For post and beam designs, the roof can be entirely finished before the bales are put in place. For load-bearing designs, it will have to come after the walls are up.

Any protective covers at the tops of your walls should be completely waterproof. This does not include most hardware store tarpaulins. Polyethylene sheeting — as used for vapor barriers — is a good choice, but any waterproof membrane will do. If you only have cheap tarps, double them up before you use them.

Tarpaulins and housewraps can be used to protect the sides of your walls. Cheap tarpaulins are quite adequate for the short term. They can be stapled to the top plate or fascia boards or to truss ends if the fascia is not in place. They should also be well anchored at the bottom; staple them to the foundation curb or weigh them down with tires, concrete blocks, or heavy lumber.

This well-tarped house is secured with creative anchors.

It can take several hours to put tarps up well, so leave yourself enough time to do a good job. If you will need to work on your walls again, make the tarps easy to roll up or remove. Otherwise, make the arrangement permanent enough to resist high winds and driving rains.

Typar or Tyvek housewrap also makes excellent bale wall protection, especially if you will not be plastering for some time. These materials come in rolls wide enough to match the height of a typical exterior wall and can be fastened easily with staples or thin strips of wood. They resist UV rays better than tarpaulins and are more water resistant. Sealed with appropriate tape or caulking, they provide enough of an air barrier to lend the bale walls some insulation value before the plaster coat is applied.

Celebrate!

Raising bale walls is a remarkably satisfying task. Even though you're bound to be physically exhausted, stand back and admire your work. You have cause for pride. Be sure to put down your tools, brush the loose straw from your clothes, and enjoy the moment!

From Timid Newcomer to Power Tool Aficionado

"I'll never forget arriving at my first straw bale-related job site. We were to whack down a barn to provide the posts and beams for the house. I arrived a day later than the first work crew, so everybody else was already dirty, grubby, and experienced. I felt severely inadequate, unprepared, nervous — that is, until I took my first crack at a wall with a sledge hammer! Soon I, too, became an expert, guiding the newcomers and doling out jobs.

From that first act of demolition, I was present for every possible aspect of the straw bale project, my work schedule permitting. I especially loved the gut-slugging jobs, such as hauling heavy beams, digging impossible holes in the ground, etc. At the straw bale work sites I've been involved in, no one cares what sex you are, they just appreciate/need your help. There are jobs to be done, and whoever wants to claim them, does.

The most exciting thing I did, though, was to use power tools. I'd used hammers and hand-saws a-plenty, but power tools were a whole new ball game. I have now had a brief introduction to cutting with a skill saw — interestingly, I recently heard on a radio talk show that the skill saw was invented by a Quaker woman, who thought of the invention while watching her spinning wheel go round. I've used a persuader, a power nailer, and other splendid tools.

However, my claim to fame has been to be in charge of the mortar mixer! I take great pleasure in knowing exactly how much cement, lime, and shovels of sand make a good mix, and it feels good for my five foot one inch frame to haul heavy bags, watch my mix form, and then pour it into the waiting wheelbarrow or stucco sprayer. I was most proud this summer, when I was hired as part of a plastering crew, to arrive on site with my sparkling new tools — my very own hammer,

a swanky yellow staple gun (which the boys liked so much they drooled over it), a multi-tool, my own chemical respirator, ear muffs, etc.. I was a bit miffed when the plaster sprayer covered my new tools with concrete splashes, but the boys insist it's cooler to have broken-in tools. I'm not so sure I agree, but I must admit, the other day when I pulled out my staple gun, I looked at the concrete chunks somewhat fondly.

The best part of working on the straw bale construction projects I've been involved in is that I've been able to have valid input into decision making and problem solving. The wall-raising is reminiscent of the old barn raising projects of the past, with huge shared meals and festivities afterwards. I've seen volunteers from 10 years old to 84 years old, men and women alike, people of all kinds of abilities come together and help out. For me, I can't imagine any other way I'd want to spend my summers off, than working up a good, dirty sweat playing with power tools on a straw bale project."

— Tina Therien

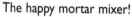

The happy mortar mixer!

CHAPTER 18

Plastering Your Bale Walls

The job of plastering your bale walls is a considerable undertaking. Whether you do it yourself or hire others to the job for you, the choices you make at this stage will have a critical impact on the way your house looks and performs.

The plaster coating — sometimes referred to as 'stucco' — that is applied to your bale walls seals the straw against air movement, pest penetration, rain, and snow. The plaster coating and method of application you choose will define the final visual appearance of your home and create the 'feel' of both the exterior and interior walls.

Plaster finishes can be beautiful, strong, and adaptable both outside (as shown in adjacent photos) and inside (as shown in photos below). It is possible to achieve many different finishes, while creating a wall with the structural strength to stand for several generations.

John Marrow

ABOUT PLASTER

A Time-Honored Finish

Plasters of various kinds have been used to finish buildings for centuries. The correct kind of plaster can provide a durable layer of protection from the elements, and a wide range of textures, colors, and surfaces can be achieved. From a rough, devil-may-care amateur application to the most meticulous professional job, plaster finishing allows for all kinds of approaches.

Examine a wide variety of plastered buildings — both modern and historic — and you'll soon develop a sense of the variety of finishes you can

Courtesy of Ross Kembar, Architect

achieve with different plasters. It is possible to get very creative with your plaster, so don't worry if you look around and find most plaster finishes boring.

A Workout for the Mind and Body

Plastering permits the use of a wider array of materials and techniques than any other element of your straw bale house. There is no single best combination of ingredients and application techniques. You will have to consider cost, climatic appropriateness, embodied energy, availability of materials, desired finish, building code requirements, your attitude toward plasterers — especially amateurs — and speed of application and curing.

Plastering is one of the most labor-intensive activities in straw bale construction. Whether you apply by hand or by machine, the sheer physical effort required to plaster a building surprises many people. Be prepared to put in a lot of effort yourself or to pay well for the people you hire to make the effort for you. Plastering is the one area in straw bale building in which the amount of necessary effort and materials can exceed those of conventional construction.

What Is Plaster?

People are often confused by the terms that are used to describe the coating used to seal straw bale walls. All plasters use an aggregate — which is simply the technical word for sand — to provide most of the volume of material in the plaster. The aggregate is bonded by another ingredient, or combination of ingredients, and it is these bonding agents that distinguish each kind of plaster. When mixed with water, the bonding agents become pliable and allow the plaster to be applied to the walls and worked to create the desired finish. When the bonding agent cures or dries, it hardens and provides a strong surface capable of withstanding weather and structural forces. Cement, clay, lime, and gypsum are the most common varieties of plaster. Each offers its own particular advantages and disadvantages when used in conjunction with straw bale walls.

USING THE FOUR BASIC PLASTERS

Cement/Lime

Durability

The most widely used plasters in modern construction are cement-based. Cement/lime plasters create hard, durable surfaces and offer impressive strength. Cement and straw bond well together, and most bale structures tend to have some form of cement plaster as the exterior finish.

Cost

Cement and lime are widely available and their cost is relatively low.

Mixing and application

There are plenty of available resources pertaining to the proper mixing and application of cement and lime that are useful for novice plasterers. Because cement is the same wherever you buy it, standard mix formulas can be used. There are likely to be many experienced cement plasterers in your area should you wish to consult or hire professionals.

Code compliance

Cement/lime plaster may be the only exterior plaster recognized by your building code. A great deal of testing has been done on cement products to ensure their suitability for various applications.

Embodied energy

Cement is created from ground limestone, clay, alumina, and other minerals that are heated together in kilns and then ground to create a powder. The mining and burning of cement absorb large amounts of energy and may not be appropriate if you are attempting to build with a minimum of impact on the environment.

Quality of finish

Cement plasters create a very hard surface and often feel abrasive. Finishes can range from the smoothly troweled to the highly textured. A local masonry supply outlet can likely provide you with examples of different application techniques. Cement plasters can support the use of pebble finishes, in which large aggregate is used on the top coat to create a variety of looks. You can also embed tile, stone, wood, and other elements in a cement plaster.

Cement plasters respond well to the addition of pigments. White cement and/or white sand can be used in the top coat to brighten pigments. Lime washes can also be used, as can traditional paints, although paints are prone to cracking and flaking and can act as an unintentional vapor barrier.

A sponged finish on a white Portland cement wall. Leftover plaster was used to make tiles.

Other factors

Cement is corrosive to skin. Care must be taken when you are working with it to ensure that correct breathing apparatus is worn and that skin is not exposed to wet cement. The reliability, code-compliance, and strength of cement plasters make them a practical choice.

Clay or Earth-based Plasters (Adobe)

Earth-based plasters are made using local soil that has a naturally occurring balance of sand to clay. For centuries, such plasters have protected buildings from the elements.

Durability

Historically, earth-based plasters were repaired or entirely re-surfaced regularly — a maintenance schedule that may not suit modern builders. Unlike other plasters, clay-based varieties do not undergo a chemical change when curing. When water is added back into hardened clay plasters, they soften and can erode. If they are used indoors or in dry climates, this is not necessarily a problem, but where driving rains or snow can be expected regularly, such plasters can benefit from natural or chemical stabilizers to prevent erosion.

Cost and availability

If suitable soils exist on your building site or in the local area, earth plasters can be very inexpensive. Where local soil requires modification in the amounts of sand and/or clay, costs rise. The use of natural or chemical binders — chopped straw, cement, or emulsified asphalt — will also add to the cost. It is possible to use commercially-prepared clays to make earthen plasters, with per bag costs similar to cement and lime. For indoor applications where additives are less necessary, earth plasters offer unbeatable cost savings. If you live in an area with normal to high rainfall, don't forget to consider the personal cost of regular maintenance.

Mixing and application

Due to infinite variations in local soil conditions, generic recipes cannot be used for mixing earth plasters. You will have to do some experimenting to ensure that your particular mix is the strongest it can be. Earth-based plasters bond very well with straw and are easy to apply. Because they are not caustic, hand application is possible. Most builders using earth plasters do not use any form of wire reinforcement but, rather, use the natural bond between straw and earth to increase the strength of the plaster.

Code compliance

Earth plasters are more likely to be acceptable in areas where they have been used traditionally. Local building codes may require that you apply earth plasters over a minimum application of cement or gypsum or may disallow them altogether.

Embodied energy

Where site soil is used, the embodied energy for earth plasters will be very low. Even with the use of additional additives, earth plasters are more environmentally-friendly than any of the alternatives.

Quality of finish

An earthen plaster dries with a softer feel than cement and has different acoustical properties. Color and texture will vary with soil type and method of application, and its finish can be very beautiful and blend well with the curves and bumps of a straw bale wall. Pigments, lime washes, natural sealants, and paints can all be used to color earthen plasters. Earthen plasters can have a tendency to 'dust', especially if brushed by moving bodies. Sealant can be used to minimize this dusting. You can blend natural elements like stones, pebbles, twigs, bark, and ceramics into earthen plasters, and sculpting and relief work are also possible.

Other factors

Your willingness to experiment will dictate whether or not earth plasters are for you. There are mines of information about earth plasters that you can tap for information and inspiration, but the variability of soil will mean that, in the end, it's up to you and your dirt to come to an agreement.

Lime Plasters

Lime plasters have fallen out of common use since the invention of cement, but they have a long and proven history and can work well with straw bales.

Durability

Properly applied, lime plasters can be long-lasting. As cracks appear, it is possible to hea' them by rubbing in fresh lime putty. Lime does not offer the same kind of water resistance that a cement plaster does, but it can be a suitable exterior finish in most climates.

Cost and availability

Lime is quite widely available and costs about the same as bagged cement. Talk to someone who has used several brands of lime — all are not created equal — and find out which will work best for you. Expect to encounter raised eyebrows and skepticism when you let it be known you are trying to mix a lime plaster!

Mixing and application

A traditional lime plaster uses only lime, sand, and water. The lime must first be made into putty by soaking it in water for anywhere from 24 hours to several years. Lime plaster hardens by exposure to the air, not chemically, and it takes a long time to set into a hard surface. It is traditionally applied in successive, thin coats to allow each layer to have maximum exposure to the air. Modern additives — including cement and gypsum — have been used to speed up the curing process.

The highly pliable nature of lime putty makes it relatively easy to work with, and it is often applied directly to the bales without the use of any reinforcing mesh. Working with lime requires caution. It is highly caustic, and correct breathing equipment must be used when you are mixing dry lime.

Code compliance

Lime plasters are quite rare in modern construction. This kind of plaster is unlikely to be covered by building codes, but familiarity with it as a finishing material and historical precedent may allow for its use.

Embodied energy

The production of quicklime requires plenty of energy to burn the limestone, though the mining practices used to extract limestone are not terribly destructive. Limestone is common and accessible and does not require deep pit- or strip-mining. Local small-scale lime production, now rare, is relatively sustainable. (Many homestead farms had a lime kiln in the back-fifty).

Quality of finish

Lime plasters have a softer feel than cement and are naturally brighter. Pigments will work well with lime.

Other factors

Lime is commercially packaged for many applications; plaster-making is only one application. Be sure to find lime that is meant specifically for plastering or masonry purposes — agricultural lime does not make good plaster. Pure lime putty can be mixed and stored indefinitely, since it will not cure as long as it's protected from exposure to air. This means you can always have some on hand for repairing cracks or creating additions. There are relatively few modern resources available to those who wish to use lime plasters, so expect to take some time to experiment with formulation and application.

Lime plasters are among the most breathable finishes available. This means that more air and moisture can pass through the plaster. This can be beneficial in that it allows any trapped moisture to exit the bales; it also means that more moisture can penetrate when humidity and temperature conditions are conducive. Lime plasters tend to discourage the growth of mold and mildew and can also repel many breeds of insects.

Gypsum Plasters

Gypsum plasters are often what comes to mind when the term 'plaster' is used. In older homes, plaster and lath was the most common interior wall finish. Gypsum is also the main ingredient used in making modern drywall — Gyproc — and drywall compound.

Durability

Gypsum plasters should only be used indoors, since exposure to rain will cause rapid deterioration. As an indoor plaster, it can last the lifetime of your home with no maintenance required. Anybody who has ever stripped an old home of its plaster will know how durable it can be!

Cost and availability

Gypsum plasters are manufactured by many large companies under different brand names — Structolite, Sheetrock 90, and Red Top are common brands — and most building supply stores will be able to order gypsum products if they don't already stock them regularly. Gypsum plasters are likely to be the most expensive option, especially if they are used directly from the bag without the addition of any sand. Prices tend to vary several dollars per bag for the same products, so check several sources before you buy.

Mixing and application

Gypsum plasters come in a 'just add water' form and so are easy to mix. Mixing must be done in relatively small batches, since gypsum plasters set chemically and each batch has a short workable lifetime. Some gypsum plasters include Perlite in the mixture to add volume and reduce weight for base coat applications. Fine-screened sand can also be added to base coats to give extra volume; most commercially available bags include ratios for its addition. It will take some experimentation to judge what volume to make for each batch.

Gypsum plasters are relatively easy to apply, since they are quite sticky and pliable while wet. Sculpting and relief work is very easy to do. The gypsum adheres well to bare straw or to a base coat of cement plaster, and gypsum plasters look good if you allow them to take the shape of the bales underneath. If your aim is to achieve completely straight walls, you will have to master the techniques of the old-fashioned plasterers, which can take a lot of practice to get right.

Code compliance

Gypsum plasters will be acceptable as an interior finish in most areas. They have a long history in home building, and the companies that manufacture modern varieties have testing data on strength and durability.

Embodied energy

Gypsum must be mined and heated like cement and lime, but the process requires only about one-third of the energy. Manufactured products include chemical stabilizers and agents to slow or speed the setting process.

Quality of finish

Gypsum plasters provide a soft finish but are not prone to dusting or crumbling. They create a more pleasant acoustical effect than do cement finishes. Some varieties will dry to quite a bright white finish without the addition of any paints or pigments. Gypsum plasters take regular paints very well, or any number of pigment solutions can be used to provide color. It is easy to sand a gypsum plaster finish to remove high spots and achieve a smooth finish. Patching is simple, since small batches can be easily mixed and successive layers bond well to one another.

Other factors

You might want to purchase a single bag of several different gypsum plasters and experiment to see which gives you the qualities you most prefer. The carefully engineered mixtures and the consistency of the mixes allow for generally crack-free walls. Gypsum plasters can be used as a top coat over a base of cement plaster, which can provide your interior with a softer, more pleasing finish and reduce your costs. You will have to clean your tools and mixing equipment frequently, since curing occurs very quickly.

Combination Plasters

None of the four main types of plaster has to be used on its own. It is possible to combine ingredients to make hybrid plasters or to use different plasters for different coats. Cement plasters almost always use lime or lime putty, sometimes in equal proportion to the cement. Cement can be added to lime putty or to earth plasters. Clay can be added to cement, lime to earth, clay to gypsum, gypsum to lime. However, before you make unorthodox combinations, it is best to do some research or try some experiments — before you are committed to covering your entire house!

Check Your Local Area

Depending on where you live, plaster finishes may still be common on frame-walled and block-walled buildings, and you may find many professional plasterers available for hire or consultation. Check out plastered buildings in your area, and talk to homeowners and professionals for advice. Contractors building in-ground swimming pools often have a crew of experienced plasterers. Plaster finishes used to be much more widely used than they are today, so often the best advice will come from retired builders and plasterers. These people are usually glad to help revive their old practices and may be willing to help you out.

If plaster finishes are uncommon where you live, you will have to do some research to locate the materials, tools, and advice you'll need to do the job. Look for areas with climate conditions similar to yours where plaster finishes are in use.

Take Plastering Advice With a Grain of... Grain?

Plastering a straw bale wall is different from plastering a wooden or cement wall. The plaster bonds with the straw rather than creating a separate and thin layer. You will use a good deal more plaster to cover bale walls than equally-sized wood or block walls, and the consistency of your ideal mix will likely be different as well. Because plasters can 'key into' the straw, it is possible to use mixtures and ingredients — earth and lime in particular — that would not be suitable for application on wooden or concrete walls.

You may be steered away from plaster finishes by people who have seen plasters that cracked and peeled from wooden or concrete walls. Plasters on bale walls don't operate as a separate skin and so aren't affected by the same differential expansion and contraction that occurs on wooden or concrete walls. Even where cracks do appear, the plaster itself does not pull away from the wall. Often, peeling and cracking is caused by paint on the exterior surface acting as a vapor barrier to trap moisture inside the plaster; color for plaster is better achieved by tinting the plaster itself or by using breathable paints and stains.

THE PLASTERING PROCESS

It is standard practice to apply three coats of plaster to both the interior and exterior walls, and in some jurisdictions the building code will enforce this practice. Three coats will provide more than adequate protection against the elements as well as significant structural strength. The three coats together should create an average of 1-inch of coverage over the entire wall. The actual thickness of the plaster will vary from point to point, but you don't want the thinnest spots to be much less than 3/4 inch thick.

Scratch Coat

The first coat of plaster is called the scratch coat and is the most time-consuming and material-intensive coat to apply. It is forced into the straw to achieve a good bond and built up to fill in the hollow spots and irregularities of the bales. Plasterers who are experienced at covering straight walls are usually surprised at the amount of time and material it takes to build the scratch coat on a bale wall.

The scratch coat uses the strongest plaster mix with a higher amount of binder to aggregate — except in the case of lime plasters. Plaster is applied thickly enough to cover most of the straw ends and averages a thickness of $1/2$–$3/4$ inches. It is called the scratch coat because you will literally scratch the surface of the plaster with horizontal strokes once the plaster has begun to set. These scratches will afford the next coat a mechanical grip and supplement any chemical bonds that are formed.

Brown Coat

The second coat is often referred to as the brown coat. It will average $1/4$–$3/8$-inch thick and will define the overall shape of the wall. It can be applied as soon as the scratch coat has begun to set. A lot less material and time will be required to apply the brown coat. A light scratching with a broom will roughen the surface of the brown coat and help the finish coat to bond.

Color Coat or Finish Coat

The third coat is the layer that is used to create the finished look of the wall. From heavily textured pebble coats to thinly brushed color washes, the mixture and application of this coat depends largely on the finish you are trying to achieve. If you are coloring with pigment, it is added to this coat. Sometimes, special 'white' cement is used to allow colors to show up more brightly. A number of different application and finishing tools can be used to create the effect you want.

Hand Application of Plaster

Applying your own plaster by hand is one way you can drastically reduce labor costs for this time-consuming process. Mixing and applying plaster is a very basic, simple process, and the help of friends and family can be most welcome at this stage. If you spread the effort among a dozen people, it can speed up the work and make for a fun weekend of shared effort.

A natural division seems to exist in the human population: those who enjoy plastering and those who detest it. If you are among the former, you might actually have a good time putting in the effort that's required. If you are among the latter, it may be worth any price to have professionals do the work for you!

Wall Preparation

Be sure that any reinforcing mesh you require is firmly attached. Check the house for detailing so you know where you expect the plaster to go when it meets doors, windows, foundation, and roof plate. Remember that joints, edges, and corners will benefit from heavier mesh. Do any last minute trimming of straw to achieve as flat a wall surface as possible.

Sweep old bits of loose straw from the intersection of floors, walls, and window ledges, then cover the floors with plastic or drop cloths. Plastering is a messy business, and these coverings are not likely to be reusable. Tape the edges of the drop cloths at the base of the walls. The tape can be used to create a straight, even seam between the plaster.

Apply tape to window frames, door frames, and any other elements you don't wish to have plastered. Be sure to cover up window sills, since plaster dropping from above can stain them permanently.

It can be handy to pre-cut a number of metal 'pins' — for pegging down any wire mesh you find sitting too far from the straw you are plastering — and distribute them around the site. Sometimes, errant mesh can be persuaded to sit flat with a stab from a trowel.

Preparing the Site

Plastering is hard, heavy work. You want to minimize the amount of effort you expend on anything other than applying plaster to the wall, so prepare your site thoroughly. Be sure to clean up any obstacles inside and outside the house. You will need to be able to walk without impediment and to deliver wheelbarrows of fresh 'mud' to all points along the walls. Be sure to create strong, well-braced ramps wherever wheelbarrows will need to enter and exit the house, and bridge any holes or trenches that still exist on the site.

You will need to assess the best place to situate your mixing equipment. Mixing is hard, hot work so try to find a naturally shaded area. Mixing should be done close to the building and to an interior entrance way, as shown in Illustration 18.1. The mixing area must have enough room to allow for a big sand pile, stacks of bagged material, the mixing equipment itself, and for several bodies to navigate around the obstacles.

You will be using a lot of water, so be sure you can get it to the mixing site. If necessary, you may need to rent a storage tank and pump, which will also require positioning close to the mixing. A lot of water will hit the ground during mixing and cleanup, so it helps if the mixing site has good natural drainage. Don't mix in a hole!

You must also assess where difficulties may arise in reaching the tops of walls. For two-story buildings, you will almost certainly need to set up scaffolding to reach the upper walls. Proper assembly and leveling of scaffolding can be time-consuming, especially if the ground around the building is uneven. For shorter reaches, you may be able to arrange some leftover bales around the building to use as steps for reaching the tops of regular walls. It is best to have all this work done before you bring together your equipment and crew.

Illustration 18.1

By keeping all the elements for mixing plaster close together and choosing a site with good access to the building, you can reduce the amount of labor involved during plastering.

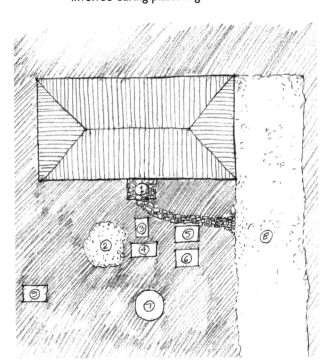

Plastering Setup

1. Entry
2. Sand
3. Stucco Sprayer
4. Mortar Mixer
5. Lime
6. Cement
7. Cistern (Raised or Uphill from Setup
8. Driveway
9. Bale Press

If you are plastering an upstairs wall inside the building, protect the stairs from the extreme wear and spills they are likely to receive. You will need to make plans for delivering plaster to the upper floor in the most practical and effortless way possible. You may want to rig up a pulley or block and tackle to make lifting heavy buckets of plaster a bit less backbreaking. Alternatively, you could set up a smaller hand-mixing station on the second floor. In general, it's a good idea to start plastering the upper floor and do the hardest work first.

Put away any tools and construction materials you won't need. Be sure you do have the tools and supplies you might need — staple gun, extra wire mesh, twine, and metal cutters — near at hand but out of the way of falling plaster.

MIXING OPTIONS

Hand-mixing

You can hand-mix plaster in a wheelbarrow if small batches are all that's needed, or you can build a mixing box from plywood or sheet metal. A wide shallow shape will work best, and the box should be placed so the contents can be easily emptied into wheelbarrows for transportation around the site. If you are using bagged materials, creating a 'bag splitter' over the mixing box is a good idea, as shown in Illustration 18.2.

The best tool for mixing plaster is a mortar hoe. These can be purchased at masonry supply stores or can be made by creating holes in a standard garden hoe. You will also need a good spade for shoveling sand and other bulk ingredients.

Machine Mixing

Barrel-style cement mixers make lousy plaster mixers. Don't plan to rent or use one of these machines — it's less time-consuming to mix by hand! Mortar mixers are properly designed for the task and feature rotating, paddle-like blades. These mixers are usually gasoline-powered, so be sure to have plenty of gas and oil on hand to keep your operation running. Mortar mixers come in different sizes and are identified by the number of cubic feet of material they can handle. Larger mixers will enable you to create mixes using full bags of material rather than shovelfuls. Make sure your mixer is set up to allow easy dumping into waiting wheelbarrows — you may have to raise the machine onto a platform or blocks.

The mixer takes a central location between the water supply (in this case a large tank) the bags of cement and lime, and the mound of sand. Scaffolding is ready to assist the plasterers to reach the higher portions of the wall.

Illustration 18.2
A bag splitter can be fashioned from leftover lumber on-site. It is a help when half bags of material are required.

PLASTERING EQUIPMENT

Safety Equipment

You must take reasonable precautions when working with plaster. Anyone who is involved in the mixing of plaster should wear quality respiration equipment. It is inevitable that clouds of cement, lime, clay, and sand will be in the air. Don't invite the stuff into your lungs. Eye protection is likewise recommended for all mixers and plasterers. Splatters occur at the mixing station and when plaster is applied to bare straw — keep it out of your eyes. Quality work gloves are a must, and each person may want two or three pairs, since they are bound to get soaked. Industrial quality rubber gloves are another option. The mixing, moving, and application of plaster is hard physical work. Be aware of the onset of fatigue and take breaks as required. Injury is most likely to occur when you become exhausted.

Wheelbarrows

You will need at least two good strong wheelbarrows for transporting plaster from the mixing site. The more plasterers you have, the more wheelbarrows you'll need. Some wheelbarrows are shaped specifically with a deep, narrow profile for dumping cement and plaster; cheap wheelbarrows will collapse with a heavy load of plaster on board. Wheelbarrows can be rented from most building supply or rental centers.

Shovels

It is best to have a different shovel for each ingredient you are adding to your plaster mix, and if you intend to use a shovel to help do the mixing keep it separate from the dry ingredients. If you do use multiple shovels, be sure they are of similar size, since most of your measuring will be done by the shovelful.

Mortarboards

A flat sheet of steel or wood can be mounted on a bucket or a milk crate to make a mortarboard. This board can act as a transfer station between wheelbarrow and individual plasterer, allowing one wheelbarrow to deliver to multiple users.

Trowels

Every plasterer has a favorite trowel by which he or she swears. Try to have a good selection of trowels on hand. Rounded-edge swimming pool trowels can be easier to use on wavy bale surfaces, since sharp-cornered ones will tend to dig in and scratch where lumps and bumps are encountered. Trowels in a range of lengths and widths will be handy, as will putty knives. A triangular brick trowel can be handy for reaching into tight spaces and can also be used instead of a hawk to load a trowel with plaster.

Illustration 18.3
Some of the tools of the plasterer's trade.

Clean trowels are essential. If there is plaster residue on the troweling surface, it will be much more difficult to apply the plaster. Rinse your trowels frequently during use and clean them thoroughly with a brush every time you take a break.

Hawks

Any flat piece of wood or steel mounted on a handle can serve as a hawk, as shown in Illustration 18.3. The hawk is used to carry a load of plaster to the wall. From there, the plaster is cut from the hawk and applied to the wall with the trowel. You will be holding your hawk all day, and on it will be a remarkably heavy load of plaster. Be sure the handle suits your grip and that the hawk is not too large for you to comfortably hold and maneuver it. Some store-bought hawks come with a foam pad at the top of the handle — an idea you'll appreciate by the end of the day!

Sponges

Quality sponges can come in handy as a finishing tool, especially for your top coat of plaster — sponged surfaces tend to crack less. Sponges are also handy for cleaning up spills.

Buckets

Buckets can be used to carry rinsing water for each plasterer, to move plaster around the site, to scoop sand or other ingredients, to hold up mortarboards, etc. Try to have lots on hand!

Cleanup Tools

The best cleaning device for plaster covered equipment is a plastic toilet brush, but any kind of stiff durable brush will do. For stubborn cleanups, a stainless steel wire brush is ideal. Cleanup brushes will spend most of their day soaking in water, so plastic handles are better than wood. The more brushes you have, the more people can help with cleanup at the end of the day!

Water Barrels

Most typical garden hoses do not deliver water fast enough to keep up with mixing demands. If you have several large barrels on hand, it allows you to continuously fill the barrels and then use a bucket to add water to your mix in a faster, more measured way.

Water Storage Tank

If you do not have a reliable source of water at your site, you can rent a large storage tank and have it filled. The bigger the tank the better, so go for a size of at least 1000 gallons and expect to have it filled more than once. Be sure to check if water can be delivered on a weekend — there is nothing worse than to have a plastering crew on hand and no water left by Sunday!

MIX FORMULAS

Nothing is so sacred to a plasterer as his or her particular mix formula! What follows are general recipes to use as a starting place for your own custom formula. Be sure to talk to plasterers in your region or those who have experience with your particular kind of plaster before you settle on a formula. If you are making a unique mix, be sure to do some experimenting — on straw bales! — before starting to plaster your entire building.

A note on measurements: all the recipes below are ratios of one ingredient to the next. The most common measurement is the 'shovelful.' Of course, every shovel and every shoveler is going to produce a different shovelful, but as long as the same person is attempting to make the same sized shovelful every time, the system works!

Cement/Lime Plaster

1 part cement
1 part lime (mason's/stucco lime)
5 to 7 parts fine-screened sand

This mix is used with five parts sand for the scratch coat, six parts sand for the brown coat, and seven parts sand for the top coat. Bagged clays are possible replacements for the lime in cement plasters. They make for a good sticky plaster, are non-caustic, and have a lower embodied energy.

Earth Plaster

The use of earth plasters is a subject and skill unto itself, and it is beyond the scope of this book to do more than introduce some basic information. There is no precise formula guaranteed to be suitable for your particular soil conditions. There are good resources and knowledgeable people willing to help you produce a suitable earth plaster if you choose to go this route.

The basic rule is that too much clay content will cause cracking as the plaster dries and too little clay will result in a weak crumbly finished plaster. As a rule of thumb, 65–85 percent of your mixture will be sand, and the remaining 15–35 percent will be clay. Of course, chopped straw or other natural binders are often used as well and are not included in these percentages.

To test your soil conditions, remove some topsoil and put it in a jar, filling the jar about halfway. Add water and shake the mixture vigorously. As the soil settles out of the water, it will separate into three layers with sand on the bottom, clay in the middle, and silt on top. Take samples from several different areas of your site since — soil conditions can vary dramatically in a matter of a pace or two — and label them well. You'll be able to tell from your samples if you have to import sand or clay for your mix.

Only experimentation will lead you to the right mix formula. Start combining natural and/or added ingredients with water and apply them to the sides of bales. When they dry, test them for crumbling and cracking. Too much cracking and you've got too much clay to sand; too crumbly and it's the other way around.

Stabilizers are often an essential part of an earth plaster. Once you have a good formula, you can decide on a stabilizer. Emulsified asphalt is most common, but cement has also been used. Experiment with proportions by spraying water onto a dried test patch and seeing how it resists erosion compared to an unstabilized mix.

Habib John Gonzalez, a bale builder in British Columbia, suggests this recipe as a starting place:

>   5 parts sand
>   5 parts clay
>   1 part cement
>   ½ part lime

Lime Plaster

>   1 part lime putty
>   1 ½–5 parts sand

Use the maximum amount of sand for the scratch coat and work down to the minimum amount of sand for the top coat.

Lime putty is created by mixing 1 bag of lime with 10–12 gallons of water — batches can be made in 55-gallon barrels. The mixture is allowed to soak for a period of one week to several years. As long as the top of the mixture is covered with water, it will last indefinitely.

Many different stabilizers can be added to lime plasters. The most common is cement, which is added at a ratio of approximately one part cement to four parts lime.

Lime water, a thin mixture of 2–3 percent lime to water, is often sprayed onto the straw before the lime plaster is applied. The lime-dampened straw will bond better and make a stronger plaster. The caustic nature of lime water may help to retard the growth of molds should the finished wall become chronically damp.

Gypsum Plaster

Commercial gypsum products come with precise measuring formulas on the bag. If you are adding sand, figures for acceptable sand quantities are also on the bag. Some hints for variations might come from plasterers with plenty of experience with the product — ask your supplier about plasterers who are familiar with the product.

MIXING

In most plastering crews, one person will usually emerge as the 'Mix Master' — the person most able to produce a good plaster with the least number of complaints from the plasterers. Mixing is a hard and often thankless job, but a good mixer will never let the crew run out of plaster.

Hand-mixing

Dry ingredients should be thoroughly combined before the addition of any liquid. Once the ingredients are well-mixed, push the dry mix to one side and add water to the mix-free zone. The mortar hoe can then drag the dry mix into the water slowly. When the entire mix is damp, additional water can be added until the desired consistency has been reached.

Machine Mixing

With the machine in motion, add approximately half to three-quarters of the required water followed by half the sand. When the sand is thoroughly wet, add the lime or clay, the cement, then any pigment or fibers. Continue to add the remainder of the sand followed by any required water until the desired consistency has been reached.

Measurement

For most plasters, you will be relying on your shovel to act as a large measuring spoon. Be sure to add scoops of a similar size each time, but don't worry about being excessively fussy about the size of each shovelful. If you are mixing bagged ingredients, you can determine how many of your particular shovelfuls are in a bag and then add the bags directly to the mix.

Consistency

The amount of added water will determine the stiffness of the finished mixture. Only experience will tell you what the best consistency is for you. In general, the plaster should be stiff enough to maintain itself in a blob on your mortarboard or hawk yet wet enough to be pliable under your trowel.

It's very easy to over-soak your mixture. Plaster mixtures will seem too dry until they hit their saturation point, and then they become too wet very quickly. Give your plaster enough time to thoroughly mix before adding more water, and then add water slowly a bit at a time, allowing it time to mix again. Unless you are dealing with bagged gypsum plaster, the quantity of water required will vary from batch to batch, so precise measuring is not possible. Using buckets rather than a hose for water will allow for accurate approximation, and you will very quickly get the hang of creating a desirable mix.

PREPARING THE WALLS

Filling Holes In the Wall

Before you get into full-scale plastering, you may want to make a batch of plaster to use as fill for low spots in your walls or to smooth out highly irregular areas. This can speed up the actual application of the scratch coat by minimizing the number of heavy applications required. It's also a good time to get a bit of practice measuring and making a mix and to try your hand at troweling before you face an entirely bare wall!

Misting the Walls

After all the conscious effort you have made to keep your walls dry, you are now going to contradict your good bale training and turn a hose on them!

Low spots are filled with plaster before the entire wall is attacked.

Most plasters consume water in order to cure, and dry straw will wick away too much water to allow for proper curing. Plasters affixed to damp straw further strengthen the bond between the materials.

Avoid applying a direct stream of water at the bales; rather, apply a fine mist. Careful work with a garden hose and a spray attachment will suffice, but a back-pack sprayer — as used by landscapers — is better suited for the task. You can use straight water or lime water. Only moisten the walls where plastering is about to proceed as other areas will dry out long before any plaster is applied.

Shading the Walls

Direct sunlight will cause the plaster to cure too quickly, so try to time your plastering to avoid direct sunlight on uncured plaster. If this is not possible, hang tarps to provide shade during application and curing.

Plaster and Frost

In northern climates, you will want to avoid plastering if temperatures are expected to dip below freezing within 24–48 hours of applying the plaster. The freezing of water within the plaster does all kinds of nasty things to the strength and durability of the finish. If you are plastering in questionable weather — when temperatures are flirting with the freezing point — you can hang tarps or blankets over your plastered wall. Any cement based plaster generates a small amount of heat as it cures and can help the wall keep its heat and ward off the frost.

PLASTERING

Applying the Plaster to the Walls

First-time plasterers are infamous for the creation of unintentional sidewalks of spilled plaster around the base of the wall. It's no easy feat to get a full trowel of plaster on a wall and have it stay in place! Still, with some practice, most people are able to get the hang of it and do a good job. The techniques are much easier to demonstrate than to describe in written form, so getting a lesson from someone with experience is a definite plus. (It's even better if you can convince that person to join your crew!)

If you are using a hawk, you can use the 'cut-and-swipe' technique. Place a hawk full of plaster near or directly against the wall. Using the trowel, separate a hunk of plaster, lift it onto the wall, and smear it against the surface with a smooth, curved swipe. Apply a fair bit of pressure to ensure that the plaster bonds well with the bare straw or the previous coat of plaster. Then repeat, over and over and over!

The hawk technique works well when you cannot work right next to a wheelbarrow or mortarboard full of plaster. The fully-loaded hawk is very heavy, and your arm may quickly tire of holding it. Enter a second technique, used by bricklayers and masons. With a triangular brick trowel in one hand and your wall trowel in the other, use the brick trowel to scoop some plaster

Plaster is taken from the hawk and applied to the wall with a sweeping motion of the arm.

For those working on the ground, plaster can be scooped right out of the wheelbarrow or from a mortarboard. For those on ladders or scaffolds, the hawk minimizes the number of trips up and down.

and deposit it on the wall trowel. True professionals make this look easy as they throw perfect lumps of plaster onto their trowel in a seemingly fluid and endless motion! With some practice, anybody can get the hang of this technique and use a hawk only when necessary.

Applying the Scratch Coat

Applying the scratch coat is the hardest part of plastering. The bare straw will seem to swallow remarkable amounts of plaster, and you will require fill-ups at an astounding rate. Avoid over-working the plaster by using as few strokes as possible — one is best — to achieve your best result. The brown coat will offer lots of opportunity for straightening the walls, so concentrate mainly on good, even coverage for the scratch coat. It's a good idea to keep a pair of wire-cutters in your pocket, to trim bits of string, straw, and wire that refuse to be buried beneath the plaster.

You will need to scratch the surface before it becomes too hard to do so. If the plaster crumbles and falls off the wall, you are scratching too soon. Be sure to score the plaster well, using horizontal motions.

The first coat of plaster is scratched before it cures completely. Scratching is usually horizontal, but some artistic license is certainly allowable.

Misting the Walls

Cement-based plasters consume water in order to cure. It is a good idea to mist the walls with water as they cure. Don't soak them. If water is running down the plaster, you've applied too much. You should be able to see the plaster swallowing the water.

Applying the Brown coat

It is best to apply the brown coat before the scratch coat is completely cured — hardened but still a bit damp. Use a properly adjusted mix [see recipes]. The brown coat should entirely cover the scratch coat, and pressure should be applied to each trowel stroke to press the plaster into the scratched grooves beneath. Use the brown coat to give the walls the shape you want. Add extra plaster in low areas; use less on high points. Corners can be shaped according to taste, using careful trowel work or special corner trowels. For the truly committed plasterer who really enjoys the work, the brown coat is where some real technique can be put to use!

Caulking Joints and Cracks

After the brown coat has cured, you will likely find that, due to the natural shrinkage of plaster, small openings will appear where plaster meets door and window frames and posts and beams. Before applying the top coat, it's a good idea to apply some quality outdoor caulking to these cracks — polyurethane is the most weather-resistant — to prevent air infiltration. The top coat will cover the caulking, but you may want to choose a color to match that of your top coat.

Choosing and Mixing the Top Coat

Even though it is a thin layer, the top coat creates the final look of your house. There are literally hundreds of different ways to finish the top coat of plaster. Some of these are achievable with trowel technique alone; others require the use of different aggregate, still others the use of spraying machines. Before setting your heart on a particular finish, find out how it is achieved, and make any necessary arrangements for supplies or labor.

A hand-finished top coat can look attractive, especially if it is tinted with pigment. Pigments can be purchased at reasonable cost from masonry supply stores, and they will have samples chips like you'd find with paints. Pigments are available in many colors — greens, yellows, reds, and blues — and in many shades. Unlike paints, pigments will not peel, crack, or trap unwanted moisture. It is possible to make your own natural stains or pigments to add to the top coat, though pigments manufactured for use with plasters will weaken the plaster less and have a more stable coloring. It is a good idea to experiment with pigments on leftover bales before applying a colored mix directly to your walls. The color can change dramatically as the plaster dries, and you want to achieve a mix formula that gives you the desired color when dry.

Your top coat of plaster does not have to be of the same materials as the earlier coats. Especially indoors, softer plasters can be applied as the top coat. Gypsum or earth-over-cement are popular options.

Top coat plasters are usually troweled in the same manner as earlier coats. If you like the look of hand-troweled plaster, and many people do, you can simply be more artistic with your troweling motion. For textured surfaces, trowel on the plaster and then use the trowel to pull away from the wall. This will leave a bumpy texture. Special rollers can also be used to create textured surfaces. In one of our favorite finishing techniques, we do a regular troweling of the plaster, then return with a damp sponge and rub the surface smooth as the plaster begins to set. This can create beautiful, rounded shapes. Sponging can be especially effective if you are creating curved window and door openings or

The more complicated the contours, and the more intersections, the longer the plaster application will take. The rewards, however, can be worth the effort.

If you work the curing plaster with a damp sponge, it can smooth out the surface and create soft, gentle curves.

finishing carved niches and has the added benefit of helping to eliminate small surface cracks in the plaster. Your top coat will need to be misted at least two or three times if it is a cement-based plaster.

Excessive Cracking

Some minor surface cracking is not unusual in plaster finishes. If you find that your scratch coat and/or your brown coat are cracking excessively, even when you adjust the mixtures and water content, you may want to hire a professional to give you some advice on how to solve the problem before you apply successive coats. Excessive cracking can result from too high a proportion of binder in your mix, too little water, too much water, or a curing that occurs too quickly. Applying too thick a coat may result in horizontal cracking, as the weight of the material can cause it to sag. You can fill cracks in scratch coats and brown coats with a 'soft wet' mixture; rub it with a sponge until the crack is filled. The same can be done for the top coat, but not without affecting the finished look and causing discoloration. Always try to address the root cause of any cracking before undertaking repairs.

Cleanup

It is important to clean up your tools, equipment, and site before the plaster has hardened. Trowels, buckets, shovels, wheelbarrows, mixing equipment — anything that's touched plaster should be scraped and rinsed before it becomes impossible to clean. It's easy to lose expensive tools to hardened plaster, especially if you're using cement and gypsum. Tape should be pulled off window and door frames and floors before the plaster sets. Otherwise, the tape will be hard to remove and will pull off chunks of plaster that should stay on the wall. Clean yourself well, too. Cement and lime will dry out your skin and cause painful cracking if you don't get it off. Treat yourself to a good, long bath and some lotion!

Machine Application of Plaster

A spraying machine can do the job of a whole crew of plasterers in less time. Various machines allow you to spray plaster onto your walls without you having to carry and lift all the plaster. Troweling will still be required to create an appropriate finish, but troweling is much easier if the plaster is already on the wall.

Spraying machines are not very common, and rental units are few and far between. It is likely that you will have to hire a crew that has a machine and knows how to use it. A spraying crew may or may not be familiar with straw bale walls. If not, be sure they understand the extra amounts of plaster that will be required before accepting a quote for the job. Some spraying outfits may be able to apply enough plaster in one coat to eliminate the need for a brown coat.

There are two kinds of machines for spraying plaster. Stucco sprayers pump mixed plaster through a hose and onto the wall. Gunnite machines pump dry mix that is combined with water at the nozzle. Both are suitable for straw bale walls.

Despite being faster than hand-plastering, spraying is not necessarily less physical work. Feeding the hungry machine can take two or three dedicated mixers, and the person spraying will have to be followed by at least two trowelers. Work must proceed without break or else the mixture will harden in the hoses.

You will need to prepare your site thoroughly for a machine application. The hoses are heavy and the machine is stationary, so clear paths must be made available for moving the hose around the site. Scaffolding must be provided where necessary. It is critical to tape and cover elements you don't want plastered, since sprayers are less than completely accurate!

Plaster spraying outfits tend to be expensive to hire. If you are hand-plastering with volunteer labor, your savings are significant. However, with a sprayer, the reduction in time and effort is equally significant, and a hired spraying crew will be cheaper than a hired hand-plastering crew.

You could hire a spraying outfit to apply only a base coat, which would take care of the most labor-intensive aspect of hand-application. Or you could have a specialty top coat sprayed. You might hire a sprayer for the exterior and do the interior by hand. Any combination of options is possible.

A stucco sprayer applies plaster to the bale wall, where it is troweled by hand. A sprayer can cut plastering time in half. Note the tarp ready to provide shade from the sun right after the plaster is applied.

Fun With Plaster

Plaster walls allow you to be very creative. Relief carving, artistic scratching, and sculpting are all possible. If you find the actual plastering process too exhausting to consider such artistic endeavors, you can always apply additional plaster at a later time — as long as you haven't painted or otherwise sealed the plaster.

A spraying machine is proudly displayed, with the mixer that feeds it standing by, ready to tip more plaster into the hopper.

Every Plastering Job Is Unique

As with your bale house itself, plastered walls are highly individualized, even unique. Professional plasterers can't even replicate a job. For some, this lack of a standardized finish might be distressing, and professional plasterers can do a remarkably good job of minimizing it. For many people, however, the individuality of a plastered finish on bale walls is a large part of the charm and beauty of a bale building.

The shapes and textures of a plastered bale wall can be pleasing to the eye — literally; our eyes respond better to textured surfaces than flat ones.

Corners are formed using
two trowels held in a 'V'
to create a sharp, square corner.
Corners can also be rounded
or left a bit bumpy.

The gentle play of shadow and light on an undulating wall is pleasant and changes the atmosphere of a room. Acoustically, too, plastered bale walls soften a space by eliminating the echoes found in square, straight rooms. You many find that people who visit your home have an uncontrollable urge to touch the walls. And why not? The warmth and subtlety of plaster walls are tactile and inviting!

Acrylic and Synthetic Stuccos

The recent introduction of synthetic stuccos has caused no end of debate among plasterers. Used only for top coat applications, synthetic stuccos create a waterproof finish and allow for a wider range of colors and more controlled finishing textures. Synthetics are usually chosen as an exterior finish, but if you use an exterior synthetic, you will be creating a vapor barrier on the outside of your walls. This can cause problems with moisture buildup unless the interior is treated with a vapor retardant of at least equal value. Vapor retardant can come in the form of an interior coat of synthetic stucco or as vapor-retardant paint. Synthetic stuccos are the least environmentally-friendly of all the finishing options and usually require the application of a bonding agent over the brown coat, making their application more labor-intensive than other plasters.

OTHER OPTIONS FOR SURFACING BALE WALLS

Perhaps you live in a climate where plaster finishes are less than ideal, or maybe you need to conform to appearance requirements in an urban area. Or maybe you just don't like plaster finishes. Plaster of any form does not have to be the final wall finish for your straw bale building. In fact, it is possible to apply any kind of exterior or interior siding to bale walls.

It is highly advisable to seal your bale walls with at least one coat of plaster before applying any other form of siding. Even one coat of plaster adds significant structural strength to the walls; it also acts as an excellent fire retardant and a barrier to insects and pests. The base coat of plaster can be applied by hand or by machine with no regard for finished appearance.

Unplastered walls should have at least a well-sealed vapor/air barrier. A borax treatment can be applied to the straw as a fire retardant. Bales exposed to moving air lose some of their insulation value, and fire may be able to spread along the loose ends of the straw even though the whole bales are likely to resist combustion.

Strategies for affixing other forms of siding usually use thin wooden strapping to act as attachment points. Strapping can be run vertically between the wooden bale curb and the top plate and is affixed at intervals that match building code requirements for the particular siding used. The spaces between the strapping can be filled with plaster. Wooden siding, plywood — as a base for cedar shakes — or even vinyl or aluminum siding can be attached to the strapping, as shown in Illustration 18.4; for interior walls, drywall can be mounted.

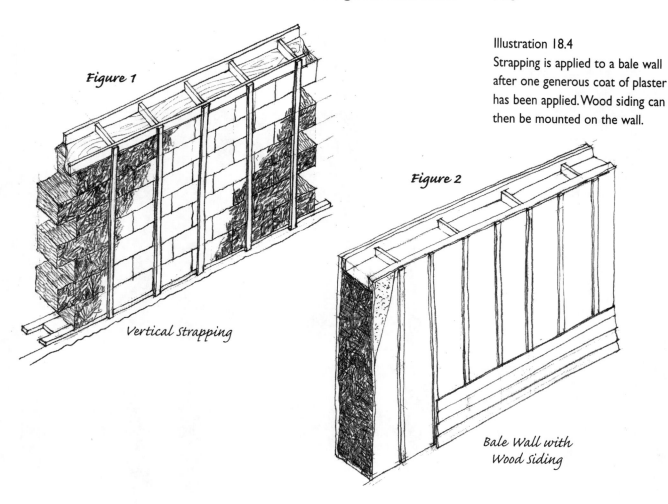

Figure 1

Vertical Strapping

Figure 2

Bale Wall with
Wood Siding

Illustration 18.4
Strapping is applied to a bale wall after one generous coat of plaster has been applied. Wood siding can then be mounted on the wall.

Brick and stone can also be used to sheath bale walls. Again, a coat of plaster is recommended. This plaster can be used to affix brick ties that stabilize the outer shell of brick or stone. Foundation design must be detailed to create a brick ledge. Your building code or a knowledgeable mason will outline applicable requirements. As with brick and stone facades over frame walls, a space must exist between the wall and the brick, and drainage must be provided at the bottom of the wall for any moisture that gets trapped. Your window and door buck design must also accommodate the requirements of brick and stone work.

Think Like Water and Fire; Think Like a Mouse

Whatever non-plaster finish you apply, it pays to take time to think about its possible penetration by rain and pests and any potential for the spreading of fire. If you apply a coat or two of plaster first, these concerns can be greatly lessened.

PLASTER MAGIC

From shaggy bales to beautiful, finished walls — the plastering process gives strength, shape, and definition to your building. It's long, hard work, but when you stand back and admire it you won't notice your tired arms quite so much!

Plaster can be worked in many ways — straight and seamless or soft and artistic — as shown by this straw bale summer kitchen in Ship Harbour, Nova Scotia.

Kim Thompson

Courtesy of Ross Kembar, Architect

Tiles and found objects can be embedded in the plaster for effect.

Light plays nicely on rounded forms.

Courtesy of Ross Kembar, Architect

REFERENCES

Portland Cement Association. *Portland Cement Plaster (Stucco) Manual.* Portland Cement Association, 1996. 1500 Don Mills Road, Ste. 703, Toronto ON M3B 3K4 Canada.

Stagg, W.D. and B.F. Pegg. *Plastering: A Craftsman's Encyclopedia.* BSP Professional Books, 1989. ISBN 0-632-02545-X.

Taylor, J.B. *Plastering.* Longman Scientific and Technical, 1990. ISBN 0-582-05634-9.

The Last Straw, #26, provides information on lime plaster. Contact: HC66 Box 119, Hillsboro NM 88042 USA. www.strawhomes.com

Van Den Branden, F. and Thomas Hartsell. *Plastering Skills.* American Technical Publishers, Inc., 1984. ISBN 0-8269-0657-5.

CHAPTER 19

Straw Bale Case Studies

There are thousands of straw bale structures of all sizes, shapes, and styles in all parts of the world. Here are some case studies written by, and summarizing the insights of the owners and/or builders of three straw bale homes.

PREFABRICATED STRAW BALE CONSTRUCTION IN INNER CITY MINNEAPOLIS

In March 1998 a joint venture between Southside Neighborhood Housing Services (SNHS) and the Community Eco-design Network (CEN), was undertaken to develop a low cost, superinsulated strawbale building system in inner city Minneapolis. SNHS is an established non-profit developer of affordable housing in south Minneapolis and CEN is a non-profit research and development corporation that focuses on northern climate strawbale and other sustainable building technologies. CEN has been developing northern climate strawbale and prefabricated plans for the last five years and partnered with SNHS to develop this demonstration project. While the costs for the demonstration house did not come in as low as anticipated, many valuable lessons were learned from the project which will enable us to consistently go below market rate housing on future projects.

The Demonstration House is a 1400 square foot, three bedroom home which was sold to a low income buyer. The combination of prefabrication and superinsulation has the potential to lower the costs of construction and produce a higher quality, energy efficient home. This building system uses a number of alternative and sustainable building components besides strawbales as insulation.

Foundation

The foundation system for the Demonstration House was a frost-protected shallow foundation with a wide concrete footing and a concrete slab, encapsulating strawbales that act as fill and slab insulation. Instead of deep frost footings, the perimeter of the slab is insulated with four feet of rigid insulation about one foot below the surface. This type of foundation is a cost-effective alternative to frost footings, although the concrete work continues to be expensive and somewhat problematic. Since the construction of the house, we have developed prefabricated wood foundations and foundations using insulated grade beams and piers which are lower in cost and can be easily prefabricated. Without the use of concrete, the foundation requires less skill to build, making it easier for volunteers and inexperienced workers to install.

Framing

The framing system in the Demonstration House was a lightweight post and beam frame made up of 3x4 'super studs' and manufactured wood I-beams, all of which are prefinished in our shop. This frame was erected in a tilt-up truss pattern and was covered with prepainted gypsum board. We build a 4 x18 gypsum mechanical chase for the electric and some of the plumbing (the first course of bales were put on edge to make room for the chase). This framing system went up fairly rapidly, although it required lots of time consuming interior trim. In the future we plan to replace the 'wall board' with precast plaster interior panels. The mechanical chases will not be used; instead we will have the electric wiring and equipment installed before the bales are stacked and run the plumbing in the floor of the house instead of the walls. We will also use a ladder truss system which uses an 18 inch deep truss set on end with the strawbales inserted between the trusses instead of the post and beam frame. This gives us a good nailing surface on both the interior and exterior and makes it easier to install the bales. We also used a vapor barrier which was installed just behind the gypsum board, a standard superinsulated building detail. We will use a vapor barrier in future projects and may use an exterior infiltration barrier just underneath the stucco.

Precast Exterior Stucco Panel System

We developed a lightweight, precast stucco panel that is used instead of conventionally applied stucco. Panels were cast at our prefabrication shop and shipped to the site.

For the Demonstration House we used a lightweight mix of perlite, Portland cement, and reinforcement filaments along with a variety of steel reinforcement. The perlite turned out to make the panel too brittle so we will use other lightweight aggregates in the future. Difficulties were encountered with the attachment of the panel to the lightweight post and beam frame (which should be taken care [of] in future projects with the ladder truss design mentioned above). Per square foot costs were hard to ascertain since this was the first time the panels were used on a large scale project. Additional research is being done [to] come up with the best reinforcement and stucco mix to make the panels both strong and lightweight. We now have molds for the panels that can be easily taken to a construction site and poured onsite rather than in a shop, saving shop expense and transportation damage. Panel cost is predicted to be less expensive than traditional stucco applied with a paid workforce.

Mechanical Systems

We are very satisfied with the performance of the infloor radiant heat system. This type of heating system will be used in future projects. The Bradford-White Combicore hot water heater (which heats both the domestic hot water and the infloor heating liquid) is an efficient unit and costs much less than a boiler. The only change will be to use an electric hot water heater or an electric heat pump instead of a natural gas [one]. Using a unit without an open flame is much more simple in a superinsulated house and lessens the need for extra ventilation and indoor air quality concerns. We have found lower cost infloor products to use in the future and will be able to lay down much of the infloor tubing ourselves, saving money on the mechanical system.

Straw Bales

Strawbales were used throughout the entire house; under the concrete slab, in the walls, and in the attic. Around 1200 bales were used in the project. Having the extra weight of strawbales in the attic adds considerable weight and the structural system has to be stronger but it is effective insulation and great for sound deadening. We have learned the following things about strawbales for construction and design purposes:

• Bales are a low cost insulation and fill material
• The bale module of 36x18 x14 inches is ideal for prefabricated systems
• Bales make an excellent insulated fill material in foundations with no lateral loads
• Bales cannot be depended upon for consistent size
• Strawbales are a superior insulator that does not settle and is very good for sound attenuation. Street noise and airplane noise is greatly reduced in the house.

Overall this was a very valuable project for us, and we learned much from it. We have made many changes to our building system based on this project. Within the next year we should have designed and built enough projects that we have a good idea what the costs are and how we compare to more conventional construction. In 1999 we are concentrating on finding contractors and training workers who can bid and build projects that use this building system. We will have three or four projects that will help us develop that workforce and further refine construction costs and techniques.

Eric D. Hart
Community Eco-design Network
PO Box 6241
Minneapolis, Minnesota 55406 USA
erichart@mtn.org
(612) 823-5216 extension 315
http://www.cedn.org

OVERVIEW OF STRAW HOUSE, SHIP HARBOUR, NOVA SCOTIA

The Straw House in Ship Harbour, Nova Scotia, was the first code-approved load-bearing straw bale building in Canada. It also pioneered two story design for straw bales, and the use of straw as floor insulation.

The house measures 1500 sq. ft. interior, 25' x 30'. It is seven bales high on the main floor and three on the second, with an exposed cathedral-style roof. The rafters in the roof are 6" x 6"

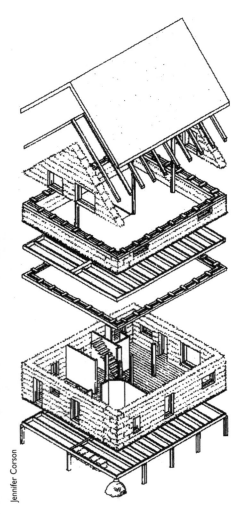

Jennifer Corson

Illustration 19.1
This exploded view of
Kim Thompson's house is an
excellent overview of the
construction of a two-story,
load-bearing design.

timbers, supported by posts cut from the property, they carry rigid R20 insulation. This design gives a clear second story.

The building rests on poles, salvaged from a disused power line that cut across the site. They are set into our rocky ground at least 4 feet deep to avoid frost heave. We had originally intended to build on slab, but given financial constraints and an interest in destroying the immediate ecosystem as little as possible, we decided to work with posts, which allowed us to experiment with putting straw in the floor as insulation between the joists.

The joists were set so that they could accommodate a half-bale jammed between them, then a tongue-and-groove spruce floor was laid out on top. Strapping was nailed into the joists from below to provide a grid to keep the bales from slipping through. We also recommend that a mesh be fixed to the joists to hold the straw in place, and to deter rodents. In climates such as ours, 6 ml polypropelene is laid out directly onto the ground, and then covered with soft ground to minimize rising damp. This floor method was fairly labor intensive, especially laying the T & G, since the straw kept creeping between the joins; this need not be a problem if one were laying a second floor on that.

The walls have half inch threaded iron rods running from the ground floor to the second floor top plate about every 3 feet as well as being pinned with three-foot lengths of sharpened bamboo every 2 feet. The rods allowed us to torque down the plates until the straw settled; both the rods and the bamboo gave extra lateral strength. Wood bracing with lengths of 2" x 6" in an X-shape were added to each of the walls to provide further lateral stability. These were later parged over.

The bale walls were covered in chicken wire for reinforcing both inside and out then two coats of parging were applied to the inside, and three to the outside. The third was a colour coat containing ferrous sulphate, which creates a warm yellow ochre colour. The interior was white washed.

There are no vapor barriers in our walls. We have built many other straw bale structures over the last five years and continue to advocate this policy. We have been monitoring the Ship Harbour walls for relative humidity and moisture content for four years, with research assistance from NRC and CMHC. The results have been very positive, most recently MC measured only 9–11%. There has been no cracking of the plaster due to any shifting in building. Where green lumber was used there were occasional fine cracks which appeared as the wood dried out. These are easily repaired.

There are things we would have done differently if we were to do it all again. Mainly they include designing straw into the roof as insulation, combining some cob with the straw bale system, parging directly onto the straw, and using all the little tricks we have learned about finish work. We learn and learn and learn....

Kim Thompson
Straw House Herbals
RR#1
Ship Harbour, NS B0J 1Y0

THE MAGWOOD/BOWEN 'EXPERIMENT IN PROGRESS'

Our house is quite far removed from anything we had initially intended when we first thought of building. The idea of building with straw started out as a joke, and terms like off-grid, passive solar, and embodied energy were just a collection of so many foreign-sounding words.

In the end, our 1500 square foot, two-story, post and beam home incorporated not only the 'laughable' straw bales, but many of the other intriguing and beneficial features we were exposed to in the course of designing, building, and living in our home.

We received building code approval based on an architect's plans, and experienced little trouble (but a fair bit of bewilderment) from our local building inspector. The house is built on an insulated, slab-on-grade foundation, with radiant floor heating in the slab. On that slab we erected a post and beam frame made from recycled barn timbers from a large pig-shed that was falling down on our property. The frame was built using a system of locally-welded steel plates and fasteners (this proved to be expensive and time-consuming; we would have been better off using traditional joinery), and the roof was framed with rough-sawn, locally-milled lumber. A galvanised steel roof tops the structure.

Because of many unexpected delays early in the building process, we found ourselves installing the bales on a December weekend. Luckily, the earlier snows had melted, and the weather was quite mild for the season. Having a roof already on the structure removed much of the anxiety of keeping the straw dry, as it was stored on the sheltered slab upon delivery.

Once the walls were up, the rest of the house was finished (though that term must be applied loosely!) before the weather improved in the spring and allowed for plastering to take place. We used gypsum plaster for the interior (sand and cement delivery were impossible due to a driveway buried in snow) and, when the weather broke for good, a cement/lime plaster on the exterior. Typar house-wrap did an excellent job of sheathing the bales for the entire winter, keeping them dry and free from snow.

When the shell of the house was finished, we were out of money. Therefore, our mechanical systems are of the simple, homemade variety. A used, air-tight woodstove provides heat, domestic hot water, and heat for the radiant floor system. Homemade solar collectors provide domestic hot water, and will soon be expanded to help out with floor heating duties as well.

We went for a long time with no electrical power, using a system of rotating car batteries to power our water pump and fill our gravity-feed tanks. Gradually, we added a small amount of solar electric capacity (160 watts), supplying a bank of used golf cart batteries. The system is adequate for lighting, home office, stereo, water pumping, and moderate VCR/TV usage. This winter, an old Volkswagen Rabbit diesel was added to the system as a back-up generator. Refrigeration is handled by a double-insulated ice box, which is vented to the outside in the winter time.

The process of building the house has changed our lives dramatically. It has met our need for low-cost living. Thanks to the straw walls and good passive solar design, we only burn an average of one cord of wood each winter, and hope to reduce that even further with the addition of active solar floor heating. Other bills (besides taxes and telephone) are non-existent. For the privilege of spending less cash, we must spend time monitoring and maintaining our systems.

In building our straw bale house, we learned just how much other stuff goes into building a home. The straw bales were the fastest, easiest, and most satisfying element of the construction process — it's all the other parts that proved expensive and time-consuming.

The use of alternative methods of heating and powering a home have made us aware of the importance of designing with these systems in mind, not adding them afterward. As integrated elements, they can be achieved much more simply.

We built the entire house with the help of friends and family, and that, more than anything, is the part we remember most fondly. We strengthened existing friendships and forged new ones around the exciting, serious, and rewarding business of building together. We made a lot of mistakes, but harbor no regrets about having thrown ourselves into making a house of straw.

Chris Magwood
c/o Camel's Back Construction
RR3 Madoc ON K0K 2K0
Cmagwood@kos.net

CHAPTER 20

Constructing With Work Parties

Many potential straw bale builders are attracted to the idea of a communal wall-raising. Work bees are a practical, inexpensive, and often fun way to build parts of a home. But it's not as simple as calling up friends and relatives and watching the work get done for you.

ALL ABOUT WORK PARTIES

What Is a Work Party?

Like the barn-raisings of earlier times, work parties are gatherings of friends, family, and community members who will help with the construction of a building. Many people are attracted by an image of building with shared effort and community spirit, and work parties have certainly played a large part in the raising of many straw bale structures. The potential exists for you to develop rewarding, meaningful work experiences and relationships that will last as long as the building itself.

Good Work Party Tasks

Certain phases of construction are better suited to work parties than others. Bale wall-raising is one good example, as is plastering. Digging for foundations and erecting a post and beam framework can also be done with many hands. Other phases of construction may require specific skills or specialized tools or will progress too slowly for work parties to be effective.

Work Parties Versus Workshops

Hands-on workshops are a popular and useful way to learn the basics of straw bale building. Workshop participants pay an instructor for the experience of helping to raise a building. It is important to recognize that volunteers and paying participants have very different expectations and needs. Hosting a workshop when what you really need are volunteers is a sure-fire way to disappoint yourself and the workshop participants. If you plan to erect your building with paying workshop participants, be sure their need for instruction, guidance, and discussion comes first.

Calling a Work Party

Your call for volunteers requires you to decide how many people you want to attend and who you want to call. It may take only a few phone calls to nearby friends and family to round up a suitable crew, or you may have to make a more public call for help. There never seems to be a shortage of willing volunteers for straw bale projects,

A volunteer work site can be a beehive of activity, with several tasks being accomplished at once. It can be a handful to supervise!

but only you can decide on the appropriate mix of friends, family, and/or strangers — and live with the interpersonal dynamics created therein!

Too many people can be more of a problem than a help. Figure out how many people you think are ideal for the task at hand, and try to limit attendance to that number. Everybody who shows up will want to do something useful and meaningful, and you don't want people to leave frustrated at not having been able to participate. Maybe you could schedule people for shifts and include more volunteers than are actually needed.

Timing

You need to prearrange dates and times for your volunteers, which puts you in the position of having to complete all the preliminary work by the appointed date. You'll need to strike a balance between setting dates early enough that volunteers can plan to attend but not so far in advance that the inevitable delays and hold-ups put you off track and cause repeated re-scheduling. Your best bet is to be pessimistic when setting dates. Figure out the timing of your project to the best of your ability, and then add several weeks to the estimate. It's better to be ready a week early and busy yourself with other project tasks than to have volunteers arrive before they can be most useful.

Have Everything Ready

The more prepared you are for your work bee, the more will get accomplished. A bale-raising won't be as successful if one or two people are hurriedly trying to build a curb for the bales to rest on or are frantically nailing together window bucks. A plastering party can grind to a halt if the chicken wire still needs to be hung. At the same time, a buck-making or chicken-wiring party can be a great success, as long as that was your intention in the first place! You need to have all the necessary materials and equipment on hand. It is a waste of everybody's time if you have to drive to the building supply store to pick up forgotten items.

Start Early

If possible, try to gather your volunteers the night before work is to commence. This will allow new people to get acquainted, and it will help to ensure an early start on the project. It takes a work party time to build serious momentum, and the later you start in the day, the less time you will have to reap the rewards of that momentum.

Instruction

Be sure your volunteers have an overall understanding of what is to be achieved. Instruct the entire group about the entire process. When the overall picture is clear, it makes the role of each individual process and function more meaningful. Talk about the tasks and the number of people required to perform them. Explain each task thoroughly. Cover everything from what to expect at the start of the task — that is, making sure the previous job has been done correctly — to what will be expected of the people working on the following stage. Let your volunteers know exactly what's expected and why.

Try to match people to tasks that suit their personalities, knowledge, and strengths. People with certain skills — especially carpentry skills — will gravitate to certain tasks. Don't forget that people may want to experiment with several tasks and try things outside their realm of experience. There is little in the construction of a bale wall — or almost any phase of construction — that is beyond the ability of most people to learn, so be flexible and allow people to choose tasks that interest them. It can be helpful to make photocopies of your task list and explanatory drawings. Give a sheet to each person so they don't have to rely on memory or repeatedly ask for help.

Supervision

As a work party supervisor, you should expect to spend most of your time acting as a trouble-shooter and not plan to do much hands-on building. Ideally, each separate crew will have a knowledgeable leader, but since this is not always possible, be sure that you circulate around the work site and keep tabs on the progress of each phase and crew. Don't be afraid to correct people in their work but do so positively. In the end, it is your building, and you should not settle for work below your standards. Always be willing to re-explain, to show by example, and to reassign people who are not enjoying their tasks. As a site supervisor you will be incredibly busy. Remember to take breaks, drink, and eat throughout the day, and encourage your volunteers to do the same.

Tools

Three people sharing one hammer will work no faster than one person with one hammer. Anticipate the number of people who will be performing each task and be sure they have adequate tools to get the job done. Ask volunteers to bring specific tools, or borrow or rent them, but don't fall short. Label tools well, since they will inevitably get mixed together and scattered over the site.

Good instruction combined with a bit of experience makes the project move ahead smoothly.

The site supervisor must constantly circulate to explain, encourage, and inspire volunteers. Note the flip chart that explains the process and breaks down each task into its component parts.

Large crews mean lots of hungry and thirsty people. Beware of big, sit-down meals, however, since they take a lot of time out of the short work day!

Food and Drink

Busy workers eat and drink a remarkable amount. Be sure there is enough food and liquid to keep everybody well fueled. For large crews, this will mean assigning somebody the specific task of feeding the crew or else arranging for catered food. Plenty of water and juice is essential, as are hot beverages when temperatures are colder. Don't forget the caffeine addicts in your crew!

Be clear with your volunteers about what will and will not be provided in the way of food and drink, especially if you cannot afford to provide for everybody's needs. It is also worthwhile to check for food allergies.

Be sure your site has provisions for all food-related amenities — running water or plenty of bottled water, refrigeration, storage, dishes, and cutlery. A well-fed crew is a happy crew and one that will gladly return again. A hungry and thirsty crew will be easily inspired to mutiny!

Accommodation

Construction is hard work, and a good sleep will keep strengths and spirits up. Let people know if they need to provide sleeping bags, pillows, bedding, tents, etc. Always be sure to have some extra sleeping gear on hand for extra people who show up or for those who forget their own. Work parties often extend into nighttime parties. Often, this is half the fun of building with volunteer crews. But don't forget to sleep or to be courteous to others who need theirs!

Safety

Work sites attended by large crews change rapidly. What was once a clear path can become an obstacle course in a matter of minutes. People will be moving large objects, using power tools, and focusing on their particular task. Everybody needs to be reminded to move slowly and carefully.

Be sure to have an adequate first aid kit, and let people know where it is located. Minor injuries will consume large numbers of Band-Aids and antiseptic creams. Serious injuries are a possibility, so have the right supplies available. Be sure that at least two people on-site know how and where to get help and how to give directions so ambulance crews or fire fighters can locate the work site.

Sunstroke and dehydration are common on summer work sites. Keep hats on heads and plenty of liquid flowing. If your site has no natural shade, put up a tent or an awning and encourage people to take breaks in the shade.

Smokers must be kept far from a straw bale work site. Provide them with distant chairs and sand-filled buckets for butts. Fire extinguishers should be placed strategically around the site, and a functioning hose and/or large barrels of water must be available in case of fire.

Realistic Expectations

Raising half a wall can either be a victory or a letdown, depending on what you expected to accomplish. Try to set your expectations carefully, and know that delays, problems, and oversights are inevitable. A good rule to follow is to estimate how long you think a task will take, then multiply that amount of time by a reality factor of two or even three!

Try to plan useful, secondary tasks that can be performed by people who are temporarily unemployed because of delays. Work parties can easily end up with a large group of people standing around a single trouble spot, offering advice and trying to help out. As supervisor, try to assign people to work out problems, and redirect others to useful jobs.

You Are the 'Cruise Director'

Your mood and attitude on the work site transfer directly into the general mood of the project and its participants, so try to stay positive and focused, even as your expectations are challenged. Temper tantrums are a no-no. You are going to be taking the job more seriously than any of your volunteers, so don't expect the same level of commitment from them as you do from yourself. Treat your volunteers with respect, and do your best to make the day fun and enjoyable.

Thank-You's

Don't let those new friends get away without finding out how to reach them. Many houses would never have been built without the dedication of volunteers. Come up with meaningful and creative ways to thank people for their help. This means having addresses and phone numbers for all your volunteers.

Good food, good company, and rewarding work are often thanks enough for a volunteer, but a card or a phone call is a positive extension of good will. Have all your volunteers come out to a non-working celebration of the project when it is finished. Hand out awards, enlarged photographs of crews and participants, or give a thank-you speech. Of course, the best way to show your appreciation is to go out and volunteer on the projects your volunteers will undertake in the future. Share the knowledge!

Taking a Straw Bale Workshop

"My mother introduced me to straw bale construction by inviting me to attend a weekend workshop at the Ecology Retreat Centre (Ontario, Canada) in May, 1998. We had no previous experience with construction but my mom is interested in possibly building one day, and after that weekend, so am I.

At first I was apprehensive about going since I knew nothing about it. So the first thing I learned that weekend was the value of new learning experiences and how these can open doors for possibilities one might otherwise not have imagined — in fact you can even make your own doors!

What does this have to do with straw bale construction? It has to do with imagining what is possible, taking risks, and potentially being involved with a building project in a direct way; a way that encourages awareness of how and where one builds; a way that encourages recognition of life style choices and their impact on, or compatibility with, one's surroundings.

Working along with others, learning something new, was primarily fun and grounding. There was a sense of accomplishment that weekend as a small group of people with ranging talents and abilities was successful in building a straw bale structure. The sense of community and camaraderie that formed in one short weekend gave other dimensions to construction than merely the nuts and bolts. It seemed to me that construction can bring people together; that a focussed group can accomplish a lot in a short period of time, and in that time people's dreams and creativity are given a chance to develop and be realized.

My mother and I both enjoyed learning about what had brought people to the workshop and what people were hoping to build some day. There was such an interesting and varied array of project plans — cottages, studios, additions, and houses to name a few. We were inspired by these projects, by the questions that were asked and shared information.

I learned that straw, which has limited uses, can be extremely purposeful, versatile, and malleable. These features of building with straw, along with the many other attributes of straw bale structures, strike me as a powerful inspiration to the imagination. For example, I particularly like the idea of incorporating rounded or curved forms into living spaces. With straw bale, these shapes are more easily attainable than with other building materials.

I liked the feel of the straw bale house we visited and in the small structure we built. The thick walls and insulation create a unique atmosphere in which sound is muffled. I felt a quietness and calmness in the way that sound was carried. There is an ironic strength to these structures that I did not anticipate from a material that, when less contained, could easily blow away in the wind.

During the workshop we learned some practical construction skills and that it's possible to be directly involved in building. But beyond the mechanics of construction there can also be other enlightening and rewarding experiences. I would encourage anyone to think of the benefits of straw bale construction and I will definitely be on-hand and on-site if and when my mom decides to build!"

— Laura Ponti-Sgargi lives and works in Toronto.

Proud workshop participants pose next to the shed they erected in a single day.

Hosting a Work Party

Our house was built over a period of 10 months, and over that time at least 50 different sets of hands participated in its construction. People volunteered for everything from helping us pick out the site to tearing down an old barn for beams, to hoisting those beams in place, raising bales, plastering, and interior finishing. Some of my strongest friendships were cemented (!) during this building process and the tears and frustrations were shared by many a willing (and sometimes unsuspecting) shoulder. A lot of wonderful memories have been built into these walls. Every time I look at the beam that holds up our roof I think of the ten bodies that hoisted that 27-foot beam up to the peak of the second floor when the crane couldn't come. A lot of sweat and hard work goes into building a house, and if that work is volunteer labor one of the best ways to reward and thank people is by taking good care of them while they work.

When Chris and I started to build, we wanted to share all the tasks and do everything equally; I didn't envision cooking and hosting to be an important part of these activities but I soon learned that it was. Many people have since commented to me that it was the food, drink, and camaraderie, as well as the learning process of building that kept them coming back. So, here are some things I learned over the many, many work parties we held:

1) *Assume that people need to be fed while they are on-site, and take the approach that you feel comfortable with. Hosting a party on a work site can be very difficult as running water, electricity, and adequate shelter can be in scarce supply. For our first work party I took on the task of cooking everything (from chili to salads to cookies) in our little trailer on site and soon learned that some things can be better purchased. It may be cheaper to cook everything from scratch, but if that's not possible look for other alternatives: have the meal catered, buy deli foods and other prepared goods, do a mix of some prepared foods and some grocery items, arrange for a pizza or other take-out meal.*

2) *Don't try to make work parties pot luck. People are providing enough of a service by offering their labor, without trying to transport and coordinate food as well.*

If water, or other liquids will be scarce on site, you can ask people to bring their own jug. As well you might want to get people to bring their own mug.

3) *Don't plan a sit down meal during the day. If possible, put out some food at a designated break hour, and leave it out for a little while, so people can break and eat when it is convenient. Make sure that you, and all on site, do take a break and get something to eat and drink. Remember that people need to eat and drink at different times — aside from the main meals, make sure there is a supply of on-the-go food: muffins, sandwiches, fruit, hard boiled eggs, granola bars, etc.*

4) *If you can't take on the task of coordinating food yourself, make sure someone is designated to do it. It is an important job!*

5) *Please don't leave all the women on the work site to coordinate food, and dishes, etc., while the men do the heavy stuff! Find some people who need a break from the sun, and assign them the job.*

6) *Is it a party or...While it is called a work party, the main reason people are there is to work, and the food and drinks should only support that, not be so enticing as to drag people away from their jobs. As well, hold off on the beer or other refreshments until people need to wind down at the end of the day.*

7) *Do think about food safety. On a work site, refrigeration can be tricky but safe food storage is very important. If you don't have refrigeration on site, try to arrange some with a neighbour, pack a lot of coolers, and plan food that keeps well. Also, you'll need to think about washing dishes, and how to do that safely and efficiently. Contact your local public health office if you want to pick up some information on food and water safety. After all, you don't want your crew coming down with salmonella!*

8) *Don't forget to get in there and get your hands dirty and have fun!*

— Julie Bowen continues to feed friends and family at her straw bale house near Cooper, Ontario.

CHAPTER 21

Other Straw Bale Projects

Throughout this book, we've concentrated on the home-building applications of straw bale construction. Of course, these techniques are easily translatable into similar structures, such as additions, garages, sheds, guest cabins, and greenhouses.

The Wellspring Retreat Center near West Bend, Wisconsin, gets a straw bale addition.

Eric Hart

OTHER BALE IDEAS

Beyond Houses

Straw bales can be used to complement houses or other structures. Fences and privacy walls can be created with bales, as shown in Illustration 21.1, as can garden and patio furniture. As long as you remember the basics of straw bale building — keep the bales from getting wet! — these projects can be tackled with creativity and inventiveness.

Industrial Buildings and Shopping Malls

Prefabricated industrial buildings may be cheap to put up, but they are expensive to heat and waste remarkable amounts of energy every year. Usually built with little or no glazing, these buildings are very well suited to straw bale construction built on prefabricated steel frames.

Shopping malls, too, are well suited to bale construction. With their straight, square walls and minimal glazing, straw bale malls could be easily erected and would lower operating costs significantly.

Public Structures

Local municipalities and volunteer groups can use straw bale construction to create any number of projects, from low-income housing to public washrooms and from band shells to schools. As die-hard northerners, it is our dream to one day build a straw bale hockey arena!

Churches, community centers, and youth recreation centers could all be built of bales with the participation of the people who will use and benefit from the finished building. By encouraging public participation in construction and by lowering lifetime operating costs, straw bale buildings make possible any number of exciting projects!

Driftless Farm near LaCrosse, Wisconsin gets a straw bale green house.

Eric Hart

Courtesy of Ross Kembar, Architect

Straw bale lawn furniture is
an organically-shaped addition
to a garden setting.

Illustration 21.1
A straw bale privacy wall and
bench seat can be a beautiful
addition to your landscaping and
a fun way for you to practice
working with bales and plaster.

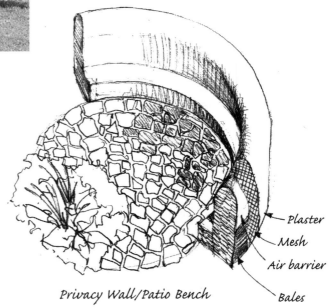

— Plaster

— Mesh

— Air barrier

— Bales

Privacy Wall/Patio Bench

Courtesy of Ross Kembar, Architect

A straw bale shed/greenhouse
is a practical and worthwhile project.

Straw Bale Youth Centre at Afton First Nations Reserve, Antigonish County, Nova Scotia

While attending a conference in British Columbia in 1996, Chief Kerry Prosper picked up information on plastered straw bale construction which was being done on the other side of the country, in Nova Scotia. When he returned home to Afton he began to research the straw bale system through the Internet and via a small business called Straw Bale Projects which works with individuals and organizations to construct buildings and programs with a commitment to sustainable living practices.

Over the next year Straw Bale Projects conducted two workshops with Afton residents. The first was a half day introductory slide show and video presentation held on the reserve and attended by about 30 people. The second took place in Ship Harbour at the Straw House with five people from Afton taking part.

There was a lot of interest in constructing something, but the right project wasn't there until the spring of 1998 when the band decided to create a space for youth on the reserve. Straw bale provided an opportunity to build a structure which was environmentally responsible, affordable, and most importantly, a system where youth could play a significant role in building their own space. The positive spin offs seemed endless.

Three young adults (age 23–26) were hired to work with Straw Bale Projects. Two more workshops were held where building designs were developed and local materials explored. The three young adults worked with reserve teens and created a youth council which in turn got many young people out to raise the walls and plaster them.

The shallow insulated slab and roof construction were contracted out. Once these were in place, it was a matter of a few weeks before the walls were up and plastered. Costs were kept low by using recycled doors and windows, and parts of the construction (such as roof insulation) were left uncompleted until such time as the youth could fundraise for them.

It can be difficult with community projects to work on the buildings only as funds become available. Sustaining the momentum of work parties over a long period is hard work. The big magic with straw bale is seeing a project realized in a matter of weeks when there is excellent organization and commitment from the community.

The straw bale Youth Centre involved many community members in the process of construction.

Afton Project details:

Built: May–June 1998

Cost: estimate $14,000 (materials only, labor was mostly donated)

Area: exterior: 30' x 33' = 990 sq.ft.
 interior: mainfloor: 27' x 30' = 810 sq.ft.
 second floor: 15 x 22' = 330 sq.ft. living space
 12 x 22 = 264 sq.ft. storage space
 total living space: 1,140 sq.ft.

Foundation: shallow, insulated slab-on-grade

Roof: asphalt shingles, fiberglass insulation

Walls: Post and beam (unmilled posts cut from reserve land); non-load-bearing straw with cement stucco finish on both exterior and interior surfaces.

Insulation value: R-40

Doors and Windows: recycled

Labor: Local contractors for foundation and roof

Design and wall construction, Straw Bale Projects, and three youth workers, with youth and adult volunteers numbering five to twenty-five on any given day.

Band Chief: Kerry Prosper

Project Liaison: Dodd Goo Goo

Band Office tel.: 1-902-386-2781

Design/builders: Straw Bale Projects
 Kim Thompson and Rod Malay
 tel.: 1-902-845-2750

CHAPTER 22

The Challenge

Throughout this book, we have tried to present as wide a range of building options as possible. We believe that straw bale structures can adapt to the needs and wants of most home builders and that the advantages of higher efficiency and lower environmental impact and cost are available to anybody who decides to build with straw bales.

STRAW BALE AS A LIFESTYLE

Many people are attracted to straw bale building specifically for its significantly lower environmental impact. The decision to stray from the wastefulness of mainstream construction can mean extra research, extra costs, or additional time as you create more sound solutions to housing needs. From passive solar gain design to naturally-based stains for finishing your walls, alternative choices are abundantly available and sometimes overwhelming in their variety. If you inform yourself before you start building, you'll know better what you want, what is available, and what you can afford.

Straw bale buildings make the adoption of renewable energy sources for both home heating and electricity viable. Fewer resources are needed to maintain a comfortable home, and with passive and active solar heating, the highly efficient straw bale house makes it possible to rely more on the sun's energy than ever before. That lowers the ongoing environmental impact of your home. As more people make these positive choices, prices for the equipment will continue to fall. Already, many of these options are affordable by most people who are considering building a house.

Straw bale building also lends itself to ideas like co-housing and communal living arrangements. Used as interior walls, straw bales can provide the kind of privacy and comfort that make such shared living possible. Of course, all these choices involve you stepping away from what's considered normal. Your lifestyle will necessarily change. Think practically about what you *really* need and want from your living space, and plan accordingly.

For too long, we who live in northern climates have been pursuing an unsustainable lifestyle, based on the over-consumption of resources. We urge you to do your best to correct this trend with the choices you make in building, heating, and powering your home.

CONCLUSION

There are very few tasks as complex, meaningful, and rewarding as building a home. We hope we've provided options and solutions to many of the issues you will face when building with bales. We are certain, however, that we haven't answered them

Straw bale interior with a 'truth window' showing straw inside the wall.

John Marrow

John Marrow

Cozy, comfy spaces created with bales have an atmosphere like no other.

all. Each individual project is full of its own challenges, and it takes a great deal of resourcefulness and diligence to work out appropriate solutions. At each turn in the process, it is possible to find people with experience and advice to help you out. For first time builders, the learning curve is very steep, and even the seasoned pros find new methods and procedures each time they build.

Straw bale building is still in its infancy. Practices and methodology will continue to improve. Some of the options outlined in this book will likely fade into disuse, while others will become predominant. Yet others are still to be invented and put to test. It is the openness to innovation and change that makes building with straw bales so exciting. We hope that the thinking we've encouraged you to do throughout this book serves as your best tool in ensuring that you are an active participant in the ongoing development of straw bale building.

Just as surely as bale building will grow and change, so too will awareness of the need to engage in more sustainable building practices in general. We've made an attempt in this book to provide some focus on the environmental issues that face builders and the choices that can be made. However, there is a lot to be improved before we can make any real claims to true sustainability for straw bale construction. Sadly, meeting building code requirements and building sustainably are often two opposing ideals. It is our hope that building officials and builders will begin to recognize more fully the need to improve practices to allow for greater sustainability. But such a change will only come about if individuals openly question and challenge prevailing trends and use their opinions and their building dollars to support more sustainable practices and products. We feel that using straw bales in construction puts an important foot in the door of the building profession, and may help bring about wider, deeper changes.

And for you, regardless of the methods or materials you've used, what can be more satisfying than to listen to the wind beat against the walls while you sit, feeling safe, secure, and warm in the house you planned and built? Good luck to you in your bale building projects, and may you thoroughly enjoy that first warm night surrounded by your straw bale walls.

The authors are always curious to know what people think of this book. Please send comments, suggestions, inquiries, project news, or resource additions to cmagwood@kos.net or strawbus@auracom.com.

The Arizona
Straw Bale Building Code

The Arizona Straw Bale Building Code was a remarkable breakthrough in the development of straw bale construction, proving that this building method could meet and/or surpass all the expectations of state and local construction authorities. It is presented here to give an indication of the practices it prescribes and as encouragement to local building officials in locales where straw bale has not been codified, to show them the risk they take in accepting straw bale designs is as minimal as with any other common building system. This code also provides a snapshot of the development of straw bale construction as it existed in the early 1990s. As such, there are many prescriptions in this code that we do not agree with, and would encourage builders to circumvent if possible. The rebar pins in the foundation, the continuous pinning of bales in the wall, the use of impaled threaded rod as a precompression system, the inclusion of a membrane on the lower third of exterior walls, the restrictions upon wall length and height, the restrictions against building two story structures; this code has frozen practices that have been disputed or disproven in the field by many builders, and does not represent an accurate picture of the current state of straw bale building nor leave room for its future development.

As straw bale innovators continue to develop suitable methodologies, this code will fall further out of date. But, for now, it represents a key step in bringing straw bale construction into more widespread practice.

CITY OF TUCSON AND
PIMA COUNTY ARIZONA BUILDING CODE
APPENDIX CHAPTER 72 STRAW-BALE STRUCTURES

SECTION 7201 — PURPOSE

The purpose of this appendix chapter is to establish minimum prescriptive standards of safety for the construction of structures which use baled straw as a load bearing or non-load bearing material.

SECTION 7202 — SCOPE

The provisions of this chapter shall apply to all structures utilizing straw-bales in the construction of wall systems. Load bearing structures shall be limited to Occupancy Groups R, Division 3 and U.

SECTION 7203 — DEFINITIONS

For the purpose of this chapter, certain terms are defined as follows:

STRAW is the dry stems of cereal grains left after the seed heads have been removed.

BALES are rectangular compressed blocks of straw, bound by strings or wire.

FLAKES are slabs of straw removed from an untied bale. Flakes are used to fill small gaps between the ends of stacked bales.

LAID FLAT refers to stacking bales so that the sides with the largest cross-sectional area are horizontal and the longest dimension of this area is parallel with the wall plane.

LAID ON-EDGE refers to stacking bales so that the sides with the largest cross-sectional area are vertical and the longest dimension of this area is horizontal and parallel with the wall plane.

SECTION 7204 — MATERIALS

7204.1   Specifications for Bales.

7204.1.1 Type of Straw. Bales of various types of straw, including, but not limited to, wheat, rice, rye, barley, oats and similar plants, shall be acceptable if they meet the minimum requirements for density, shape, moisture content, and ties.

7204.1.2 Shape. Bales shall be rectangular in shape.

7204.1.3 Dimensions. Bales used within a continuous wall shall be of consistent height and width to ensure even distribution of loads within wall systems.

7204.1.4 Ties. Bales shall be bound with ties of either polypropylene string or baling wire. Bales with broken or loose ties shall not be used unless the broken or loose ties are replaced with ties which restore the original degree of compaction of the bale.

7204.1.5 Moisture Content. Moisture content of bales, at time of installation, shall not exceed 20% of the total weight of the bale. Moisture content of bales shall be determined by one of the following:

7204.1.5.1 Field Method. A suitable moisture meter, designed for use with baled straw or hay, and equipped with a probe of sufficient length to reach the center of the bale, shall be used to determine the average moisture content of 5 bales randomly selected from the bales to be used.

7204.1.5.2 Laboratory Method. A total of 5 samples, taken from the center of each of 5 bales randomly selected from the bales to be used, shall be tested for moisture content by a recognized testing lab.

7204.1.6 Density. Bales in load-bearing structures shall have a minimum calculated dry density of 7.0 pounds per cubic foot. The calculated dry density shall be determined after reducing the actual bale weight by the weight of the moisture content, as determined in section 7204.1.5. The calculated dry density shall be determined by dividing the calculated dry weight of the bale by the volume of the bale.

7204.1.7 Custom Size Bales. Where custom-made partial bales are used, they shall be of the same density, same string or wire tension, and, where possible, use the same number of ties as the standard size bales.

SECTION 7205 — CONSTRUCTION AND GENERAL REQUIREMENTS

7205.1   General. Bale walls, when covered with plaster, drywall or stucco shall be deemed to have the equivalent fire resistive rating as wood frame construction with the same wall-finishing system.

7205.2   Wall Thickness. Nominal minimum bale wall thickness shall be 14 inches.

7205.3   Wall Height. Bale walls shall not exceed one story in height and the bale portion shall not exceed a height to width ratio of 5.5 : 1 (for example, the maximum height for the bale portion of a 23 inch thick wall would be 10 feet — 8 inches), unless the structure is designed by an engineer or architect licensed by the State to practice as such, and approved by the Building Official. Exception: In the non-load bearing exterior end walls of structures with gable or shed roofs, an approved continuous assembly shall be required at the roof bearing assembly level.

7205.4   Unsupported Wall Length. The ratio of unsupported wall length to thickness, for load bearing bale walls, shall not exceed 15.5 : 1 (for a 23 inch thick wall, the maximum unsupported length allowed is 30 feet), unless the structure is designed by an engineer or architect licensed by the State to practice as such, and approved by the Building Official.

7205.5   Allowable Loads. The allowable vertical load (live and dead load) on the top of load-bearing bale walls shall not exceed 400 pounds per square foot (psf) and the resultant load shall act at the center of the wall. Bale structures shall be designed to withstand all vertical and horizontal loads as specified in Chapter 16.

7205.6   Foundations. Foundations shall be sized to accommodate the thickness of the bale wall and the load created by the wall and roof live and dead loads. Foundation (stem) walls which support bale walls shall extend to an elevation of not less than 6 inches above adjacent ground at all points. The minimum width of the footing shall be the width of the bale it supports, except that the bales may overhang the exterior edge of the foundation by not more than 3 inches to accommodate rigid perimeter insulation. Footings shall extend a minimum of 12 inches below natural, undisturbed soil, or to frost line, whichever is lower.

7205.7   Wall and Roof Bearing Assembly Anchorage.

7205.7.1 General. Vertical reinforcing bars with a minimum diameter of 1/2", shall be embedded in the foundation a minimum depth of 6 inches, and shall extend above foundation a minimum of 12 inches. These vertical bars shall be located along the centerline of the bale wall, spaced not more than 2 feet apart. A vertical bar shall also be located within 1 foot of any opening or corner, except at locations occupied by anchor bolts.

7205.7.2 Intersecting Walls. Walls of other materials intersecting bale walls shall be attached to the bale wall by means of one or more of the following methods or an acceptable equivalent:

1. Wooden dowels at least 5/8" in diameter of sufficient length to provide 12 inches of penetration into the bale, driven through holes bored in the abutting stud, and spaced to provide one dowel connection per bale.

2. Pointed wooden stakes, at least 12 inches in length and 1-1/2" by 3-1/2" at the exposed end, fully driven into each course of bales, as anchorage points.

3. Bolted or threaded rod connection of the abutting wall, through the bale wall, to a steel nut and steel or plywood plate washer, a minimum of 6 inches square and a minimum thickness of 3/16" for steel and 1/2" for plywood, in at least three locations.

7205.7.3 Anchor Bolts. Load bearing bale walls shall be anchored to the foundation by 1/2" diameter steel anchor bolts embedded at least 7 inches in the foundation at intervals of 6 feet or less. A minimum of two anchor bolts per wall shall be provided with one bolt located within 36 inches of each end of each wall. Sections of 1/2" diameter threaded rod shall be connected to the anchor bolts, and to each other, by means of threaded coupling nuts and shall extend through the roof bearing assembly and be fastened with a steel washer and nut. Bale walls and roof bearing assemblies may be anchored to the foundation by means of other methods which are adequate to resist uplift forces resulting from the design wind load. There shall be a minimum of two points of anchorage per wall, spaced not more than 6 feet apart, with one located within 36 inches of each end of each wall. The dead load of the roof and ceiling systems will produce vertical compression of the bales. Regardless of the anchoring system used to attach the roof bearing assembly to the foundation, prior to installation of wall finish materials, bolts or straps shall be re-tightened to compensate for this compression.

7205.7.4 Moisture Barrier. A moisture barrier shall be used between the top of the foundation and the bottom of the bale wall to prevent moisture from migrating through the foundation into the bottom course of bales. This barrier shall consist of one of the following:

1. cementitious waterproof coating;

2. type 30 asphalt felt over an asphalt emulsion;

3. sheet metal flashing, sealed at joints;

4. other approved building moisture barrier. All penetrations through the moisture barrier, as well as all joints in the barrier, must be sealed with asphalt, caulking or an approved sealant.

7205.7.5 Stacking and Pinning. Bales in load-bearing walls shall be laid flat and stacked in running bond where possible, with each bale overlapping the two bales beneath it. Bales in non load-bearing walls may be laid either flat or on-edge and stacked in running bond where possible. For non-load bearing walls, bales may be laid either flat or on-edge. Bales in load bearing walls shall be laid flat and stacked in a running bond, where possible, with each bale overlapping the two bales beneath it. Overlaps shall be a minimum of 12 inches. Gaps between the ends of bales which are less than 6 inches in width can be filled by an untied flake inserted snugly into the gap. The first course of bales shall be laid by impaling the bales on the vertical bars or threaded rods, if any, extending from the foundation. When the fourth course has been laid, #4 rebar pins, or an acceptable equivalent, long enough to extend through all four courses, shall be driven down through the bales, two in each bale, located so that they do not pass within six inches of, or through the space between the ends of any two bales. The layout of these pins shall approximate the layout of the vertical bars extending from the foundation. As each subsequent course is laid, two such pins, long enough to extend through the course being laid and the three courses immediately below it, shall be driven down through each bale. This pinning method shall be continued to the top of the wall. In walls seven or eight courses high, pinning at the fifth course may be eliminated. Only full-length bales shall be used at corners of load bearing walls, unless exceptions are designed by an engineer or architect licensed by the State to practice as such, and approved by the Building Official.

Vertical #4 rebar pins, or an acceptable alternative, shall be located within 1 foot of all corners or door openings. Staples, made of #3 or larger rebar formed into a "U" shape, at least 18 inches long with two 6 inch legs, shall be used at all corners of every course, driven with one leg into the top of each abutting corner bale. In lieu of staples, corner bales may be tied together, by a method approved by the building official.

7205.7.5.1 Alternative pinning method. When the third course has been laid, vertical #4 rebar pins, or an acceptable equivalent, long enough to extend through all three courses, shall be driven down through the bales, two in each bale, located so that they do not pass within 6 inches of, or through the space between the ends of any two bales. The layout of these rebar pins shall approximate the layout of the rebar pins extending from the foundation. As each subsequent course is laid, two such pins, long enough to extend through that course and the two courses immediately below it, shall be driven down through each bale. This pinning method shall be continued to the top of the wall.

7205.7.6 Roof Bearing Assembly. Load bearing bale walls shall have a roof bearing assembly at the top of the wall to bear the roof load and to provide a means of connecting the roof structure to the foundation. The roof bearing assembly shall be continuous along the tops of structural walls. An acceptable roof bearing assembly option consists of two double 2" X 6", or larger, horizontal top plates, one located at the inner edge of the wall and the other at the outer edge. Connecting the two doubled top plates and located horizontally and perpendicular to the length of the wall shall be 2" X 6" cross members spaced no more than 72 inches center to center, and as required to align with the threaded rods extending from the anchor bolts in the foundation. The double 2" X 6" top plates shall be face nailed with 16d nails staggered at 16 inches on center, with laps and intersections face nailed with four 16d nails. The cross members shall be face nailed to the top plates with four 16d nails at each end. Corner connections shall include overlaps nailed as above or an acceptable equivalent such as plywood gussets or metal plates. Alternatives to this roof bearing assembly option must provide equal or greater vertical rigidity and provide horizontal rigidity equivalent to a continuous double 2 by 4 top plate. The connection of roof framing members to the roof bearing assembly shall comply with the appropriate sections of the UBC.

7205.7.7 Openings and Lintels. All openings in load bearing bale walls shall be a minimum of one full bale length from any outside corner, unless exceptions are designed by an engineer or architect licensed by the State to practice as such, and approved by the Building Official.

7205.7.7.1 Openings. Openings in exterior bale walls shall not exceed 50 percent of the total wall area, based on interior dimensions, where the wall is providing resistance to lateral loads, unless the structure is designed by an engineer or architect licensed by the State to practice as such, and approved by the Building Official.

7205.7.7.2 Lintels. Wall and/or roof load present above any opening shall be carried, or transferred to the bales below by one of the following: 1. a structural frame, 2. a lintel (such as an angle-iron cradle, wooden beam, wooden box beam). Lintels shall be at least twice as long as the opening is wide and extend at least 24" beyond either side of the opening. Lintels shall be centered over openings, and shall not exceed the load limitations of section 7205.5 by more than 25 percent.

7205.7.8 Moisture Protection. All weather-exposed bale walls shall be protected from water damage. An approved building moisture barrier shall be used to protect at least the bottom course of bales, but not more than the lower one-third of the vertical exterior wall surface, in order to allow natural transpiration of moisture from the bales. The moisture barrier shall have its upper edge inserted at least 6 inches into the horizontal joint between two courses of bales, and shall extend at least 3 inches below the top of the foundation. Bale walls shall have special moisture protection provided at all window sills. Unless protected by a roof, the tops of walls shall also be protected. This moisture protection shall consist of a waterproof membrane, such as asphalt-impregnated felt paper, polyethylene sheeting, or other acceptable moisture barrier, installed in such manner as to prevent water from entering the wall system at window sills or at the tops of walls.

7205.7.9 Wall Finishes. Interior and exterior surfaces of bale walls shall be protected from mechanical damage, flame, animals, and prolonged exposure to water. Bale walls adjacent to bath and shower enclosures shall be protected by a moisture barrier. Cement stucco shall be reinforced with galvanized woven wire stucco netting or an acceptable equivalent. Such reinforcement shall be secured by attachment through the wall at a maximum spacing of 24 inches horizontally and 16 inches vertically, using a method approved by the Building Official. Where bales abut other materials the plaster/stucco shall be reinforced with galvanized expanded metal lath, or an acceptable equivalent, extending a minimum of 6 inches onto the bales. Earthen and lime-based plasters may be applied directly onto the exterior and interior surface of bale walls without reinforcement, except where applied over materials other than straw. Weather-exposed earthen plasters shall be stabilized using a method approved by the building official. Lime based plasters may be applied directly onto the exterior surface of bale walls without reinforcement, except where applied over materials other than straw.

7205.7.10 Electrical. All wiring within or on bale walls shall meet all provisions of the National Electrical Code adopted by this jurisdiction. Type NM or UF cable may be used, or wiring may be run in metallic or non-metallic conduit systems. Electrical boxes shall be securely attached to wooden stakes driven a minimum of 12 inches into the bales, or an acceptable equivalent.

7205.7.11 Plumbing. Water or gas pipes within bale walls shall be encased in a continuous pipe sleeve to prevent leakage within the wall. Where pipes are mounted on bale walls, they shall be isolated from the bales by a moisture barrier.

SHB Agra's Report on Fire Testing

In 1993, as part of the testing commissioned by the New Mexico-based Straw Bale Construction Association which eventually led to the inclusion of straw bale in the New Mexico building code, fire testing was undertaken on a straw bale wall panel by SHB Agra, Inc.

"Transmission of heat through the unreinforced [unplastered] straw bale during this test was not sufficient to raise the average temperature at the exterior face of this wall to 250F above the initial temperature (the governing criteria for ASTM E-119). The highest average temperature recorded on the unexposed face of the unreinforced straw was 52.8F at thirty minutes. Transmission of heat through the wall did not exceed the allowable limit for any single thermocouple. Additionally, there was no penetration of flames or hot gases through the unreinforced straw bale wall during the thirty minute test.

The burning characteristics of the unreinforced straw bales were observed through observation ports during the test. The test panel was also examined after it was removed from the combustion chamber. The straw was observed to burn slowly, and the charred material tended to remain in place. The residual charred material appeared to protect the underlying straw from heat and ventilation, thereby delaying combustion.

The maximum temperature recorded inside the furnace was 1,691F at thirty minutes. Upon removal, the bales did not burst into flames, but slowly smoldered. The fire was easily extinguished with a small quantity of water.

After the unplastered bales passed the 30 minute fire test, plastered bales were tested to more closely simulate real-life burning characteristics on finished walls, with the following results:

The highest temperature recorded on the exterior face of the stuccoed straw bales after 120 minutes of exposure was 63.1F, less than a 10 degree rise in temperature. The highest average furnace temperature recorded during this period was 1,942F, however at least one thermocouple recorded temperatures exceeding 2,000F. There was no penetration of flames or hot gases through the stuccoed straw bale wall.

The burning characteristics of the stuccoed straw bales was also observed. The reaction consisted of initial cracking of the stucco surface as the heat was applied, with little further evidence of distress."

INDEX

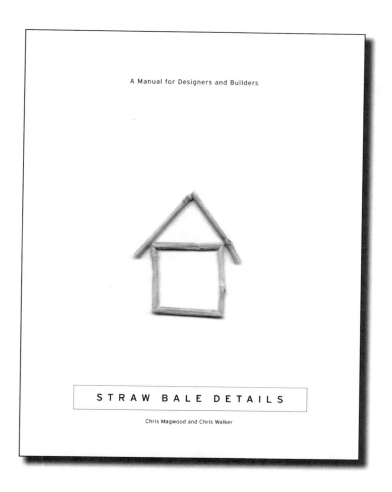

Peter Mack

Several years ago, a colleague (ironically his last name is Hay) told Peter about mortared straw bale structures for barns, sheds, etc. The idea was forgotten until he read about it in *Fine Homebuilding* about five years ago. At that point, he set to work with a few friends building two straw bale walls on an existing foundation, and was duly impressed. Convinced that this must be the ideal annually renewable building material he had been looking for, he was hooked

A founding member and coordinator of the Straw Bale Co-op of Ontario, Peter has coordinated and written for the Straw Bale Co-op quarterly newsletter, both of which have been idle of late due to an over-busy construction schedule. He harbors a passion for learning, and feels strongly about ecological and political issues. He describes the best part of his life as having been spent learning appropriate technologies, sampling many trades; he has finally settled on straw bale construction which satisfies his conscience, holds his interest, and provides a great creative outlet, all at the same time.

Since Peter and Chris Magwood co-founded Camel's Back Construction, interest in their work has been steadily climbing, and they've been happily building homes, studios, and other buildings as well as consulting and teaching ever since. Pete Mack and partner Tina Therien currently live in a former blacksmith's house in the hamlet of Warsaw. They are always on the lookout for the right piece of property to build on. — What kind of home do you suppose?

Peter Mack
PO Box 61
Warsaw, ON K0L 3A0

Chris Magwood

After making almost every possible straw bale mistake in the creation of his own home — so he says — Chris was seriously infected with the desire to make more straw bale buildings, and to make them better and better. He has been involved with many straw bale homes, outbuildings and theoretical jam sessions in the years since. Enough, in fact, that his passion has turned into his full-time occupation.

Having also committed a number of independent energy crimes and *faux pas* on his own home, he is equally obsessed with better integrating solar, wind, and micro-hydro energy and heating systems into building design. There are so many simple, cost-effective ways to lighten our impact on the environment that he believes it simply makes no sense to ignore them.

Chris' involvement in writing this book arose from his experiences facing the tough and insightful questions of clients and from the newcomers and building professionals who have attended their hands-on workshops. These people have collectively taught him that there's always a new way to approach a problem and that there is always an unexpected question waiting to be asked.

For the foreseeable future, there is nothing Chris would rather do than consider those questions and give the answers the form and dimension (and hopefully the grace and beauty) of a straw bale building.

Chris Magwood
Camel's Back Construction
RR 3 Madoc, ON K0K 2K0
E-mail: cmagwood@kos.net
www.mwsolutions.com/straw

BOOKS TO BUILD A NEW SOCIETY

New Society Publishers' mission is to publish books that contribute
in fundamental ways to building an ecologically sustainable and just
society, and to do so with the least possible impact on the environment,
in a manner that models that vision.

We specialize in:

sustainable living

ecological design and planning

environment and justice

nonviolence

resistance and community

the feminist transformation

progressive leadership

accountable economics

conscientious commerce, and

educational and parenting resources

For a full catalog, call 1-800-567-6772, or visit our web site at
www.newsociety.com

NEW SOCIETY PUBLISHERS